SHE WIELDS A PEN

AMERICAN WOMEN POETS OF
THE 19TH CENTURY

A little Road - not
made of Man -
Enabled of the Eye -
Accessible to Thill of Bee -
Or Cart of Butterfly -

If Town it have - beyond
itself -
'Tis that - I cannot say -
I only *know - no* Curricle
that rumble there
*Bear Me -

+ besides + Vehicle + hold.
+. Sigh -

SHE WIELDS A PEN

AMERICAN WOMEN POETS OF THE 19TH CENTURY

Selected and edited by
JANET GRAY
Princeton University

Consultant Editor for this volume
CHRISTOPHER BIGSBY
University of East Anglia

J. M. Dent   London

T 20769

This edition first published in Great Britain by
J. M. Dent, 1997
a division of the Orion Publishing Group,
Orion House, 5 Upper St Martin's Lane,
London WC2H 9EA

Frontispiece: 'A little Road – not made of Man', from Fascicle 34,
The Manuscript Books of Emily Dickinson 1830–1886
© The President and Fellows of Harvard College, The Houghton Library

A CIP catalogue record for this book
is available upon request.

Filmset by Selwood Systems, Midsomer Norton
Printed and bound in Great Britain by
Butler & Tanner Ltd, Frome & London

ISBN 0 460 87859 X

CONTENTS

NOTE ON THE EDITOR

JANET GRAY was born in Altadena, California, the second of three daughters of Quaker parents, whose convictions immersed the family in social service and the civil rights and anti-war movements. She was educated at public schools except for four years when her family lived in Korea, where her mother tutored her, and India, where she attended boarding school. After graduating from Earlham College in 1970, she worked in the peace movement, then edited an alternative journal, *New Pasadena*, published to support grassroots community organisations. For twelve years she operated a typing and editing business while taking part in the Los Angeles poetry scene, performing in clubs, theatres and libraries. Her first book of poems, *To Pull Out the Peachboy*, was published in 1981; subsequent volumes include *Flaming Tail Out of the Ground Near Your Farm* (1987) and *A Hundred Flowers* (1993). Having earned a Master's degree at Middlebury College's summer school, she entered the doctoral programme of Princeton University in 1988, where her research concentrated on British and American women poets of the nineteenth century. She has taught British and American literature and Women's Studies at Princeton and Trenton State College.

CHRONOLOGY OF THE POETS' LIVES AND TIMES

Year	Poets' Lives	Cultural and Historical Background
1800		Average number of births per woman: 7; population 5.3 million
1808		Foreign slave trade ends
1812		US declares war on England
1815	Lydia Huntley Sigourney (24), *Moral Pieces in Prose and Verse*	1812 war ends. Ojibwa forced to cede lands to the US
1816		African Methodist Episcopal Church founded
1816–21		Indiana, Mississippi, Illinois, Alabama, Maine, Missouri admitted to the Union
1820		Congress sets pattern of slave and free states with the Missouri Compromise
1820–30		Industrial towns develop; factories in Lowell, Massachusetts hire 'mill girls'
1826	Jane Johnston Schoolcraft (26) publishes poems and prose in the first edition of *The Literary Voyager or Muzzeniegun*	
1828	Eliza Follen (40) becomes editor of Sunday School publication, *Christian Teacher's Manual*	

Year	Poets' Lives	Cultural and Historical Background
1831	Female Literary Association of Philadelphia founded; Sarah Louisa Forten (17) is a member	William Lloyd Garrison founds abolitionist newspaper *The Liberator*
1832	Caroline Gilman (38) begins publication of the youth journal *Rose Bud*; Frances Kemble (23) tours the US playing Shakespearean roles	
1833	Eliza Follen (45), *Little Songs, for Little Boys and Girls*	Philadelphia Female Anti-Slavery Society founded; Oberlin College, first coeducational, multiracial college in the US, founded
1834	The pseudonym Ada is identified in *The Liberator* as 'a young and intelligent lady of color'	
1834–7		English writer Harriet Martineau tours North America and writes *Society in America*
1835	Lucy Larcom (11) goes to work in a textile mill in Lowell, Massachusetts	
1836		Wesleyan College, first chartered women's college, opens in Macon, Georgia
1836–7		Arkansas and Michigan admitted to the Union
1837	Sarah Josepha Hale (49) becomes editor of *Godey's Lady's Book*	First Anti-Slavery Convention of American Women held in New York City
1838		Cherokees expelled from eastern states begin the 'Trail of Tears' towards

Year	Poets' Lives	Cultural and Historical Background
1838		Midwestern reservations – a quarter die en route
1839		First Married Women's Property Act passed in Mississippi; other states follow
1840	Lydia Huntley Sigourney (49) tours Europe, received as a celebrity; Mary Dana Shindler (30) begins a prolific poetic career	
1840–60		First major wave of immigration brings 4.5 million new arrivals to the US, most from Western Europe
1841	Ann Plato (20?) publishes her essays and poems	New York *Tribune*, one of the first general-interest newspapers, founded
1842	Penina Moise (45) becomes superintendent of religious education at Beth Elohim, Charleston, South Carolina	Charles Dickens tours the US giving readings from his works
1843	The Ware sisters, Catherine Ana Warfield (27) and Eleanor Percy Lee (23) publish their first collaborative book of poems	
1844	Margaret Fuller (34), *Summer on the Lakes*; she begins writing criticism for the New York *Tribune*	
1845	Margaret Fuller, *Woman in the Nineteenth Century*	Thoreau begins residence at Walden Pond in Massachusetts; Poe, *The Raven and Other Poems*; Slogan 'Manifest Destiny' is

Year	Poets' Lives	Cultural and Historical Background
1845		coined to justify westward expansion
1845–50		Florida, Texas, Iowa, Wisconsin, California admitted to the Union
1846		Sewing machine patented; Congress declares war on Mexico to support interests of slaveholding American settlers in Mexican territory
1847		John Greenleaf Whittier becomes editor of abolitionist paper *The National Era*
1848	Frances Kemble (39) is divorced, losing custody of her two children	Seneca Falls Convention, the first women's rights convention, meets in New York State; war with Mexico ends with treaty of Guadalupe Hidalgo, ceding California, Utah, Arizona and New Mexico to US; Thomas Buchanan Read edits *The Female Poets of America* with 71 poets; Rufus Wilmot Griswold edits *The Female Poets of America* with 91 poets
1849	Ina Coolbrith (7) crosses the continent on the Overland Trail	Gold discovered in California; rush for gold rapidly increases the population
1850	Alice Cary (30) and Phoebe Cary (26) leave Ohio for New York City	First national convention on woman suffrage held in Worcester, Massachusetts; Fugitive Slave Act requires Northerners to aid in the capture of escaped slaves;

Year	Poets' Lives	Cultural and Historical Background
1850		California admitted to the Union; Susan Warner's *The Wide, Wide World* breaks sales records for American fiction
1851	Elizabeth Oakes-Smith (45) becomes the first woman lecturer on the lyceum circuit; Louisa May Alcott (19) receives her first acceptance notice from a publisher	Sojourner Truth delivers her speech 'Ain't I a Woman' at a women's rights convention in Akron, Ohio
1852		Harriet Beecher Stowe, *Uncle Tom's Cabin*, abolitionist novel which sets new sales records
1853		Gadsden Treaty with Mexico adds Texas and other lands to US
1854	Sarah Josepha Hale (66), *Woman's Record*, an encyclopedia of notable women; Achsa Sprague (26) begins her career as a travelling spiritualist; Frances Ellen Watkins Harper (29) joins the Underground Railroad, begins her career as a travelling lecturer and publishes *Poems on Miscellaneous Subjects*	Kansas–Nebraska Act repeals Missouri Compromise provision that no slavery should exist in territories north of the Mason-Dixon line
1855		Whitman, *Leaves of Grass*; Longfellow, *The Song of Hiawatha*
1857		US Supreme Court upholds the Fugitive Slave Law and denies citizenship to blacks

Year	Poets' Lives	Cultural and Historical Background
1857		in Dred Scott decision; Elizabeth Barrett Browning, *Aurora Leigh*
1858	Harriet Prescott (Spofford) (23) sends her first short story to *Atlantic Monthly*	
1858–9		Admission of Minnesota and Oregon
1859		Abolitionist John Brown convicted of treason for raid on a federal arsenal
1860–1900		14 million immigrants enter the US, including increasing numbers of southern and eastern Europeans
1860	Elizabeth Akers Allen (28), 'Rock Me to Sleep', appears in *Saturday Evening Post* and becomes sensationally popular	Average number of births per woman: 5.2; population: 31.4 million
1861	Ina Coolbrith (19) leaves her husband following his attempt on her life; Adah Isaacs Menken (22?) gives her first performance as Byronic heroine Mazeppa in Albany, New York	Admission of Kansas; Southern states secede from the Union; Civil War begins with Confederate capture of Fort Sumter in Charleston, South Carolina; Harriet Jacob's *Incidents in the Life of a Slave Girl*, first published slave narrative by a woman
1862	Elizabeth Drew Barstow Stoddard (39), *The Morgesons*; Julia Ward Howe (43), 'Battle-Hymn of the Republic', published in *Atlantic Monthly*; Emily Dickinson	Homestead Act grants 160 acres to each permanent settler in the west for a nominal fee; Battle of Cinco de Mayo; Mexican troops under Zaragoza check French forces at Puebla

Year	Poets' Lives	Cultural and Historical Background
1862	(32) writes 366 poems and submits four to *Atlantic Monthly*	
1863		Lincoln issues Emancipation Proclamation, freeing slaves
1864	Frances Crosby van Alstyne (44) begins selling hymns to gospel music publishers; Sarah M. B. Piatt (28) publishes her first of seventeen volumes of poetry	
1865	Lucy Larcom (41) becomes editor of *Our Young Folks*; Margaret Preston (45), *Beechenbrook: A Rhyme of the War*; poems of the Zaragoza clubs published in the San Francisco newspaper *El Nuevo Mundo*	Passage of Thirteenth Amendment abolishing slavery; Lincoln assassinated days after the Confederacy surrenders
1866		With land grants, railway companies begin rapid expansion of rail systems in the west
1867	Mary Eliza Tucker Lambert (29) publishes two books of poetry	Reconstruction Act, aimed at guaranteeing black male suffrage, passes over President Johnson's veto
1868	Louisa May Alcott (36), *Little Women*	Fourteenth Amendment grants citizenship to everyone born or naturalised in the US
1869	First women's club founded in New York City. Elizabeth Oakes-Smith (63) is a	Founding of National Women's Suffrage Association and American

Year	Poets' Lives	Cultural and Historical Background
1869	founder and Alice Cary (49) president	Women's Suffrage Association; railroads connect east and west coasts
1870	Gail Hamilton (Mary Abigail Dodge) (37), *A Battle of the Books*; Louisa May Alcott (38) flees her career to rest in Switzerland; Rose Hartwick Thorpe (20), 'Curfew Must Not Ring Tonight'	Fifteenth Amendment passed protecting male voting rights regardless of race
1871	Julia Ward Howe (52) becomes President of Woman's International Peace Association	
1872	Sarah C. Woolsey (Susan Coolidge) (37), *What Katy Did*	Sixteen women arrested in New York for trying to vote
1873	Mary Mapes Dodge (42) founding editor of *St Nicholas*, magazine for children; Lizette Woodworth Reese (17) begins her fifty-year career as an English teacher	Comstock Law outlawing mailing of birth control information passed -- it remains until 1971
1874	Ina Coolbrith (32) begins her forty-year career as a San Francisco Bay area librarian	Women's Christian Temperance Union founded; Emerson edits *Parnassus*, including only five contemporary American poets; Pawnee move from their ancient lands on the Platte River, Nebraska, to a reservation in Indian Territory, now Oklahoma
1875		John Greenleaf Whittier

Year	Poets' Lives	Cultural and Historical Background
1875		edits *Songs of Three Centuries*, including more than 20 American women poets
1876	Henrietta Cordelia Ray (27), 'Lincoln', read at the unveiling of the Freedmen's Monument	Sioux defending holy places defeat General Custer at the Battle of Little Bighorn
1877	Sarah Josepha Hale (89) retires from editorship of *Godey's Lady's Book*	Seventieth birthday celebration for Whittier at *Atlantic Monthly* – no women invited
1878–98		An estimated 10,000 African Americans lynched
1879	Constance Fenimore Woolson (39) expatriates from the US to Europe	Bureau of Ethnology created by Congress
1880	Mollie E. Moore Davis (28) settles in New Orleans with Confederate Major husband; Owl Woman (40?) begins receiving healing songs from the spirit world	
1881	Helen Hunt Jackson (51) distributes copies of *A Century of Dishonor* to every member of Congress	
1882		Wilde makes lecture tour of the US; era of immigration restriction begins with Chinese Exclusion Act; Russian Jews massacred in pogroms in Nizhniy-Novgorod
1883	Emma Lazarus (34), 'The New Colossus'; Ella Wheeler Wilcox (33),	

Year	Poets' Lives	Cultural and Historical Background
1883	*Poems of Passion*	
1884	Helen Hunt Jackson (53), *Ramona*	Longfellow becomes first American poet commemorated in Westminster Abbey, London
1885	Charlotte Perkins Stetson Gilman (25) is given 'rest cure' for post-partum depression	Bryn Mawr College founded, first women's college to offer graduate studies
1886	Emily Dickinson's sister Lavinia discovers manuscript books of poems in Emily's cabinet after her death aged 56	Police and striking workers clash in Chicago's Haymarket Square – anarchist leaders convicted of bombing the square; Statue of Liberty unveiled in the harbour of New York
1887	Hawaiian princess Lili'uokalani (49) pays state visit to Queen Victoria and President Cleveland; Edith M. Thomas (33) moves from Ohio to New York for her literary career	Dawes Severalty Act allocates land parcels to Native American households, forcing cultural change
1888	Julia Ward Howe (69) tours the west as a lecturer	
1890	Josephine Delphine Henderson Heard (29), *Morning Glories*, possibly the first book of poems by an African American woman in nearly twenty years; Emily Pauline Johnson (29) begins her twenty-year international performing career; Emily Dickinson publishes first collection of poems	Wyoming enters the Union as the first state with full woman's suffrage; Sherman Anti-Trust Act passed in response to the growth of monopolistic corporations

Year	Poets' Lives	Cultural and Historical Background
1891	Henrietta Cordelia Ray (42) earns a Master of Pedagogy from the University of the City of New York	
1892	Frances Ellen Watkins Harper (67), *Iola Leroy*, first novel about Reconstruction by an African American; Charlotte Perkins Stetson Gilman (32), *The Yellow Wall Paper*	Founding of Colored Women's League
1893	Queen Lili'uokalani (55) deposed by American residents of Hawaii	
1894	Ella Higginson (32), *A Bunch of Western Clover*	
1895		Gelett Burgess begins publication of nonsense magazine *The Lark* in San Francisco
1896		Founding of the National Association of Colored Women, a federation of African American women's clubs; Supreme Court rules in Plessy v. Ferguson that 'separate but equal' racial segregation is justified
1897	Mary Weston Fordham (35?), *Magnolia Leaves*, endorsed by Booker T. Washington; Voltairine de Cleyre (31) tours the UK addressing labour organisations on anarchism	
1898	Charlotte Perkins Stetson	*US annexes Hawaii;*

Year	Poets' Lives	Cultural and Historical Background
1898	Gilman (38), *Women and Economics*	*Spanish–American War* results in US annexation of Philippines, Puerto Rico and Guam and occupation of Cuba
1900	Carolyn Wells (38), *Idle Idyls*; Priscilla Jane Thompson (29), *Ethiope Lays*	Average number of births per woman: 3.6; population: 76 million

INTRODUCTION

A black woman sits cradling a white infant in the corner of a modest middle-class parlour. She gazes into the distance through a window. In the centre of the room a white woman reads from a bright little book, her attention enfolding her audience of toddlers, a girl and a boy. Overseeing all, a young white patriarch stands, hands in pockets, as if he has nothing to do but signify his position in the household. The cover illustration for this anthology captures a certain scene in the history of American women's literary endeavour, a scene especially characteristic of the eastern states in the decades before the Civil War. Print culture linked such private spaces, and women writers, editors and readers used print to construct roles for themselves in shaping the young nation. The red book might hold poems by Eliza Follen, Sarah Josepha Hale or Lydia Huntley Sigourney, pioneers of American children's literature. Reading to her children, the mother enacts what became known as 'republican motherhood', the mission of forming a new kind of citizen – an aim that keeps her at home but calls on her creativity, intellect and autonomy. It is a political role, different from her husband's but, as the painting shows, central – and dependent on the nurse's relieving her of the physical work of nurture. For the moment, the scenes in which the black woman's voice will be heard lie elsewhere, far from the reading of the little red book.

The images that could be painted representing the creative lives of the authors in *She Wields A Pen* are multiple, a function of a vast array of locales, cultures, social settings and historical moments. Jane Johnston Schoolcraft could be depicted at a table in her Irish father's fur-trading post in the far north, on the shore of Lake Superior. Homer's *Iliad* would lie open on the table with Schoolcraft's notes on Ojibwa oral lore placed next to it, as she worked at translating the story of her warrior grandfather into a form that readers educated in European literary traditions could appreciate. A festive gathering of the Hawaiian royal court's poetry club could be shown from Lili'uokalani's life. Or she could appear far from home, in a room in Washington, DC, writing a journal entry in English with mingled

Hawaiian poetic words to disguise her reflections about US political aggression in her beloved native land. Merced Gonzáles and her sister members of the Zaragoza Clubs could appear around a banquet table in the old adobe village of Los Angeles, cups lifted in a toast to the heroes of Mexican resistance to French occupation. Sarah Louisa Forten could be shown, a young woman in her teens, at a biracial women's literary meeting, or in her family's hospitable parlour in Philadelphia. Others in the parlour, besides her parents and sisters, could include the abolitionists Frederick Douglass, John Greenleaf Whittier and Angelina Grimké, with whom Sarah might be deep in conversation. Priscilla Thompson could be shown inside a print shop in a small Ohio city, her manuscript 'Ethiope Lays' set on the counter, paying the shop's owner to make it into a book. Emily Dickinson would appear alone at a busy desk in a closed room; there would be a stack of letters ready to mail, and she would be collating sheets of poetry, needle and thread at hand with which to stitch them together.

Making a poem occurs amid other work – the daily labour of sustaining life and connection, the society's work of shaping, extending and re-evaluating itself. And poems by women come about as instances of the positions that women occupy in daily life and social institutions, whether in acceptance of dominant notions of what women should be and do, in resistance, or as agents of change. During the nineteenth century, in American as in other Western cultures where the middle class had come to dominate social values, women were expected to attend to private life – running the home, meeting family members' daily physical needs, overseeing life-cycle events, building communities. However, home and community could not be taken for granted everywhere in the US. The nation as it came to be constituted over the century was a vast, varied terrain occupied by exiles, captives and emigrés, so that underlying any shared American idea of belonging in a particular place was a voluminous and heterogeneous story of uprooting. Home had to be fabricated for American culture, community to be invented over great expanses, social ideals and class structures redefined and histories retold – whether to emphasise continuity with or radical breakage from the heritage of lands now far away. These were needs that gave American print culture an urgency specific to its national scene. They were also missions consistent with women's prescribed roles – the basis on which women editors, writers and readers formed a distinctive female public sphere through print.

The poetry in this anthology, with few exceptions, appeared in print in the context of social purposes beyond the making of poems. By the end of the century, a shift in ideals of citizenship from communal moral authority to professional expertise set the stage for American literary culture's acceptance of the idea that poetry is an autonomous discipline responsible only to its own tradition and craft. Though women participated in shaping this poetic, its rise occurred as the influence of female print culture declined, and in time literary critics and scholars used it to eliminate nearly all nineteenth-century women poets from the American literary canon. The recovery of women's poetry has proceeded slowly, in part because of the persisting authority of this poetic. *She Wields A Pen* represents the aspiration to restore some of the plenitude of women's poetic production as well as the history of debate surrounding it. Projects of literary revision, however, require more than a knowledge of history; they come about because an audience arrives on the scene that is asking new questions, seeking to change the present by recovering forgotten dimensions of the past.

Emily Dickinson is the most securely canonical of all nineteenth-century American women poets in English – the only one whose works have been anthologised as frequently as those of forty-five men, from Thomas Wyatt to Randall Jarrell. A century after Dickinson stopped trying to publish her poems, she was the only nineteenth-century American woman recognised as either a true poet or a contributor to the formation of a distinctive national literature. Paradoxically, Dickinson gained this position in part because her life and works were unrepresentative of women writers of her age. Dickinson's status was secured as a distinctly modern poetics gained authority, an approach to poetic evaluation centred on the notions that a poet is an exceptionally gifted person who rises above the literary marketplace and that poetry is a discipline unto itself, answerable only to its own formal rules. In the case of the reclusive Dickinson, the idea that poetry is a solitary, internal art converged with another idea that became entrenched in Western bourgeois culture during the nineteenth century: that women belong in the private spaces of the home. Much of Dickinson's appeal to feminist critics since the 1960s turned on the combination of these ideas: exposing the anguish of women's confinement to the domestic sphere, she seized freedoms through the separate world of imagination. Yet the nineteenth-century gender system was not wholly disabling to women writers. Social sanctions did restrict women's entry into higher education, politics and the professions, and suspicion clung to the reputations of women who entered the public sphere. The figure of a suicidal fallen woman adrift in the modern urban landscape, appearing frequently in nineteenth-century art and literature (for example, in Julia Ward Howe's 'Lyrics of the Street'), symbolises this association between public women and degraded sexuality. Women writers had to contend with sexist attitudes and institutions, but such social sanctions did not keep them out of print. Women pioneered writing as a paying occupation, and for most of the century, women writers and readers dominated the American literary marketplace.

Any one story about American women's poetry during the century is necessarily partial, a starting place from which to explore differing stories. However, it holds true for most of the poets in this anthology that poetry was not a discipline unto itself. Women wrote in the context of their participation in groups and movements whose purposes extended beyond literary production. The Sunday School movement, begun late in the eighteenth century and established as an institution in the 1830s, provided impetus for the creation of a body of children's poetry. Eliza Follen, Sarah Josepha Hale and Penina Moise all produced verse for use in children's religious education. The growth of the radical anti-slavery movement in the 1830s opened both print and public speaking venues for women and the occasion, rare through much of American literary history, for African American writers (such as Sarah Louisa Forten and Frances Harper) to draw recognition from the white press. Abolitionist writers developed sentimentality, a rhetoric associated with 'feminine' emotionalism, into a powerful political instrument: they invoked confrontative representations of the conditions of enslaved women and children to rouse revulsion against slavery and forge bonds of sympathetic identification between races. Women were engaged throughout the century in fierce criticism of the government's treatment of tribal people, but they also took part in shaping representations of Native Americans that accommodated the rapidly expanding nation. This divided agenda appears in Lydia Huntley Sigourney's 'Indian Names': the poem is engrossed with Native Americans' endurance as words on a map – badges of white guilt – but it situates the aboriginal people themselves in the prehistory of a traumatic encounter rather than in the living present. The women's club movement organised after the Civil War pursued literary study alongside philanthropy and civic activism. Black women's clubs were, in addition, at the vanguard of efforts to uplift the race – an important context for late-nineteenth-century African American poets such as Henrietta Cordelia Ray, who promoted cultural ideals with little obvious reference to race.

In the last quarter of the century, poetics showed signs of change. Antebellum poet Hannah F. Gould had taught children about theology and revolution through nature poems; Mary Mapes Dodge, an influential postbellum author and editor, addressed children of an urban middle class, protected from nature, labour, politics and religion. Childhood was becoming a separate discursive world with its own rules, as was poetry. Child's and poet's voices converge in the simplified diction and vivid images of Sarah Piatt and Lizette Woodworth Reese, precursors of the women modernists of the early twentieth century (such as Amy Lowell, Sarah Teasdale, Louise Bogan and Edna St Vincent Millay). Political poetry thrived, but its vanguard weapon was irony (as in Charlotte Perkins Stetson Gilman's poems), a hallmark of modernist poetics. Even Frances Densmore's sparse translation of Owl Woman's healing songs looks like modernist poetry compared with earlier cross-cultural writing, such as Schoolcraft's 'Otagamiad'. Reviewers had begun to distinguish between 'real' poetry and various lesser categories. The poetics that would eventually canonise only Dickinson was gaining sway – and the women's club movement had laid groundwork for it. In their study of literary texts, particularly those of Shakespeare, women's club members were seeking personal growth, aiming to recapitulate the history that they believed great cultural works captured: the history of the self's emancipation from both oppressive institutions and self-defeating individual desires. Drawing on Romantic literary theory – not yet accepted in academia – they turned to works of literary 'genius' for models of an ideal, transcendent self. The clubs developed methods for closely studying literary form, a practice that academic critics later adopted, elaborated and linked to masculine toughness (see, for example, the critical background on Louise Imogen Guiney), using the criteria of fixed, universal value to eliminate all but a very few women writers from the literary canon.

A two-stage transformation affecting the relationship between print and oral culture over the course of the century generated the conditions for the rising influence of the idea that poetry is a discipline unto itself. In the first stage, ideals of citizenship shifted their focus from communal to individual moral authority; in the second, from exemplary individuals to experts whose authority was assumed morally neutral. Early in the century, public life was idealised as a sphere of oratorical debate and consensus based on the Roman model of republicanism. Classically consisting of the professions of law, politics and the clergy, this oral culture was almost exclusively a white male sphere, while women's oral transmission of culture took place within families and local communities. However, from about 1820 to 1870, an alternative, female public sphere thrived in print under the leadership of women editors, among whom Sarah Josepha Hale was the most influential (see The Poets and Their Critics for a discussion of Hale's poetics). Its mission complemented that of the male public sphere but adapted values associated with women's lives to public discourse. Forging the stories and icons of national identity, women writers and editors gave primacy to everyday life and human connection, building networks of community – centred on women and children – over the expanding geographical spread of Euro-American culture. By constructing a public voice through texts, female print culture took part in the first transformation described above, for print – in which speaker and addressee must imagine one another – cultivates individual interior life. Women represented in this anthology who did speak in face-to-face public forums, too, illustrate this first transformation. Elizabeth Oakes-Smith and Frances Harper engaged in political argument in their public speaking, but other poets in this anthology performed under the auspices of the increasingly centralised entertainment industry. By mid century female performers in whom audiences could recognise idealised versions of themselves were attracting large and devoted audiences. Kemble's sonnet 'To Shakspeare' represents her public readings of his plays as almost a spiritualist act invoking his presence and approval. (In her twenty-year career, Kemble set the stage for the women's clubs reverential study of Shakespeare.) For Achsa Sprague, the performance of poetry *was* a spiritualist event, in which the poet modelled a vanguard moral subjectivity in touch with transcendent essences.

A corresponding set of transformations took place in the aims and practices of the American publishing industry. Early in the century, artisan-publishers regarded print as an instrument of God, a revolutionary weapon for creating a democratic nation and abolishing the remnants of feudal mentality. By 1850, publishing had become established as a viable business. A rapidly growing population, high literacy, increased leisure, the extension of railways and technological developments that made printing cheaper all contributed to a tenfold growth in American publishing from 1830 to 1850. Work roles within the press became specialised, and publishers envisioned themselves not as artisans but as patrons. Although business was profitable, these 'gentlemen publishers' considered themselves public servants and moral guardians rather than businessmen. When entrepreneurial capitalism boomed following the Civil War, publishing lagged behind other industries as publishers resisted overtly commercial practices. Publishers whose primary aim was high sales, who cared little about promoting moral values, began to appear by the 1880s – representatives of the ascendancy of the specialist. Even faced with such competitors, many publishers and authors continued to mask their commercial aspirations, asserting the noncommercial value of their books; *real* literature rose above the marketplace.

The rift between literary and commercial value appeared amid a complex of cultural rifts formed around class, region, gender and ethnicity, resulting in multiple layers that cultural entrepreneurs assumed appealed to the tastes of different groups (summed up as low-, middle- and high-brow). These rifts were evident by 1850 but took different forms by the late 1800s, as two distinctive formats for poetry – the luxury book and the slender volume – illustrate. Artisan publishers early in the century had hailed cheaper printing as an advance that would further democratise literature by making it available to all classes. The cost of periodicals did drop, but the average cost of books remained at about a day's wages for working people. Publishers took advantage of improvements in print technology to increase their production of large luxury books (such as Lydia Huntley Sigourney's *Illustrated Poems*, 1856), investing in heavy paper, colour artwork, leather binding and gold trim. Poetry in this format was a status commodity for the upper classes. Slender volumes appeared in increasing numbers in the 1880s and 1890s, packaging the works of such critically esteemed poets as Lizette Woodworth Reese. Artful but unostentatious, they presented their contents as quality rather than quantity, for consumption by an elite of taste rather than wealth. In between times, Gail Hamilton attacked the gentlemen publishers' practice of avoiding financial talk and Helen Hunt Jackson insisted poetic skill should have a dollar value – both struggling to redefine and preserve the link between merit and money that had made writing, even writing poetry, a paying career for so many women. But in the era of expertise, being an expert at writing poetry paradoxically became an avocation. Selling enough books to support oneself and being praised by critics as a true poet became almost mutually exclusive; one could not have both popularity with a mass audience and recognition as a refiner of taste (a puzzle that plagued the careers of some turn-of-the-century poets, such as Louise Imogen Guiney and Ella Wheeler Wilcox).

The era of expertise also edged women writers out of the processes by which literary works achieve a lasting place in cultural memory. Following on other postbellum businesses and professions, publishing became aggressively competitive; the 'feminine' values on which female print culture thrived had no place in this masculinised world. Women published, but they were largely excluded from the collegial networks among publishers, critics and academics through which enduring reputations, and thus literary canons, are made. Two poetry anthologies published by male veterans of American letters in the mid-1870s, as the influence of female print culture declined, illustrate women poets' status in different approaches to the making of mixed-gender canons. Calling his selection *Parnassus* in keeping with his lofty idea of poetry, Ralph Waldo Emerson included only five of his female contemporaries. John Greenleaf Whittier included at least twenty American women poets in *Songs of Three Centuries*, admitting to eclectic if moralistic taste. Neither man struck on a canon that would endure to the present – neither anthology included Dickinson or Whitman. As a pair, however, these collections illustrate that late-nineteenth-century American literary culture found more room for women poets in poetry conceived as a miscellany of performing voices than in poetry conceived as a singular transcendent pinnacle. Ironically, when the publishers of *Atlantic Monthly* threw a seventieth birthday party for Whittier in 1877, they did not think to invite any women – even though the guest of honour had encouraged, collaborated with, and advanced the careers of more women writers than had any other man. In the early decades of the twentieth century, literary critics continued the process of edging women out; by the 1940s, a canon of American literature had formed centred on the heroic individualism of the common man in his pursuit of freedom from social constraints. The imaginative mode that dominated female print culture, which envisioned the loss of human connections as the greatest tragedy, was dismissed, ridiculed and largely forgotten.

As late-twentieth-century scholars recognised early in the feminist project of recovering forgotten women writers, challenging the processes of canonisation requires interrogating the criteria of value that literary canons embody. The recovery of women's prose has proceeded much more quickly than that of poetry, in part because the persisting authority of the notion that poetry is a separate field of expertise, unrelated to the world in which it is produced, has restricted our ability to read poetry. Focused as it is on the individual as an expert and on the poem as an intricate made object, this poetic implies that the printed page has an inherent value that supersedes the uses a particular community might make of the words on it; and this implication, in turn, contributes to a long-range forgetting of poetry's vital cultural roles. To see through the authority of the printed text, we need to open up our poetics, our theories of literary making. We need to explore not just the formal qualities of the text itself but the cultural work that such an utterance, localised in time and space, might do.

Searching through volume upon volume of poetry by nineteenth-century American women, I looked for forms associated with the English poetic canon (the sonnet was by far the most common) and for forms associated with folk culture and oral performance – forms built on repetition, simple stanzas and narratives, phrases and situations that would have been familiar to the audience. I chose recitation pieces and hymns that enjoyed extraordinary popularity. I looked for women's representations of the continent's varied natural landscape and modern city scenes. I looked for poems associated with the everyday and life-cycle events – traditional areas of women's culture – and for poems that challenged the distinction between private and public life. I chose poems by women about women, reflecting differing arguments and iconographies from the era that both gave rise to the movement for women's suffrage and impeded its success. I looked for pleasure and desire and their places in the gender system. I looked for humour, since nineteenth-century women poets have been stereotyped as overwhelmingly grim, and children's verse, usually removed to a separate category. I selected poems about the century's historical events, looking for ideologies that supported and ideologies that challenged dominant political and economic structures. I have included poems on performance and print culture and observations about reading, writing and the media. Because our recovery of nineteenth-century texts is too easily dependent on a publishing industry centralised in the northeastern states, I searched for poets excluded because of race, region and language.

This volume reflects my hope of its contributing both to the recuperation of women poets and to other allied projects: restoring the history of conflict over literary value and reframing American literature as a comparative discipline comprising heterogeneous cultures. All of these projects are relatively new and growing – my selection reflects the conviction that now is a time for extending our knowledge, not narrowing the field. This introduction has emphasised historical factors surrounding women's production of poetry in the nineteenth century, but projects of literary revision do not rely solely on knowing historical facts. They come about because changes occur in how people understand the present; different questions, different perspectives take precedence in their explorations of history. To restore forgotten dimensions of the past, we must ask our own questions, reading as participants in the ongoing process of cultural reevaluation. Much of value lies beyond the limits of this book; much of this is becoming accessible through the internet (see, for instance, the site on nineteenth-century American women writers at http://clever.net/19cwww). As it stands, *She Wields A Pen* begins and ends as it does deliberately. Praising nonsense in the first poem, Eliza Follen praises not chaotic absurdity but responsiveness to difference and change. In the last poem, invoking her father's story of an 'uncanny object' that damns a tyrant, Priscilla Thompson invokes the lasting dignity of stories about how people have resisted oppression.

JANET GRAY

References

Secondary sources drawn upon in the Introduction are listed in Suggestions for Further Reading (pp. 365–369) under the categories 'Nineteenth-Century American Literary History', 'Gender in Nineteenth-Century American Cultural History' and 'Issues and Methods in Women's Literary History'.

NOTE ON THE TEXTS

'Lines on Nonsense', 'For the Fourth of July', 'Children in Slavery': Mrs [Eliza] Lee Follen, *Poems* (Boston: William Crosby & Co., 1839).

'Mary's Lamb': Sarah Josepha Hale, *Poems for Our Children: designed for Families, Sabbath Schools and Infant Schools, Written to Inculcate Moral Truths and Virtuous Sentiments* (Boston: Marsh, Capen & Lyon, 1830); selection from 'Three Hours; or, The Vigil of Love': Sarah Josepha Hale, *Three Hours; or, The Vigil of Love: and Other Poems* (Philadelphia: Carey & Hart, 1848).

'Apprehension', 'The Butterfly's Dream', 'The Child's Address to the Kentucky Mummy': Miss H. F. Gould, *Poems*, vol. 1 (Boston: Hilliard, Gray & Co., 1836).

'Death of an Infant': *Poems* by the author of 'Moral Pieces in Prose and Verse' [Lydia Huntley Sigourney] (Boston, Hartford, New York, 1827); 'Indian Names': *Poems* (Philadelphia, 1834); 'Poetry', 'The Western Emigrant': *Zinzendorff and Other Poems* (New York: Leavitt, Lord & Co., Boston: Crocker & Brewster, 1836); 'Erin's Daughter': *The Western Home and Other Poems* (Philadelphia, 1854).

'What Will Be Your Destiny?': Mrs [Caroline] Gilman, *Oracles for Youth* (New York: Putnam, 1852).

'To Persecuted Foreigners', 'The Newspaper': Penina Moise, *Secular and Religious Works of Penina Moise, with Brief Sketch of Her Life*, compiled and published by Charleston Section, Council of Jewish Women (Charleston, SC: Nicholas G. Duffy, Printer, 1911).

'Otagamiad': Jane Johnston Schoolcraft, Philip P. Mason, ed., *The Literary Voyager or Muzzenyegun* (East Lansing: Michigan State University Press, 1962). Quotation marks have been corrected for consistency.

Selection from 'The Sinless Child': Mrs Seba [Elizabeth Oakes] Smith, *The Sinless Child and Other Poems* (New York: Wiley & Putnam; Boston: W. D. Ticknor, 1853).

'Sonnet', 'To Shakspeare', 'Sonnet', 'Faith', 'Sonnet': Frances Anne Kemble, *Poems* (Boston: Ticknor & Fields, 1859).

'Meditations', 'The One in All', 'Lines Written in Boston on a Beautiful Autumnal Day': Margaret Fuller, *Life Without and Life Within*, ed. Arthur Fuller (Boston: Brown, Taggard & Chase, 1860).

'Real Comfort': Mary S. B. Dana [Shindler], *The Parted Family and Other Poems* (New York: Dayton & Saxton; Boston: Saxton & Peirce, 1842).

Selection from 'Female Scriptural Characters', 'Woman's Rights': Rebekah Gumpert Hyneman, *The Leper and Other Poems* (Philadelphia: A. Hart, 1853).

'An Appeal to Women': Ada, *The Liberator*, vol. 4, no. 5 (1 April 1834), p. 20; 'The Scroll is Open': *The Liberator*, vol. 7, no. 7 (11 February 1839), p. 28.

'The Sun-Struck Eagle', 'Forests and Caverns': [Catherine Ana Warfield and Eleanor Percy Lee], *The Wife of Leon and Other Poems. By Two Sisters of the West* (New York: C. Appleton & Co.; Philadelphia: George S. Appleton, 1844).

'Battle-Hymn of the Republic', selections from 'Lyrics of the Street', 'The House of Rest': Julia Ward Howe, *Later Lyrics* (Boston: Lee & Shepard, 1887).

'Advice to Young Ladies', 'The True Friend': Ann Plato, *Essays; Including Biographies and Miscellaneous Pieces, in Prose and Poetry* (Hartford, printed for the author, 1841; New York and Oxford: Oxford University Press, 1988).

'The Window Just Over the Street', 'In Bonds', 'The West Country', 'Telling Fortunes': *The Poetical Works of Alice and Phoebe Cary with a Memorial of Their Lives*, ed. Mary Clemmer (New York: Hurd & Houghton; Cambridge: The Riverside Press, 1877).

'Erinna's Spinning': Margaret J. Preston, *Old Song and New* (Philadelphia: J. B. Lippincott & Co., 1870).

'The Mandan Chief': Frances Jane Crosby [van Alstyne], *The Blind Girl and Other Poems* (New York: Wiley & Putnam, 1844); 'Let Me Die on the Prairie', 'On Hearing a Description of a Prairie', 'Thoughts in Midnight Hours': Frances Jane Crosby [van Alstyne], *Monterey and Other Poems* (New York: R. Craighead, 1851); 'We Are Going', 'Blessed Assurance', 'I Am Thine, O Lord': Frances Jane Crosby [van Alstyne], *Bells at Evening and Other Verses* (4th ed.; New York and Chicago: Biglow & Main, 1902).

'The House by the Sea', 'Nameless Pain', 'The Wife Speaks', 'One morn I left him in his bed', 'Before the Mirror', 'Above the Tree': Elizabeth Stoddard, *Poems* (Boston and New York: Houghton Mifflin Co., 1895).

'Homes for All', 'Harvest Gathering', 'Shakespearian Readings': *The Poems of Alice and Phoebe Cary* (New York: Hurst & Co. Publishers, 1850).

'A Little Cavalier', 'What the Train Ran Over': *The Poetical Works of Lucy Larcom* (Boston and New York: Houghton Mifflin Co., 1884).

Selection from 'Aunt Chloe': *Complete Poems of Frances E. W. Harper*, ed. Maryemma Graham (New York and Oxford: Oxford University Press, 1988).

'Schemhammphorasch', 'Che Sara Sara', 'A Hospital Soliloquy': Rose Terry Cooke, *Poems* (New York: Geo. Gottsberger Peck, 1888).

Selection from 'The Poet': Achsa W. Sprague, *The Poet and Other Poems* (Boston: William White & Co., 1864).

'Fascicle 34': transcribed from *The Manuscript Books of Emily Dickinson*, ed. R. W. Franklin (Cambridge, Mass. and London: Belknap Press of Harvard University Press, 1981). Poems correspond to nos. 645, 646, 647, 649, 650, 651, 648, 478, 754, 710, 755, 756, 690, 757, 758, 711, 993, 675 in *The Complete Poems of Emily Dickinson*, ed. Thomas H. Johnson (Boston: Little, Brown & Co., 1955).

'Solitude', 'Distance', 'My House Not Made with Hands', 'My Strawberry': Helen Hunt Jackson, *Verses* (Boston: Roberts Brothers, 1877); 'Emigravit', 'Opportunity': Helen Hunt Jackson, *Sonnets and Lyrics* (Boston: Roberts Brothers, 1886).

'The Mayor of Scuttleton', 'Fire in the window', 'Someone in the garden', 'The Moon came late', 'Shepherd John', 'Early to bed', 'The Way To Do It', 'Poor Crow!', 'The Wooden Horse', 'Tinker, come bring your solder', 'Taking Time to Grow': Mary Mapes Dodge, *Rhymes and Jingles* (New York: Scribner, Armstrong & Co., 1875).

'The Lay of a Golden Goose': *Louisa May Alcott: Her Life, Letters and Journals*, ed. Ednah D. Cheney (Boston: Roberts Brothers, 1889).

'Street Music': Florence Percy [Elizabeth Akers Allen], *Forest Buds, from the Woods of Maine* (Boston: Brown, Bazin & Co., Portland, Maine: Francis

Blake, 1856); 'Rock Me to Sleep', 'In the Defences': *Poems by Elizabeth Akers* (Boston: Ticknor and Fields, 1867).

'Note': Gail Hamilton [Mary Abigail Dodge], *Chips, Fragments and Vestiges*, ed. H. Augusta Dodge (Boston: Lee and Shepard, 1902).

'A Home', 'My Rights': Susan Coolidge [Sarah C. Woolsey], *Verses* (Boston: Roberts Brothers, 1880).

'Magdalen': Harriet Prescott Spofford, *Poems* (Boston: Houghton Mifflin Co., 1882); 'The Tryst': Harriet Prescott Spofford, *In Titian's Garden* (Boston: Copeland and Day, 1897).

'The Palace-Burner': Sarah M. B. Piatt, *A Voyage to the Fortunate Isles and Other Poems* (Boston: Houghton Mifflin Co., 1886); 'The Witch in the Glass': Sarah M. B. Piatt, *The Witch in the Glass, etc.* (Boston and New York: Houghton Mifflin Co., 1889); 'A Child's Party': Sarah M. B. Piatt, *Child's World Ballads and Other Poems* (Westminster: Archibald Constable & Co., 1895).

Selections from 'Loew's Bridge: A Broadway Idyl': Mary Eliza Tucker Lambert, *Loew's Bridge, a Broadway Idyl* (New York: M. Doolady, Publisher, 1867); reprinted in *Collected Black Women's Poetry*, vol. 1, ed. Joan R. Sherman (New York and Oxford: Oxford University Press, 1988).

'Aloha'oe', 'Sanoe', 'Ku'u Pua I Paoakalani', 'Ka Waiapo Lani': papers of Queen Lili'uokalani are held in the Archives of Hawaii and the Bernice Pauahi Bishop Museum, Honolulu. New translations of 'Sanoe' and 'Ku'u Pua I Paoakalani' are used by permission of the translators, Kawika McGuire and Sue Nance.

'Judith': Adah Isaacs Menken, *Infelicia* (Philadelphia: J. B. Lippincott & Co., 1873); reprinted in *Collected Black Women's Poetry*, vol. 1, ed. Joan R. Sherman (New York and Oxford: Oxford University Press, 1988).

'Songs for the Four Parts of the Night': Frances Densmore, [Owl Woman], *Papago Music*, Bulletin 90 of the Bureau of American Ethnology (Washington, DC: US Government Printing Office, 1929).

Selections from 'Two Women': Constance Fenimore Woolson, *Two Women* (New York: D. Appleton & Co., 1877).

'Longing', 'My "Cloth of Gold"', 'Ownership', 'Lines': Ina Coolbrith, *Wings of Sunset* (Boston and New York: Houghton Mifflin Co., 1929).

'How Long?', 'Success', 'The New Colossus', 'Long Island Sound', 'City

Visions', '1492', selection from 'On the Voyage to Jerusalem': *The Poems of Emma Lazarus*, vols. 1 & 2 (Boston and New York: Houghton Mifflin Co., 1889).

'Self-Mastery', 'The Quest of the Ideal', 'An Ocean Musing', 'The Tireless Sculptor', 'Toussaint L'Ouverture': Henrietta Cordelia Ray, *Poems* (New York: The Grafton Press, 1910); reprinted in *Collected Black Women's Poetry*, vol. 3, ed. Joan R. Sherman (New York and Oxford: Oxford University Press, 1988).

'Communism', 'Solitude': Ella Wheeler Wilcox, *Poems of Passion* (Chicago: W. B. Conkey Co., 1883); 'Burdened', 'In the Night': Ella Wheeler Wilcox, *Maurine and Other Poems* (Chicago: W. B. Conkey Co., 1888); 'No Classes!', 'Woman', 'My Grave': *Poems of Pleasure* (Chicago: Morrill Higgins & Co., 1892).

'Curfew Must Not Ring Tonight': Rose Hartwick Thorpe, *Ringing Ballads* (Boston: D. Lothrop, 1887).

'Going Out and Coming In', 'Cry of a People': Mollie E. Moore [Davis], *Poems* (Houston, Texas: E. H. Cushing, 1872).

'Cries of the Newsboy': Edith M. Thomas, *In Sunshine Land* (Boston and New York: Houghton Mifflin Co., 1893).

'Mid-March': Lizette Woodworth Reese, *A Branch of May* (1887; reprinted Portland, Maine: Thomas Bird Mosher, 1920); 'Telling the Bees', 'Indian Summer', 'A Street Scene', 'An Old Belle', 'The Day Before Spring', 'Trust', 'Mystery', 'Reserve': Lizette Woodworth Reese, *A Quiet Road* (Boston and New York: Houghton Mifflin Co., 1896).

Selections from 'Héroes del Cinco de Mayo' and 'Homenajes de gratitud': *The World of Early Chicano Poetry, 1846–1910*, vol. 1, *California Poetry, 1855–81*, compiled, edited and translated by Luis A. Torres (Encino, California: Floricanto Press, 1994). Used by permission of the translator.

'Homes', 'The Anti-Suffragists', 'The Mother's Charge', 'Christian Virtues': Charlotte Perkins [Stetson] Gilman, *In This Our World*, 5th ed. (Boston: Small, Maynard & Co., 1914).

'To Clements' Ferry', 'Tennyson's Poems', 'Thine Own', 'Love Letters', 'The Black Sampson': Josephine Delphine [Henderson] Heard, *Morning Glories* (Philadelphia, PA: published by the author, 1890); reprinted in *Collected Black Women's Poetry*, vol. 4, ed. Joan R. Sherman (New York: Oxford University Press, 1988).

'Marshlands', 'Joe', 'Wave-Won': E. Pauline Johnson, *The White Wampum* (London: John Lane; Toronto: Copp Clark Co.; Boston: Lamson, Wolffe & Co., 1895).

'Down Stream', 'Garden Chidings', 'A Reason for Silence', 'John Brown: A Paradox', 'The Atoning Yesterday': Louise Imogen Guiney, *The White Sail* (Boston: Ticknor & Co., 1887).

'Atlanta Exposition Ode', 'Serenade', 'The Coming Woman': Mary Weston Fordham, *Magnolia Leaves* (Charleston, SC: Walker, Evans & Cogswell Co., 1897); reprinted in *Collected Black Women's Poetry*, vol. 2, ed. Joan R. Sherman (New York: Oxford University Press, 1988).

'Four-Leaf Clover', 'Eve', 'Moonrise in the Rockies', 'Dawn on the Willamette', 'A Dream of Sappho', 'The Opal Sea', 'Dawn', 'The Statue': Ella Higginson, *When the Birds Go North Again* (New York: The Macmillan Co., 1898, 1912).

'Fate', 'The Poster Girl's Defence', 'A Pastoral in Posters', 'The Original Summer Girl', 'A Problem', 'Of Modern Books': Carolyn Wells, *Idle Idyls* (New York: Dodd, Mead & Co., 1900).

'Out of the Darkness', 'Love's Compensation': *Selected Works of Voltairine de Cleyre*, ed. Alexander Berkman (New York: Mother Earth Publishing Association, 1914).

'Freedom at McNealy's', 'My Father's Story': Priscilla Jane Thompson, *Ethiope Lays* (printed by the author, Rossmoyne, Ohio, 1900); reprinted in *Collected Black Women's Poetry*, vol. 2, ed. Joan R. Sherman (New York: Oxford University Press, 1988).

SHE WIELDS A PEN

AMERICAN WOMEN POETS OF THE 19TH CENTURY

ELIZA LEE FOLLEN
1787–1860

ELIZA LEE FOLLEN was the fifth of thirteen children in a prominent Boston family. Her father was engaged in international trade and diplomacy. Her intellectually accomplished mother assured that her daughters were well educated. In 1819, after the death of their father, Eliza and two of her sisters established their own household. She belonged to a group that founded a Sunday school and met regularly to discuss religious issues. Through this group she met Charles Follen, who had fled Germany because of official opposition to his democratic views. They married in 1828; their only child, a son, was born in 1830. Both Follens were outspoken early members of the Massachusetts anti-slavery movement. Following Charles's death in 1840, Eliza broadened her activism and publishing, becoming one of Boston's most revered citizens. From 1828–30 she edited the *Christian Teacher's Manual* and from 1843–50 *The Child's Friend*, both Sunday school publications. She also published editions of the writings of Fénelon, a seventeenth-century French liberal theorist, and of Charles Follen. Other writings include *The Skeptic* (1835) and *Sketches of Married Life* (1838). Her *Poems* (1839) includes abolitionist verse, hymns, verse renderings of Psalms and translations from German.

Lines on Nonsense

Yes, nonsense is a treasure!
　I love it from my heart;
The only earthly pleasure
　That never will depart.

But, as for stupid reason,
　That stalking, ten-foot rule,

She's always out of season,
    A tedious, testy fool.

She's like a walking steeple,
    With a clock for face and eyes,
Still bawling to all people,
    Time bids us to be wise.

While nonsense on the spire
    A weathercock you'll find,
Than reason soaring higher,
    And changing with the wind.

The clock too oft deceives,
    Says what it cannot prove;
While every one believes
    The vane that turns above.

Reason oft speaks unbidden,
    And chides us to our face;
For which she should be chidden,
    And taught to know her place.

While nonsense smiles and chatters,
    And says such charming things,
Like youthful hope she flatters;
    And like a syren sings.

Her charm's from fancy borrowed,
    For she is fancy's pet;
Her name is on her forehead,
    In rainbow colors set.

Then, nonsense let us cherish,
    Far, far from reason's light;
Lest in her light she perish,
    And vanish from our sight.

                                    1839

For the Fourth of July

My country, that nobly could dare
    The hand of oppression to brave,
O, how the foul stain canst thou bear,
    Of being the land of the slave?

His groans, and the clank of his chains
    Shall rise with the shouts of the free,
And turn into discord the strains
    They raise, God of mercy, to thee.

The proud knee at his altar we bend,
    On God as our Father we call:
We call him our Father and Friend,
    And forget he's the Father of all.

His children he does not forget;
    His mercy, his power can save;
And, sure as God liveth, he yet
    Will liberty give to the slave.

O talk not of freedom and peace!
    With the blood of the slave on our sod:
Till the groans of the negro shall cease,
    Hope not for a blessing from God.

He asks, – am not I a man?
    He pleads, – am not I a brother?
Then dare not, and hope not you can
    The cry of humanity smother.

'T will be heard from the south to the north,
    In our halls, and in poverty's shed:
It will go like a hurricane forth,
    And wake up the living and dead.

The dead whom the white man has slain,
    They cry from the ground and the waves:
They once cried for mercy in vain,
    They plead for their brothers the slaves.

O! let them my country be heard!
    Be the land of the free and the brave!

And send forth the glorious word,
   This is not the land of the slave!

1839

Children in Slavery

When children play the livelong day,
   Like birds and butterflies;
As free and gay, sport life away,
   And know not care nor sighs:
Then earth and air seem fresh and fair,
   All peace below, above:
Life's flowers are there, and everywhere
   Is innocence and love.

When children pray with fear all day,
   A blight must be at hand:
Then joys decay, and birds of prey
   Are hovering o'er the land:
When young hearts weep as they go to sleep,
   Then all the world seems sad:
The flesh must creep, and woes are deep
   When children are not glad.

1839

SARAH JOSEPHA HALE
1788–1879

SARAH JOSEPHA HALE was born in Newport, New Hampshire, daughter of a tavern keeper, and educated by her mother and brother. She ran a school from 1806 to 1813, then married a lawyer, David Hale, who gave her the equivalent of a college education. Widowed with five children in 1822, she turned to literary activity for income. The success of her novel *Northwood* (1827) led to her becoming editor of *Ladies' Magazine* of Boston in 1828. In 1837, this journal merged into *Godey's Lady's Book* of Philadelphia. Hale's editorship (1837–77) made her one of the most influential American women of the mid-nineteenth century, an arbiter of taste in dress, architecture and literature, and a publicist for women's education, women's property rights, professions for women, early childhood education, public health and other progressive causes. Yet she opposed suffrage and women's public speaking. Hale promoted American women writers through *Godey's* and other channels. Her writings include *Poems for Our Children* (1830) ('Mary's Lamb' appeared first in this Sunday school book and circulated widely thereafter); *Flora's Interpreter, or, The American Book of Flowers and Sentiments*, which ran to fourteen editions; *Three Hours; or, The Vigil of Love; and Other Poems* (1848); and *Woman's Record* (1854), an encyclopedia of distinguished women throughout history, with the largest part devoted to living American women writers. (Several of her entries are cited in the The Poets and Their Critics section of this book; see especially her comments on Hannah F. Gould.) Hale also published etiquette books and cookbooks and edited the letters of Lady Mary Wortley Montagu and Madame de Sévigné.

Mary's Lamb

Mary had a little lamb,
   Its fleece was white as snow,
And every where that Mary went
   The lamb was sure to go;
He followed her to school one day—
   That was against the rule,
It made the children laugh and play,
   To see a lamb at school.

And so the Teacher turned him out,
   But still he lingered near,
And waited patiently about,
   Till Mary did appear;
And then he ran to her, and laid
   His head upon her arm,
As if he said – 'I'm not afraid—
   You'll keep me from all harm.'

'What makes the lamb love Mary so?'
   The eager children cry—
'O, Mary loves the lamb, you know,'
   The Teacher did reply;—
'And you each gentle animal
   In confidence may bind,
And make them follow at your call,
   If you are always *kind*.'

1830

from THREE HOURS; OR, THE VIGIL OF LOVE

from *First Hour*

A blessing on the printer's art!
Books are the Mentors of the heart.
The burning soul, the burdened mind,

In books alone companions find.
We never speak our deepest feelings;
Our holiest hopes have no revealings,
Save in the gleams that light the face,
Or fancies that the pen may trace:
And hence to books the heart must turn,
When with unspoken thoughts we yearn;
And gather from the silent page
The just reproof, the counsel sage,
The consolation kind and true
   That soothes and heals the wounded heart,
As on the broken plant the dew
Calls forth fresh leaves and buds to view,
   More lovely as the old depart.

And when, with gloomy fears oppressed,
The trembling-hearted fain would rest,
No opiate like a book, that charms,
By its deep spell, the mind's alarms;
Opening, as Genius has the key,
Some haunt of mirth, or mystery,
Or trusting faith, or tender love,
As vista to the heaven above,
Where the lone wandering one may come,
Refreshed and glad, as though at home;
And feel the soul has wells of joy,
   Like springs that gush in cavern's gloom,
And hopes like gold without alloy,
   Or diamonds buried in a tomb.

But there's a fever of the soul,
Beyond this opiate control;
When the book-charm its influence loses,
The mind will wander where it chooses:
We see the page, but never heed,
Or thought is busy while we read;
And strange revealings fill the gloom—
A song of joy, or dirge of doom
Seems writ on every page we turn,
With spirit lore we fain would learn.

                    1848

HANNAH F. GOULD
1789–1865

HANNAH F. GOULD was born in Lancaster, Massachusetts and in 1808 moved with her family to Newburyport, where she lived the rest of her life. Her mother died when Hannah was a child. For many years she devoted herself to keeping house and providing companionship for her father, a Revolutionary war veteran. She began writing poetry in her thirties, first entertaining Newburyport citizens with mock-epitaphs of local celebrities, then contributing pieces to magazines and annuals. Her first book, *Poems* (1832), was published by her friends without her knowledge. It sold well, was reprinted in 1833 and 1835 and expanded in 1836. Ten other volumes followed between 1844 and 1870. In addition to children's poetry, she wrote religious, historical, commemorative and abolitionist poems, many of which appeared in *The Liberator*.

Apprehension

'Oh! sister, he is so swift and tall,
Though I want the ride, he will spoil it all,
For, when he sets out, he will let me fall,
    And give me a bump, I know!
Mamma, what was it I heard you say,
About the world's hobbies, the other day,
How some would get on and gallop away,
    To end with an overthrow?'

'I said, little prattler, the world was a race,
That many would mount with a smile on the face,
And ride to their ruin, or fall in disgrace:
    That him, who was deaf to fear,
And did not look out for a rein or a guide,
His courser might cast on the highway side,

In the mud, rocks and brambles, to end his ride,
    Perchance with a sigh and a tear!'

'Oh! sister, sister! I fear to try;
For Brutus's back is so live and high!
It creeps at my touch – and he winks his eye—
    I'm sure he is going to jump!
Come! dear mother, tell us some more
About the world's ride, as you did before,
Who helped it up – and all how it bore
    The fall, and got over the bump!'

The Butterfly's Dream

A tulip, just opened, had offered to hold
    A butterfly, gaudy and gay;
And, rocked in a cradle of crimson and gold,
    The careless young slumberer lay.

For the butterfly slept, as such thoughtless ones will,
    At ease, and reclining on flowers,
If ever they study, 't is how they may kill
    The best of their mid-summer hours.

And the butterfly dreamed, as is often the case
    With *indolent* lovers of change,
Who, keeping the body at ease in its place,
    Give fancy permission to range.

He dreamed that he saw, what he could but despise,
    The swarm from a neighbouring hive;
Which, having come out for their winter supplies,
    Had made the whole garden alive.

He looked with disgust, as the proud often do,
    On the diligent movements of those,
Who, keeping both present and future in view,
    Improve every hour as it goes.

As the brisk little alchymists passed to and fro,
    With anger the butterfly swelled;

And called them mechanics – a rabble too low
   To come near the station he held.

'Away from my presence!' said he, in his sleep,
   'Ye humble plebeians! nor dare
Come here with your colorless winglets to sweep
   The king of this brilliant parterre!'

He thought, at these words, that together they flew,
   And, facing about, made a stand;
And then, to a terrible army they grew,
   And fenced him on every hand.

Like hosts of huge giants, his numberless foes
   Seemed spreading to measureless size:
Their wings with a mighty expansion arose,
   And stretched like a veil o'er the skies.

Their eyes seemed like little volcanoes, for fire,—
   Their hum, to a cannon-peal grown,—
Farina to bullets was rolled in their ire,
   And, he thought, hurled at him and his throne.

He tried to cry quarter! his voice would not sound,
   His head ached – his throne reeled and fell;
His enemy cheered, as he came to the ground,
   And cried, 'King Papilio, farewell!'

His fall chased the vision – the sleeper awoke,
   The wonderful dream to expound;
The lightning's bright flash from the thunder-cloud broke,
   And hail-stones were rattling around.

He'd slumbered so long, that now, over his head,
   The tempest's artillery rolled;
The tulip was shattered – the whirl-blast had fled,
   And borne off its crimson and gold.

'T is said, for the fall and the pelting, combined
   With suppressed ebullitions of pride,
This vain son of summer no balsam could find,
   But he crept under covert and died.

The Child's Address to the Kentucky Mummy

And now, Mistress Mummy, since thus you've been found
   By the world, that has long done without you,
In your snug little hiding-place far under ground—
Be pleased to speak out, as we gather around,
   And let us hear something about you!

By the style of your dress you are not Madam Eve—
   You of course had a father and mother;
No more of your line have we power to conceive,
As you furnish us nothing by which to believe
   You had husband, child, sister, or brother.

We know you have lived, though we cannot tell when,
   And that too by eating and drinking,
To judge by your teeth, and the lips you *had then*;
And we see you are one of the children of men,
   Though long from their looks you've been shrinking.

Who was it that made you a cavern so deep,
   Refused your poor head a last pillow,
And bade you *sit still* when you'd sunken to sleep,
And they'd bound you and muffled you up in a heap
   Of clothes made of hempen and willow?

Say, whose was the ear that could hear with delight
   The musical trinket found nigh you?
And who had the eye that was pleased with the sight
Of this form (whose queer face might be brown, red, or white,)
   Trick'd out in the jewels kept by you?

LYDIA HUNTLEY SIGOURNEY
1791–1865

LYDIA HUNTLEY SIGOURNEY was born in Norwich, Connecticut, the only daughter of a gardener. Her mother encouraged her learning and her father's employer arranged for her to attend boarding school. With financial assistance from a wealthy New England family, she established a school for young women in Hartford in 1814 and the following year published her first book. In 1819 she married a wealthy businessman, Charles Sigourney, a widower with three children. Respecting his qualms about publicity, she published anonymously until the family suffered financial collapse around 1830. Sigourney's publications thereafter under her own name built a career of unprecedented popularity and influence. Over sixty-five volumes bear her name. *Godey's Lady's Book* paid $500 annually for permission to list her name as an editor. Other journals paid her well for any contribution. On earnings from revisions and reprints, she travelled to Europe in 1840, where she was received as a celebrity and met such notables as Maria Edgeworth, William Wordsworth and Thomas Carlyle. She recorded these travels in *Pleasant Memories of Pleasant Lands* (1842). Many of Sigourney's poems reflect her interest in Native Americans. *Traits of the Aborigines of America* (1822) draws on the ethnography of Henry Rowe Schoolcraft. The long title poems of both *Zinzendorff and Other Poems* (1833) and *Pocahontas and Other Poems* (1841) concern Native American themes. Sigourney also wrote against slavery, in support of charitable causes, in sympathy with people displaced from their homelands and in mourning for the deaths of friends and notables. Her memoirs, *Letters of a Life*, were published posthumously (1866).

Death of an Infant

Death found strange beauty on that cherub brow,
And dash'd it out. – There was a tint of rose
O'er cheek and lip; – he touch'd the veins with ice,
And the rose faded. – Forth from those blue eyes
There spake a wistful tenderness, – a doubt
Whether to grieve or sleep, which Innocence
Alone can wear. – With ruthless haste he bound
The silken fringes of their curtaining lids
Forever. – There had been a murmuring sound
With which the babe would claim its mother's ear,
Charming her even to tears. – The spoiler set
His seal of silence. – But there beam'd a smile,
So fix'd and holy from that marble brow, –
Death gazed and left it there; – he dared not steal
The signet-ring of Heaven.

1827

Indian Names

'How can the red men be forgotten, while so many of
our states and territories, bays, lakes, and rivers, are
indelibly stamped by names of their giving?'

Ye say they all have passed away,
    That noble race and brave,
That their light canoes have vanished
    From off the crested wave;
That 'mid the forests where they roamed
    There rings no hunter shout,
But their name is on your waters,
    Ye may not wash it out.

'Tis where Ontario's billow
    Like Ocean's surge is curled,
Where strong Niagara's thunders wake
    The echo of the world.

Where red Missouri bringeth
  Rich tribute from the west,
And Rappahannock sweetly sleeps
  On green Virginia's breast.

Ye say their cone-like cabins,
  That clustered o'er the vale,
Have fled away like withered leaves
  Before the autumn gale,
But their memory liveth on your hills,
  Their baptism on your shore,
Your everlasting rivers speak
  Their dialect of yore.

Old Massachusetts wears it,
  Within her lordly crown,
And broad Ohio bears it,
  Amid his young renown;
Connecticut hath wreathed it
  Where her quiet foliage waves,
And bold Kentucky breathed it hoarse
  Through all her ancient caves.

Wachuset hides its lingering voice
  Within his rocky heart,
And Alleghany graves its tone
  Throughout his lofty chart;
Monadnock on his forehead hoar
  Doth seal the sacred trust,
Your mountains build their monument,
  Though ye destroy their dust.

Ye call these red-browned brethren
  The insects of an hour,
Crushed like the noteless worm amid
  The regions of their power;
Ye drive them from their father's lands,
  Ye break of faith the seal,
But can ye from the court of Heaven
  Exclude their last appeal?

Ye see their unresisting tribes,
  With toilsome step and slow,

On through the trackless desert pass
   A caravan of woe;
Think ye the Eternal's ear is deaf?
   His sleepless vision dim?
Think ye the *soul's blood* may not cry
   From that far land to him?

1834

Poetry

Morn on her rosy couch awoke,
   Enchantment led the hour,
And mirth and music drank the dews
   That freshen'd Beauty's flower,
Then from her bower of deep delight,
   I heard a young girl sing,
'Oh, speak no ill of poetry,
   For 'tis a holy thing.'

The Sun in noon-day heat rose high,
   And on with heaving breast,
I saw a weary pilgrim toil
   Unpitied and unblest,
Yet still in trembling measures flow'd
   Forth from a broken string,
'Oh, speak no ill of poetry,
   For 'tis a holy thing.'

'Twas night, and Death the curtains drew,
   'Mid agony severe,
While there a willing spirit went
   Home to a glorious sphere,
Yet still it sigh'd, even when was spread
   The waiting Angel's wing,
'Oh, speak no ill of poetry,
   For 'tis a holy thing.'

1836

The Western Emigrant

An axe rang sharply 'mid those forest shades
Which from creation toward the skies had tower'd
In unshorn beauty. There, with vigorous arm
Wrought a bold emigrant, and by his side
His little son, with question and response,
Beguiled the toil.
                              'Boy, thou hast never seen
Such glorious trees. Hark, when their giant trunks
Fall, how the firm earth groans. Rememberest thou
The mighty river, on whose breast we sail'd,
So many days, on toward the setting sun?
Our own Connecticut, compar'd to that,
Was but a creeping stream.'
                              'Father, the brook
That by our door went singing, where I launch'd
My tiny boat, with my young playmates round,
When school was o'er, is dearer far to me,
Than all these bold, broad waters. To my eye
They are as strangers. And those little trees
My mother nurtur'd in the garden bound,
Of our first home, from whence the fragrant peach
Hung in its ripening gold, were fairer sure,
Than this dark forest, shutting out the day.'
—'What, ho! – my little girl,' and with light step
A fairy creature hasted toward her sire,
And setting down the basket that contain'd
His noon-repast, look'd upward to his face
With sweet, confiding smile.
                              'See, dearest, see,
That bright-wing'd paroquet, and hear the song
Of yon gay red-bird, echoing through the trees,
Making rich music. Didst thou ever hear,
In far New England, such a mellow tone?'
—'I had a robin that did take the crumbs
Each night and morning, and his chirping voice
Still made me joyful, as I went to tend
My snow-drops. I was always laughing then
In that first home. I should be happier now
Methinks, if I could find among these dells

The same fresh violets.'
                Slow night drew on,
And round the rude hut of the Emigrant
The wrathful spirit of the rising storm
Spake bitter things. His weary children slept,
And he, with head declin'd, sat listening long
To the swoln waters of the Illinois,
Dashing against their shores.
                   Starting he spake,—
'Wife! did I see thee brush away a tear?
'Twas even so. Thy heart was with the halls
Of thy nativity. Their sparkling lights,
Carpets, and sofas, and admiring guests,
Befit thee better than these rugged walls
Of shapeless logs, and this lone, hermit home.'
  'No – no. All was so still around, methought
Upon mine ear that echoed hymn did steal,
Which 'mid the Church where erst we paid our vows,
So tuneful peal'd. But tenderly thy voice
Dissolv'd the illusion.'
             And the gentle smile
Lighting her brow, the fond caress that sooth'd
Her waking infant, reassur'd his soul
That wheresoe'er our best affections dwell,
And strike a healthful root, is happiness.
Content, and placid, to his rest he sank,
But dreams, those wild magicians, that do play
Such pranks when reason slumbers, tireless wrought
Their will with him.
           Up rose the thronging mart
Of his own native city, – roof and spire,
All glittering bright, in fancy's frost-work ray.
The steed his boyhood nurtur'd proudly neigh'd,
The favorite dog came frisking round his feet,
With shrill and joyous bark, – familiar doors
Flew open, – greeting hands with his were link'd
In friendship's grasp, – he heard the keen debate
From congregated haunts, where mind with mind
Doth blend and brighten, – and till morning rov'd
'Mid the loved scenery of his native land.

                               1836

Erin's Daughter

Poor Erin's daughter cross'd the main
   In youth's unfolding prime,
A lot of servitude to bear
   In this our western clime.

And when the drear heart-sickness came
   Beneath a stranger sky,
Tears on her nightly pillow lay,
   But morning saw them dry.

For still with earnest hope she strove
   Her distant home to cheer,
And from her parents lift the load
   Of poverty severe.

To them with liberal hand she sent
   Her all – her hard-earn'd store –
A rapture thrilling through her soul,
   She ne'er had felt before.

E'en mid her quiet slumbers gleam'd
   A cabin's lighted pane,
A board with simple plenty crown'd,
   A loved and loving train.

And so her life of earnest toil
   With secret joy was blest,
For the sweet warmth of filial love
   Made sunshine in her breast.

But bitter tidings o'er the wave
   With fearful echo sped;
Gaunt famine o'er her home had strode,
   And all were with the dead!

All gone! – her brothers in their glee,
   Her sisters young and fair;
And Erin's daughter bow'd her down
   In desolate despair.

1854

CAROLINE GILMAN
1794–1888

CAROLINE GILMAN was the daughter of a Boston shipwright. She married Unitarian pastor Samuel Gilman in 1819, moved to Charleston, South Carolina, and had seven children. From 1832 to 1842, she published the first American weekly journal for young people, *Rose Bud* (later *The Southern Rose*), which circulated widely and made her the best-known woman writer of the South. Humorous sketches about the management of a middle-class household and its servants, written for the *Rose*, were republished as *Recollections of a New England Bride* (1834). Other publications include *Recollections of a Southern Matron* (1837), a chapter of which English journalist Harriet Martineau included in her *Society in America* (1837); *The Lady's Annual Register and Housewife's Memorandum Book, for 1838*, a manual for housekeepers; *Love's Progress* (1840), a domestic novel; children's books, including *The Little Wreath of Stories and Poems for Children* (1847); and *Verses of a Lifetime* (1849), which includes descriptions of Southern landscape, dramatic pieces and romantic ballads. Two unusual contributions are *Oracles from the Poets* (1845) and *The Sibyl, or, New Oracles from the Poets* (1847), in which Gilman adapted extracts from the works of poets as a fortune-telling parlour game. *Oracles for Youth* (1852) follows the same pattern but the verse is Gilman's. Her views on gender were progressive but her position on slavery was not. Although the Gilmans bought, educated and freed several young black men, Caroline Gilman justified slavery in her writings and supported the Confederacy during the Civil War.

from ORACLES FOR YOUTH

Directions

Let some one hold the book, and ask one of the questions. The answers being all numbered, the girl or boy who is questioned chooses a number, and the person who holds the book reads the answer to which that number belongs, aloud. For instance:

Question. What is your character?
Answer.   I choose No. 3.

Questioner reads aloud:

No. 3. Gentle tempered, sweet and kind,
        To no angry word inclined.

What Will Be Your Destiny?

FORTY-THREE ANSWERS

1. Just as you think you've gained great wealth,
   Something will make you *lose your health*.

2. Your hair will be white in a single night,
   From having *an unexpected fright*.

3. *You* will enjoy a *sweet old age*,
   So kind and pure, so long and sage.

4. *You* will fall down at eighty-four,
   And break a dozen ribs or more.

5. You will finish your days *with God for your friend*:
   Who would not be glad of so blissful an end?

6. You will be *ever absorbed in books*,
   And never give a thought to looks.

7. *In peace and plenty* you will lie,
   And in the arms of friendship die.

8. You will have cause for *many tears*,
   To cloud the beauty of your years.

9. Ah, is it so? when you are old,
   You will be very poor, I'm told.

10. In the night-time *you will weep*,
    And your painful vigils keep.

11. *Nothing dreadful, nothing sad,*
    Comes to you; for this I'm glad.

12. You always will have an *excellent table,*
    And full of horses will keep your stable.

13. The Sibyl says *you'll die in Rome,*
    Which for a time will be your home.

14. Your *plenty and peace*
    Will never cease.

15. You will suddenly *die in the crowded street,*
    If the age of a hundred years you meet.

16. *You will ride in your carriage-and-four,*
    And be very kind to the suffering poor.

17. Never murmur, never care,
    You will be a millionaire.

18. *Sick at heart, and sick at head,*
    You will wish that you were dead.

19. As the might of God you see,
    Religious you will ever be.

20. To *California you will go*
    To get the shining gold, you know.

21. Brightest pleasures you will see,
    And happiness your portion be.

22. *Love will gild your joyous life,*
    Free from pain and care and strife.

23. Don't despond, and do not care,
    You will be a nabob's heir.

24. To California you will be sent,
    But will return as poor as you went.

25. *A missionary you will be,*
    Far o'er the billows of the sea.

26. It is your destiny to rule,
    And you *will keep a village school.*

27. *Balls and parties* you will find
    Alone are suited to your mind.

28. Through the vista of the years
    I see you *mourning and in tears.*

29. *A country life* at length you'll lead,
    Rejoicing in your ambling steed.

30. Fair in the *wild and prairied west,*
    Your tired frame at length you'll rest.

31. *A public singer's* place you'll take,
    And a sensation you will make.

32. You'll only love *your native home,*
    From which you will not care to roam.

33. *A great pianist,* you will gain
    Bright laurels from the admiring train.

34. *A kitchen garden* you will keep,
    And sell fresh vegetables cheap.

35. To *higher virtues you will rise,*
    Until you're ready for the skies.

36. To the *city's crowded street*
    You'll direct your willing feet.

37. *In digging in a worn-out field*
    You'll see a box, securely sealed,
        Half buried in the ground;
    And therein jewels bright, and gold,
    And bank-notes, in large bundles rolled,
        Will joyfully be found.

38. *A music teacher* you will be,
    This is your tuneful destiny.

39. *You will travel* in your prime,
    And view the works of art sublime.

40. You *will journey the whole world o'er,*
    And gather relics from every shore.

41. The most of your time will be passed *on the sea,*
    But wherever you are, you will happy be.

42. On an *island will you live,*
    And nice pleasure-parties give.

43. You will spend your leisure hours,
    In a garden *tending flowers.*

PENINA MOISE
1797–1880

PENINA MOISE, youngest of six children, lived throughout her life in Charleston, South Carolina. Her parents had fled Haiti and lost considerable wealth in 1791, when revolution resulted in the island's being ruled for a time by former slaves. When Moise was twelve her father died. She and her siblings left school to work. She refused offers of marriage and devoted her life to religious service and writing. Her book of poems, *Fancy's Sketch Book*, was published in 1833. Thereafter she published in Northern and Southern periodicals, including the Charleston *Courier*, Jewish journals and *Godey's Lady's Book*. Her most enduring literary accomplishment was to write nearly all of *Hymns Written for the Use of Hebrew Congregations* (1856), the first Reform Jewish hymnal published in the United States. Some of her hymns are still used. Starting in 1842 Moise was superintendent of Beth Elohim school, an early Jewish entrant in the movement for children's religious education. She composed instructional poems, songs and recitations for Beth Elohim and for the school she founded with her sister and a niece during the Civil War. Nearly blind, Moise taught elocution and oral reading. Moise became housebound by neuralgia but exercised by walking around her bed while playing mental word games. She wrote at night on a chalk slate, which her niece deciphered in the morning. Beloved in her community, Moise supervised young couples' courtships in her parlour. Volunteers regularly read to Moise and a Friday afternoon literary salon, attended by the Charleston intelligentsia, met at her house.

To Persecuted Foreigners

From the Southern Patriot, 23 February 1820
23 Years Old

Fly from the soil whose desolating creed,
Outraging faith, makes human victims bleed,
Welcome! where every Muse has reared a shrine,
The respect of wild Freedom to refine.

Upon OUR Chieftain's brow no crown appears;
No gems are mingled with his silver hairs.
Enough that Laurels bloom amid its snows,
Enriched with these, the sage all else foregoes.

If thou art one of that oppressed race,
Whose name's a proverb, and whose lot's disgrace,
Brave the Atlantic – Hope's broad anchor weigh,
A Western Sun will gild your future day.

Zeal is not blind in this our temp'rate soil;
She has no scourge to make the soul recoil.
Her darkness vanished when our stars did flash;
Her red arm, grasped by Reason, dropt the lash.

Our Union, Liberty and Peace imparts,
Stampt on our standards, graven on our hearts;
The first, from crush'd Ambition's ruin rose,
The last, on Victory's field spontaneous grows.

Rise, then, elastic from Oppression's tread,
Come and repose on Plenty's flowery bed.
Oh! not as Strangers shall welcome be,
Come to the homes and bosoms of the free.

The Newspaper

To a Venetian coin, the first Gazetta
For its generic title became debtor.

Whither excursive Fancy tends thy Flight?
Like Eastern Caliph masking thee at night,
By Vezier memory attended still,
Thou pertly pryest in each domicil.
Woe! to the Caitiff then who in his cups,
Unconscious with sublimity he sups,
Shall vow in Bacchanalian truth or fun
Thou art not kindred to the glorious sun!
I fear thee not, clandestine ambulator!
Thou most sophistical and specious traitor
To Truth and Reason, those imperial twins
Whose Empire with thy Martyrdom begins.
What is thy drift in brandishing a flag,
Whose motto is a metamorphosed rag!
As by those motley streaks of white and jet,
I trace that aboriginal Gazette,
The British prototype of '65
From which all modern journals we derive.
At first confined to faction's revelations,
Mere politics, or plodding speculations.
Now to a semi-cyclopedia risen
Which the assembled arts, delight to dizen.
Its grand mosaic ground work ever graced
With polished gems of miscellaneous taste.
Philosophy his portico regains
In columns where profoundest science reigns.
While in relief a neighboring sphere discloses
Clio's with Nature's kind exotic roses.
A curious melange of mental food
In fragments thus promiscuously strewed;
Rising Aeronauts, and sinking funds,
Fearful phenomena of stars or suns.
Men in the stocks, uneasy as old Kent,
Others appalled by fluctuating rent.
New ministers to preach, and spirit lamps,
Foreign intelligence from Courts and Camps

Don-Pedro – and a fresh supply of leeches
A ball that blackens, and a wash that bleaches,
Here, Hymen's herald to the world declares
When Love triumphant at his shrine appears.
There, tenderness bereaved, its tribute brings
And Hope's crushed odours on Death's altar flings.
Advertisements of various commodities,
And anecdotes of Irish whims and oddities.
Bills of mortality, and Board of Health,
A fine green turtle – and a miser's wealth.
The prices current – a cheap hasty pudding,
Detected fallacies – and falcon-hooding,
Arrivals and departures – births and deaths,
A dreadful Storm – and artificial wreaths,
One fugitive forsakes the Cotton pod,
In terror of the Supervisor's rod.
Another dreading critic castigation,
Flies from the fields of rich imagination.
Thus from discordant interests Genius hurled
The elements that form this typic world.

JANE JOHNSTON SCHOOLCRAFT
(BAME-WA-WA-GE-ZHIK-A-QUAY)
1800–41

JANE JOHNSTON SCHOOLCRAFT was one of eight children of an Irish fur trader and an influential Chippewa or Ojibwa (alternate spellings of the same word) woman, daughter of tribal leader Waub Ojeeb (White Fisher). Jane grew up in Sault Ste Marie and returned there after being educated in Ireland. She learned tribal lore from her mother and spoke Ojibwa fluently. War Department agent Henry Rowe Schoolcraft boarded with the Johnston family when he arrived in 1822, assigned to gain tribal cooperation in new policies concerning control of the Great Lakes area established after the War of 1812. The Johnstons assisted him in researching Indian culture. Jane helped him compile a Chippewa vocabulary and drew his interest towards tales and legends. They married in 1823. With her husband, beginning in 1826, Schoolcraft published *The Literary Voyager or Muzzeniegun* ('printed document or book'), a weekly magazine distributed in eastern cities as well as locally, with articles on Ojibwa culture, history and biography. Her writings, including Christian devotional poems, tributes to her grandfather and poems on the death of her son, appeared in the magazine under the pseudonyms Rosa and Leelinau. Jane Johnston Schoolcraft became widely known as 'the northern Pocahontas' and was sought out by travelling intellectuals, among them British authors Harriet Martineau and Anna B. Jameson.

Otagamiad

In northern climes there liv'd a chief of fame,
LaPointe his dwelling, and Ojeeg his name,
Who oft in war had rais'd the battle cry,
And brav'd the rigors of an Arctic sky;
Nor less in peace those daring talents shone,
That rais'd him to his simple forest throne,

Alike endow'd with skill, such heaven's reward,
To wield the oaken sceptre, and to guard.
Now round his tent, the willing chieftains wait,
The gathering council, and the stern debate –
Hunters, & warriors circle round the green,
Age sits sedate, & youth fills up the scene,
While careful hands, with flint & steel prepare,
The sacred fire – the type of public care.

'Warriors and friends' – the chief of chiefs oppress'd,
With rising cares, his burning thoughts express'd.
'Long have our lands been hem'd around by foes,
Whose secret ire, no check or limit knows,
Whose public faith, so often pledg'd in vain,
'Twere base for freemen e'er to trust again.
Watch'd in their tracks our trusting hunters fall,
By ambush'd arrow, or avenging ball;
Our subtil foes lie hid in every pass,
Screen'd in the thicket, shelter'd in the grass,
They pierce our forests, & they cross our lines,
No treaty binds them, & no stream confines
And every spring that clothes the leafy plain,
We mourn our brethren, or our children slain.
Delay but swells our woes, as rivers wild,
Heap on their banks the earth they first despoil'd.
Oh chieftains! listen to my warning voice,
War – war or slavery is our only choice.
No longer sit, with head & arms declin'd,
The charms of ease still ling'ring in the mind;
No longer hope, that justice will be given
If ye neglect the proper means of heaven:
Fear – and fear only, makes our foemen just
Or shun the path of conquest, rage or lust,
Nor think the lands we own, our sons shall share,
If we forget the noble rites of war.
Choose then with wisdom, nor by more delay,
Put off the great – the all important day.
Upon yourselves alone, your fate depends,
'Tis warlike acts that make a nation friends
'Tis warlike acts that prop a falling throne,
And makes peace, glory, empire, all our own.

Oh friends! think deeply on my counsel – words
I sound no peaceful cry of summer birds!
No whispering dream of bliss without allay
Or idle strain of mute, inglorious joy
Let my bold voice arouse your slumb'ring hearts,
And answer warriors' – with uplifted darts,
Thick crowding arrows, bristled o'er the plain,
And joyous warriors rais'd the battle strain.

   All but Camudẃa, join'd the shouting throng,
Camudẃa, fam'd for eloquence of tongue
Whose breast resolv'd the coming strife with pain,
And peace still hop'd, by peaceful arts to gain.
'Friends' – he reply'd – 'our ruler's words are just,
Fear breeds respect and bridles rage or lust,
But in our haste, by rude and sudden hate,
To prop our own, or crush our neighbors state
Valor itself, should not disdain the skill
By pliant speech, to gain our purpos'd will.
The foe may yet, be reason'd into right.
And if we fail in speech – we still may fight.
At least, one further effort, be our care,
I will myself, the daring message bear,
I give my body, to the mission free,
And if I fall, my country, 'tis for thee!
The wife and child, shall lisp my song of fame,
And all who value peace, repeat my name!'

   ''Tis well' – Baimwáwa placidly replied,
'To cast our eyes, with care to either side,
Lest in our pride, to bring a rival low,
Our own fair fields shall fall beneath the foe.
Great is the stake, nor should we lightly yield,
Our ancient league by many a battle seal'd.
The deeds of other days before my eyes,
In all their friendship, love and faith arise,
When hand in hand with him we rov'd the wood,
Swept the long vale, or stem'd the boiling flood.
In the same war path, march'd with ready blade,
And liv'd, and fought, and triumph'd with his aid.
When the same tongue, express'd our joys and pains,
And the same blood ran freely thro' our veins?'

'Not we – not we' – in rage Keewaydin spoke,
'Strong ties have sever'd, or old friendships broke,
Back on themselves the baseless charge must fall,
They sunder'd name, league, language, rites and all.
They, with our firm allies, the Gallic race,
First broke the league, by secret arts and base,
Then play'd the warrior – call'd our bands a clog,
And earn'd their proper title, Fox and Dog.
Next to the false Dacota gave the hand,
And leagued in war, our own destruction plan'd.
Do any doubt the words I now advance,
Here is my breast' – he yelled & shook his lance.

'Rage' – interposed the sage Canowakeed,
'Ne'er prompted wit, or bid the council speed
For other aims, be here our highest end,
Such gentle aims as rivet friend to friend.
If harsher fires, in ardent bosoms glow,
At least restrain them, till we meet the foe,
Calm judgment here, demands the care of all,
For if we judge amiss, ourselves shall fall.
Beside, what boasts it, that ye here repeat,
The current tale of ancient scaith or heat,
Love, loss, or bicker, welcome or retort,
Once giv'n in earnest, or return'd sport
Or how, or when, this hapless feud arose,
That made our firmest friends, our firmest foes.
That so it is, by causes new or old,
There are no strangers present, to be told,
Each for himself, both knows & feels & sees,
The growing evils of a heartless peace,
And the sole question, of this high debate,
Is – shall we longer suffer – longer wait,
Or, with heroic will, for strife prepare,
And try the hazard of a gen'ral war!'

ELIZABETH OAKES-SMITH
1806–93

ELIZABETH OAKES-SMITH was born in North Yarmouth, Maine. Her father, a ship's captain, died when she was two and the family moved to Portland, Maine. In 1823, still a teenager, she married Seba Smith, editor of a Portland newspaper, at the urging of her mother. She assisted her husband and, in the 1830s, published her essays, stories and sketches of historical women in his newspaper, gaining entry into Portland's literary circle. When he went bankrupt in 1837, she began writing professionally. Her first novel was *Riches Without Wings* (1838). In 1839 they moved to New York, where Oakes-Smith wrote for prominent literary journals, including *Godey's Lady's Book* and *The Southern Literary Messenger*. She wrote poetry, prose sketches, travel narratives, literary and theatre criticism, children's literature and frontier tales. Later novels include *The Salamander* (1848), a transcendentalist meditation; *The Newsboy* (1854), a reform novel; and *Bertha and Lily* (1854), the story of an intellectual woman who bears an illegitimate child. A leader at the Seneca Falls conference for women's rights in 1848, Oakes-Smith was the first woman to lecture on the lyceum circuit beginning in 1851 and a founding member of the first women's club in New York (1869). She became pastor of a church in Canastoga, New York, in 1877. Her feminist articles for the New York *Tribune* were collected in *Woman and Her Needs* (1851).

from THE SINLESS CHILD

PART VI

It is the noon of summer, and the noonday of Eva's earthly existence. She hath held communion with all that is great and beautiful in nature, till it hath become a part of her being; till her spirit hath acquired strength and maturity, and been reared to a beautiful and harmonious temple, in which the true and the good delight to dwell. Then cometh the mystery of womanhood; its gentle going forth of the affections seeking for that holiest of companionship, a kindred spirit, responding to all its finer essences, and yet lifting it above itself. Eva had listened to this voice of her woman's nature; and sweet visions had visited her pillow. Unknown to the external vision, there was one ever present to the soul; and when he erred, she had felt a lowly sorrow that, while it still more perfected her own nature, went forth to swell likewise the amount of good in the great universe of God. At length Albert Linne, a gay youth, whose errors are those of an ardent and inexperienced nature, rather than of an assenting will, meets Eva sleeping under the canopy of the great woods, and he is at once awed by the purity that enshrouds her. He is lifted to the contemplation of the good – to a sense of the wants of his better nature. Eva awakes and recognises the spirit that for ever and ever is to be one with hers; that is to complete that mystic marriage, known in the Paradise of God; that marriage of soul with soul. Eva the pure minded, the lofty in thought, and great in soul, recoiled not from the errors of him who was to be made mete for the kingdom of Heaven, through her gentle agency, for the mission of the good and the lovely, is not to the good, but to the sinful. The mission of woman, is to the erring of man.

'Tis the summer prime, when the noiseless air
   In perfumed chalice lies,
And the bee goes by with a lazy hum
   Beneath the sleeping skies:
When the brook is low, and the ripples bright,
   As down the stream they go;
The pebbles are dry on the upper side,
   And dark and wet below.

The tree that stood where the soil's athirst,
   And the mulleins first appear,

Hath a dry and rusty colored bark,
   And its leaves are curled and sere;
But the dog-wood and the hazel bush,
   Have clustered round the brook—
Their roots have stricken deep beneath,
   And they have a verdant look.

To the juicy leaf the grasshopper clings,
   And he gnaws it like a file,
The naked stalks are withering by,
   Where he has been erewhile.
The cricket hops on the glistering rock,
   Or pipes in the faded grass,
The beetle's wings are folded mute,
   Where the steps of the idler pass.

The widow donned her russet robe,
   Her cap of snowy hue,
And o'er her staid maternal form
   A sober mantle threw;
And she, while fresh the morning light,
   Hath gone to pass the day,
And ease an ailing neighbour's pain
   Across the meadow way.

Young Eva closed the cottage door;
   And wooed by bird and flower,
She loitered on beneath the wood,
   Till came the noon-tide hour.
The sloping bank is cool and green,
   Beside the sparkling rill;
The cloud that slumbers in the sky,
   Is painted on the hill.

The spirits poised their purple wings
   O'er blossom, brook and dell,
And loitered in the quiet nook
   As if they loved it well.
Young Eva laid one snowy arm
   Upon a violet bank,
And pillow'd there her downy cheek
   While she to slumber sank.

A smile is on her gentle lip,
   For she the angels saw,
And felt their wings a covert make
   As round her head they draw.
A maiden's sleep, how pure it is!
   The innocent repose
That knows no dark nor troublous dream,
   Nor love's wild waking knows!

A huntsman's whistle; and anon
   The dogs came fawning round,
And now they raise the pendent ear,
   And crouch along the ground.
The hunter leaped the shrunken brook,
   The dogs hold back with awe,
For they upon the violet bank
   The slumbering maiden saw.

A reckless youth was Albert Linne,
   With licensed oath and jest,
Who little cared for woman's fame,
   Or peaceful maiden's rest.
Like things to him, were broken vows—
   The blush, the sigh, the tear;
What hinders he should steal a kiss,
   From sleeping damsel here?

He looks, yet stays his eager foot;
   For, on that spotless brow,
And that closed lid, a something rests
   He never saw till now;
He gazes, yet he shrinks with awe
   From that fair, wondrous face,
Those limbs so quietly disposed,
   With more than maiden grace.

He seats himself upon the bank
   And turns his face away,
And Albert Linne, the hair-brained youth,
   Wished in his heart to pray.
But thronging came his former life,
   What once he called delight,

The goblet, oath, and stolen joy,
  How palled they on his sight!

He looked within his very soul,
  Its hidden chamber saw,
Inscribed with records dark and deep
  Of many a broken law.
No more he thinks of maiden fair,
  No more of ravished kiss,
Forgets he that pure sleeper nigh
  Hath brought his thoughts to this?

Now Eva opens her child-like eyes
  And lifts her tranquil head,
And Albert, like a guilty thing
  Had from her presence fled.
But Eva held her kindly hand
  And bade him stay awhile;—
He dared not look upon her eyes,
  He only marked her smile;

And that so pure and winning beamed,
  So calm and holy too,
That o'er his troubled thoughts at once
  A quiet charm it threw.
Light thought, light words were all forgot,
  He breathed a holier air,
He felt the power of womanhood—
  Its purity was there.

And soft beneath their silken fringe
  Beamed Eva's dove-like eyes,
That seemed to claim a sisterhood,
  With something in the skies.
Her gentle voice a part become
  Of air, and brook, and bird,
And Albert listened, as if he
  Such music only heard.

O Eva! thou the pure in heart,
  Why falls thy trembling voice?
A blush is on thy maiden cheek,
  And yet thine eyes rejoice.

Another glory wakes for thee
   Where'er thine eyes may rest;
And deeper, holier thoughts arise
   Within thy peaceful breast.

Thine eyelids droop in tenderness,
   New smiles thy lips combine,
For thou dost feel another soul
   Is blending into thine.
Thou upward raisest thy meek eyes,
   And it is sweet to thee;
To feel the weakness of thy sex,
   Is more than majesty.

To feel thy shrinking nature claim
   The stronger arm and brow;
Thy weapons, smiles, and tears, and prayers,
   And blushes such as now.
A woman, gentle Eva thou,
   Thy lot were incomplete,
Did not all sympathies of soul
   Within thy being meet.

Those deep, dark eyes, that open brow,
   That proud and manly air,
How have they mingled with thy dreams
   And with thine earnest prayer!
And how hast thou, all timidly,
   Cast down thy maiden eye,
When visions have revealed to thee
   That figure standing nigh!

Two spirits launched companionless
   A kindred essence sought,
And one in all its wanderings
   Of such as Eva thought.
The good, the beautiful, the true,
   Should nestle in his heart,
Should lure him by her gentle voice,
   To choose the better part.

And he that kindred being sought,
   Had searched with restless care

For that true, earnest, woman-soul
   Among the bright and fair—
He might not rest, he felt for him,
   One such had been created,
Whose maiden soul in quietude
   For his call meekly waited.

And oft when beaming eyes were nigh,
   And beauty's lip was smiling,
And bird-like tones were breathing round
   The fevered sense beguiling;
He felt this was not what he sought—
   The soul such mockery spurned,
And evermore with aching zeal,
   For that one being yearned.

And she whose loving soul went forth
   Wherever beauty dwelt;
Who with the truthful and the good
   A genial essence felt,
Oh! often in her solitude,
   By her own soul oppressed,
She fain had nestled like a dove
   Within one stranger breast.

Though higher, holier far than those
   Who listening to her voice,
A something caught of better things,
   That make the heart rejoice;
Yet *teaching* thus her spirit lone
   Aweary would have knelt,
And *learned* with child-like reverence,
   Where deeper wisdom dwelt.

And now that will of stronger growth,
   That spirit firmer made,
Instinctive holds her own in check,
   Her timid footsteps stayed;
And Eva in her maidenhood,
   Half trembles with new fear,
And on her lip that strange, deep smile,
   The handmaid of a tear.

While doubting thus, a seraph stayed
  His radiant course awhile;
And with a heavenly sympathy,
  Looked on with beaming smile:
And thus his words of spirit-love
  Trust and assurance brought,
And bade her where the soul finds birth,
  To weakly question not.

Content to feel – care not to know,
  The sacred source whence its arise–
Respect in *modesty* of *soul*,
  This mystery of mysteries:
Mere mind with all its subtle arts,
  Hath only learned when thus it gazed
The inmost veil of human hearts,
  E'en to themselves must not be raised.

Her trusting hand, then Eva laid
  In that of Albert Linne,
And for one trembling moment turned
  Her gentle thoughts within.
Deep tenderness was in the glance
  That rested on his face,
As if her woman-heart had found
  Its own abiding place.

And when she turned her to depart
  Her voice more liquid grew,
'Dear youth, thy thoughts and mine are one;
  One source their being drew!
And they must mingle evermore;–
  Thy thoughts of love and me,
Will, as a light, thy footsteps guide
  To life and mystery.'

And then she bent her timid eyes,
  And as beside she knelt,
The pressure of her sinless lips
  Upon his brow he felt.
Low, heart-breathed words she uttered then:
  For him she breathed a prayer;

He turned to look upon her face,—
The maiden was not there!

1843

FRANCES ANNE KEMBLE
1809–93

FRANCES ANNE KEMBLE was born into a London theatre family. In 1832 she began a two-year performing tour of the United States with her father and her aunt, who had educated her in Paris. Pierce Butler, a Philadelphian whose family owned plantations in Georgia, fell in love with her and stalked her until she agreed to marry him. Against her husband's objections, she published *Journal of a Residence in America* (1835), critical of American institutions, to provide for her dying aunt. Visiting Georgia in 1838–9, she kept a journal on the conditions of slavery and intervened with overseers on the slaves' behalf, taking particular interest in slave women. Her *Journal of a Residence on a Georgia Plantation, 1838–1839*, was published in 1863 as part of the effort to persuade Britain not to enter the Civil War on the side of the South. The Butler family banned her from the plantation, her husband tried to control her by withholding their two daughters, and in 1845 she sailed to England alone. In 1848, Butler divorced Kemble on the grounds of desertion. She supported herself thereafter by publishing and by touring, for twenty years, through Britain and the United States, presenting solo dramatic readings of Shakespeare plays. Admirers judged her the best portrayer not only of female characters, but of Lear, Macbeth and Falstaff.

Sonnet

What is my lady like? thou fain would'st know—
A rosy chaplet of fresh apple bloom,
Bound with blue ribbon, lying on the snow:
What is my lady like? the violet gloom
Of evening, with deep orange light below.
She's like the noonday smell of a pine wood,
She's like the sounding of a stormy flood,

She's like a mountain-top high in the skies,
To which the day its earliest light doth lend;
She's like a pleasant path without an end;
Like a strange secret, and a sweet surprise;
Like a sharp axe of doom, wreathed with blush roses,
A casket full of gems whose key one loses;
Like a hard saying, wonderful and wise.

To Shakspeare

Oft, when my lips I open to rehearse
Thy wondrous spells of wisdom, and of power,
And that my voice, and thy immortal verse,
On listening ears, and hearts, I mingled pour,
I shrink dismayed – and awful doth appear
The vain presumption of my own weak deed;
Thy glorious spirit seems to mine so near,
That suddenly I tremble as I read –
Thee an invisible auditor I fear:
Oh, if it might be so, my master dear!
With what beseeching would I pray to thee,
To make me equal to my noble task,
Succor from thee, how humbly would I ask,
Thy worthiest works to utter worthily.

Sonnet

Cover me with your everlasting arms,
    Ye guardian giants of this solitude!
    From the ill-sight of men, and from the rude,
Tumultuous din of yon wild world's alarms!
Oh, knit your mighty limbs around, above,
    And close me in for ever! let me dwell
    With the wood spirits, in the darkest cell
That ever with your verdant locks ye wove.
    The air is full of countless voices, joined

In one eternal hymn; the whispering wind,
The shuddering leaves, the hidden water springs,
The work-song of the bees, whose honeyed wings
Hang in the golden tresses of the lime,
Or buried lie in purple beds of thyme.

Faith

Better trust all, and be deceived,
   And weep that trust, and that deceiving;
Than doubt one heart, that, if believed,
   Had blessed one's life with true believing.

Oh, in this mocking world, too fast
   The doubting fiend o'ertakes our youth!
Better be cheated to the last,
   Than lose the blessèd hope of truth.

Sonnet

Thou poisonous laurel leaf, that in the soil
   Of life, which I am doomed to till full sore,
Spring'st like a noisome weed! I do not toil
   For thee, and yet thou still com'st darkening o'er
      My plot of earth with thy unwelcome shade.
Thou nightshade of the soul, beneath whose boughs
   All fair and gentle buds hang withering,
Why hast thou wreathed thyself around my brows,
   Casting from thence the blossoms of my spring,
      Breathing on youth's sweet roses till they fade?
Alas! thou art an evil weed of woe,
   Watered with tears and watched with sleepless care,
   Seldom doth envy thy green glories spare;
And yet men covet thee – ah, wherefore do they so!

MARGARET FULLER
1810–50

MARGARET FULLER was born in Cambridgeport, Massachusetts, oldest of nine children. Her father, a lawyer and legislator, educated her as young men were educated. When her father died in 1835, she assumed responsibility for her younger siblings' education. She became associated with the transcendentalists Ralph Waldo Emerson, with whose aid she founded the journal *Dial* in 1840, and Bronson Alcott, in whose school she taught from 1836–7. From 1837–9, while teaching in Providence, Rhode Island, she began writing criticism and translating German literature. In 1839 she moved to Boston where she conducted a series of seminars for women at a bookshop. She was the first woman to study at Harvard and produced her first book, *Summer on the Lakes* (1844; reprinted 1991), based on her research. This book, which calls attention to exploitation of Native Americans, abuse of the environment, and mistreatment of pioneer women, prompted Horace Greeley to invite her to write for his newspaper, the New York *Tribune*. *Papers on Literature and Art* (1846) collects her articles for the *Tribune*. Fuller's *Woman in the Nineteenth Century* (1845; reprinted 1980) is a landmark of feminist theory. Its call for the removal of gender barriers inspired participants at the Seneca Falls women's rights convention in 1848. Travelling in Europe as a foreign correspondent starting in 1846, Fuller met George Sand and several British writers, including Elizabeth Barrett Browning. Settling in Rome, Fuller involved herself in the cause of Italian revolution. In 1847 she married Giovanni Angelo Ossoli, a nobleman who joined the short-lived Roman republican revolution, and had a son. They fled to Florence after the revolution failed. Sailing to New York, all three died in a shipwreck.

Meditations

Sunday, 12 May 1833

The clouds are marshalling across the sky,
Leaving their deepest tints upon yon range
Of soul-alluring hills. The breeze comes softly,
Laden with tribute that a hundred orchards
Now in their fullest blossom send, in thanks
For this refreshing shower. The birds pour forth
In heightened melody the notes of praise
They had suspended while God's voice was speaking,
And his eye flashing down upon his world.
I sigh, half-charmed, half-pained. My sense is living,
And, taking in this freshened beauty, tells
Its pleasure to the mind. The mind replies,
And strives to wake the heart in turn, repeating
Poetic sentiments from many a record
Which other souls have left, when stirred and satisfied
By scenes as fair, as fragrant. But the heart
Sends back a hollow echo to the call
Of outward things, – and its once bright companion,
Who erst would have been answered by a stream
Of life-fraught treasures, thankful to be summoned, –
Can now rouse nothing better than this echo;
Unmeaning voice, which mocks their softened accents.
Content thee, beautiful world! and hush, still busy mind!
My heart hath sealed its fountains. To the things
Of Time they shall be oped no more. Too long,
Too often were they poured forth: part have sunk
Into the desert; part profaned and swollen
By bitter waters, mixed by those who feigned
They asked them for refreshment, which, turned back,
Have broken and o'erflowed their former urns.
So when ye talk of *pleasure*, lonely world,
And busy mind, ye ne'er again shall move me
To answer ye, though still your calls have power
To jar me through, and cause dull aching *here*.

Not so the voice which hailed me from the depths
Of yon dark-bosomed cloud, now vanishing
Before the sun ye greet. It touched my centre,

The voice of the Eternal, calling me
To feel his other worlds; to feel that if
I could deserve a home, I still might find it
In other spheres, – and bade me not despair,
Though 'want of harmony' and 'aching void'
Are terms invented by the men of this,
Which I may not forget.
                           In former times
I loved to see the lightnings flash athwart
The stooping heavens; I loved to hear the thunder
Call to the seas and mountains; for I thought
'Tis thus man's flashing fancy doth enkindle
The firmament of mind; 'tis thus his eloquence
Calls unto the soul's depths and heights; and still
I deified the creature, nor remembered
The Creator in his works.
                           Ah now how different!
The proud delight of that keen sympathy
Is gone; no longer riding on the wave,
But whelmed beneath it: my own plans and works,
Or, as the Scriptures phrase it, my *inventions*
No longer interpose 'twixt me and Heaven.

Today, for the first time, I felt the Deity,
And uttered prayer on hearing thunder. This
Must be thy will, – for finer, higher spirits
Have gone through this same process, – yet I think
There was religion in that strong delight,
Those sounds, those thoughts of power imparted. True,
I did not say, 'He is the Lord thy God,'
But I had feeling of his essence. But
' 'Twas pride by which the angels fell.' So be it!
But O, might I but see a little onward!
Father, I cannot be a spirit of power;
May I be active as a spirit of love,
Since thou hast ta'en me from that path which Nature
Seemed to appoint, O, deign to ope another,
Where I may walk with thought and hope assured;
'Lord, I believe; help thou mine unbelief!'
Had I but faith like that which fired Novalis,
I too could bear that the heart 'fall in ashes,'

While the freed spirit rises from beneath them,
With heavenward-look, and Phoenix-plumes upsoaring!

The One in All

There are who separate the eternal light
In forms of man and woman, day and night;
They cannot bear that God be essence quite.

Existence is as deep a verity:
Without the dual, where is unity?
And the 'I am' cannot forbear to be;

But from its primal nature forced to frame
Mysteries, destinies of various name,
Is forced to give what it has taught to claim.

Thus love must answer to its own unrest;
The bad commands us to expect the best,
And hope of its own prospects is the test.

And dost thou seek to find the one in two?
Only upon the old can build the new;
The symbol which you seek is found in you.

The heart and mind, the wisdom and the will,
The man and woman, must be severed still,
And Christ must reconcile the good and ill.

There are to whom each symbol is a mask;
The life of love is a mysterious task;
They want no answer, for they would not ask.

A single thought transfuses every form;
The sunny day is changed into the storm,
For light is dark, hard soft, and cold is warm.

One presence fills and floods the whole serene;
Nothing can be, nothing has ever been,
Except the one truth that creates the scene.

Does the heart beat, – that is a seeming only;
You cannot be alone, though you are lonely;
The All is neutralized in the One only.

You ask *a* faith, – they are content with faith;
You ask to have, – but they reply, 'IT hath.'
There is no end, and there need be no path.

The day wears heavily, – why, then, ignore it;
Peace is the soul's desire, – such thoughts restore it;
The truth thou art, – it needs not to implore it.

The Presence all thy fancies supersedes,
All that is done which thou wouldst seek in deeds,
The wealth obliterates all seeming needs.

Both these are true, and if they are at strife,
The mystery bears the one name of *Life*,
That, slowly spelled, will yet compose the strife.

The men of old say, 'Live twelve thousand years,
And see the end of all that here appears,
And Moxen* shall absorb thy smiles and tears.'

These later men say, 'Live this little day.
Believe that human nature is the way,
And know both Son and Father while you pray;

And one in two, in three, and none alone,
Letting you know even as you are known,
Shall make the you and me eternal parts of one.'

To me, our destinies seem flower and fruit
Born of an ever-generating root;
The other statement I cannot dispute.

But say that Love and Life eternal seem,
And if eternal ties be but a dream,
What is the meaning of that self-same *seem*?

Your nature craves Eternity for Truth;
Eternity of Love is prayer of youth;
How, without love, would have gone forth your truth?

I do not think we are deceived to grow,
But that the crudest fancy, slightest show,
Covers some separate truth that we may know.

---

* Buddhist term for absorption into the divine mind.

In the one Truth, each separate fact is true;
Eternally in one I many view,
And destinies through destiny pursue.

This is *my* tendency; but can I say
That this my thought leads the true, only way?
I only know it constant leads, and I obey.

I only know one prayer – 'Give me the truth,
Give me that colored whiteness, ancient youth,
Complex and simple, seen in joy and truth.

Let me not by vain wishes bar my claim,
Nor soothe my hunger by an empty name,
Nor crucify the Son of man by hasty blame.

But in the earth and fire, water and air,
Live earnestly by turns without despair,
Nor seek a home till home be every where!'

Lines Written in Boston on a Beautiful Autumnal Day

As late we lived upon the gentle stream,
    Nature refused us smiles and kindly airs;
The sun but rarely deigned a pallid gleam;
    Then clouds came instantly, like glooms and tears,
Upon the timid flickerings of our hope;
    The moon, amid the thick mists of the night,
Had scarcely power her gentle eye to ope,
    And climb the heavenly steeps. A moment bright
Shimmered the hectic leaves, then rudely torn
    By winds that sobbed to see the wreck they made,
Upon the amber waves were thickly borne
    Adonis' gardens for the realms of shade,
While thoughts of beauty past all wish for livelier life forbade.
    So sped the many days of tranquil life,
    And on the stream, or by the mill's bright fire,

The wailing winds had told of distant strife,
    Still bade us for the moment yield desire
To think, to feel, the moment gave, – we needed not aspire!

Returning here, no harvest fields I see,
    Nor russèt beauty of the thoughtful year.
Where is the honey of the city bee?
    No leaves upon this muddy stream appear.
The housekeeper is getting in his coal,
    The lecturer his showiest thoughts is selling;
I hear of Major Somebody, the Pole,
    And Mr Lyell, how rocks grow, is telling;
But not a breath of thoughtful poesy
    Does any social impulse bring to me;
But many cares, sad thoughts of men unwise,
    Base yieldings, and unransomed destinies,
    Hopes uninstructed, and unhallowed ties.

Yet here the sun smiles sweet as heavenly love,
    Upon the eve of earthly severance;
The youthfulest tender clouds float all above,
    And earth lies steeped in odors like a trance.
The moon looks down as though she ne'er could leave us,
And these last trembling leaves sigh, 'Must they too deceive us?'
    Surely some life is living in this light,
    Truer than mine some soul received last night;
I cannot freely greet this beauteous day,
But does not *thy* heart swell to hail the genial ray?
I would not nature these last loving words in vain should say.

MARY S. B. DANA SHINDLER
1810–83

MARY S. B. DANA SHINDLER was born in Beaufort, South Carolina, daughter of a Congregational minister. In 1813 they moved to Charleston. She was privately educated there and in northern schools. She married Charles E. Dana in 1835 and moved with him first to New York, then to Bloomington, Iowa. He and their son died soon afterwards. She returned to Charleston, where she became well known as a poet and essayist, publishing in Northern and Southern periodicals. In 1848, after rejecting Calvinism, she married Robert D. Shindler, an Episcopal clergyman. They moved in 1850 to Upper Marlborough, Maryland, and in 1869 to Nacogdoches, Texas. Her books include *The Southern Harp* (1840), *The Northern Harp* (1841), *The Parted Family, and Other Poems* (1842), *The Temperance Lyre* (1842), *Charles Morton, or the Young Patriot* (1843), *The Young Sailor* (1844), *Forecastle Tour* (1844) and *Letters to Relatives and Friends on the Trinity* (1845). Her poems on the deaths of relatives number up to forty-five Spenserian stanzas, all penned in a day.

Real Comfort

There! I have lock'd the door
'Gainst every senseless bore!
O! 'tis a blessing to retire,
And, drawing near my cheerful fire,
To feel I am alone—
Responsible to none—
My cares behind me thrown—
Hence! vanish every one!
Now for a cozy time with my sweet Muse!
Come, lady, wake! this is no time to snooze;

When we're alone we've not an hour to lose,
We cannot always thus ourselves amuse.

I've laid my trappings by;
For now no envious eye
Looks on, my dress to criticise,
With strictures aye more nice than wise.
Clad in a flowing gown,
My hair I've taken down,
And, o'er my shoulders thrown,
It seeks my loosen'd zone;
Thus, free from all undue restraint, we sit,
My darling Muse and I, to try our wit,
While, author-like, our learned brows we knit,
And coax our brains bright sparkles to emit.

'Tis true, the silent night
Has darken'd round us quite;
But 'tis the time we love the best,
When earthly things are all at rest,
And sweet the hours glide
Down time's fast flowing tide,
Nor daylight's pomp, nor pride,
Invades our fireside;
And should, perchance, my fickle Muse be shy,
And choose to tarry in her native sky,
Why, even then, I'll not to others fly;
I think myself the best of company.

But come, consenting Muse!
We'll now a subject choose
From things below, or things above;
I have it then, it shall be – LOVE!
Which has its home, you know,
In earth and heaven too;
So, with no more ado,
I'll sing of love to you:—

SONG

Love is a tyrant, with a silken chain—
What! pouting, Miss? you toss your head in vain;

You know full well I've reason to complain,
Love serves me many a trick – Let's try again.

But not of Love I'll sing,
Who's ever on the wing,
And will not stay a moment more
Than he's caress'd, and fondled o'er;
I'll choose some nobler theme,
Commanding more esteem;
Come, come, how dull you seem!
Rouse up, you surely dream!
I've rack'd my brains until they fairly ache;
Come, help me now, sweet Muse, for pity's sake;
You know I can't a single couplet make
Worth any thing, till you my genius wake.

What! art thou drowsy still?
Come now, I'll take it ill,
If, at my need, you serve me so;
O! surely you don't mean to go!
Fold up your tiny wing,
You darling little thing!
Forget the tyrant king,
And hear me while I sing:—

SONG

Sweet Poetry! thine influence o'er me shed,
For thou canst charm when other charms have fled;
O! now you smile, and raise your lovely head;
Well, kiss me, dear! make friends; I'll go to bed.

1841

REBEKAH GUMPERT HYNEMAN
1812–75

REBEKAH GUMPERT HYNEMAN was born in Philadelphia, daughter of a Jewish father and a Christian mother. Lacking formal education, she was self-educated in scripture, the classics, poetry and languages. As an adult she chose a Jewish identity, married a Jewish man and lived according to Orthodox standards. Her husband disappeared after five years of marriage. They had two sons; one died of consumption and the other in a Confederate prison while serving in the Union cavalry. Hyneman wrote for Masonic and Jewish periodicals and published a book of stories for children. Her *The Leper and Other Poems* (1853) includes twelve sketches of women of the scriptures. Hyneman's story, 'The Lost Diamond', serialised in *The Occident and American Jewish Advocate* in 1862, tells of a woman's drawing back to Judaism a suitor who has passed as a Gentile.

from FEMALE SCRIPTURAL CHARACTERS

No. 5, Judith

Midnight in the Assyrian camp! No sound
Mingles with the light zephyr, whose faint breath
Fans the dull sleeper's cheek, and lifts the tress
Of raven hair on many a sunburnt brow,
Or revels in light playfulness around
The gorgeous canopy of Holofernes.
'Tis silence all. A murmuring rivulet,
Whose ripples scarce disturb the wakeful ear
Of the tired sentinel, goes whispering by,
And whisperingly is answered by the bough

Of palm and cedar on the mountain side.
The moon hath waned, and in its stead the pale
And melancholy stars are out upon
The midnight sky of Judea.

      Lift we now
The veil of yonder tent: what see we there?
Hush! for a sound might wake the slumberer,
Who soon must know a deeper, darker sleep.
There, on his couch, gleaming with gold, and bright
With glittering jewels, the proud conqueror lies.
Deep sleep is on him. Pause and gaze upon
A nation's dreaded scourge! The embroidered robe
Clings to a form of strength and majesty,
And the broad, massive brow, and deep-set eye,
And the compression of the closed lips,
Are all indicative of firm resolve.
He is alone: no! by the flickering beam
Of yonder lump of fretted gold, we see
Another form.

  A woman! a fair, lovely flower,
   With eye of fire and lip of pride,
   Why stands she by the hero's side,
  Thus, at the midnight hour?
  The glossy tendrils of her hair,
   Enwreathed with many a costly gem,
   Meet for a monarch's diadem –
  Float o'er her bosom fair,
  And veil – nay, grace the lovely form
   That trembles like a timid dove;
   Trembles, but not with thoughts of love.
  Ah, no! that bare white arm,
  That plucks the falchion from its place,
   And waves it glittering o'er her head,
  Attests 'tis for no love embrace
   Her steps are hither led.

  Hark! heard ye not a sudden sound?
   The drowsy sentry paused to hear,
   But the sweet brooklet, murmuring near,
   Is all that meets his startled ear,

In the dim silence round.
And ere the dull gray dawn of day
   Breaks from the chambers of the east,
The Hebrew matron takes her way
Among her native hills to pray;
   And 'tis their lord's behest
That she, unquestioned, pass to where
Her feelings pour themselves in prayer.

She leaves that scene of blood behind,
   And speeds through many a lonely dell;
But the fearful workings of her mind,
   Oh! who shall dare to tell?
She leaves that scene, but not alone –
   A severed, ghastly, gory head,
Whose glances lately met her own,
   Bears witness from the dead,
How fearfully her woman's soul
Had mocked at Nature's soft control –
   How well her mission sped!
Oh! not by woman's gentle hand
   Should blood be shed or victory won;
Yet, for her God, her love, her land,
   What hath not woman done?

Woman's Rights

It is her right, to bind with warmest ties,
   The lordly spirit of aspiring man,
Making his home an earthly paradise,
   Rich in all joys allotted to life's span;
Twining around each fibre of his heart,
   With all the gentle influence of love's might,
Seeking no joy wherein he has no part –
   This is undoubtedly – a woman's right!

It is her right to teach the infant mind,
   Training it ever upward in its course,
To root out evil passions that would bind

The upward current of his reason's force;
To lead the erring spirit gently back,
    When it has sunk in gloom of deepest night;
To point the shining path of virtue's track,
    And urge him forward. This is woman's right.

It is her right to soothe the couch of pain;
    There her pure mission upon earth to prove,
To calm with gentle care the frenzied brain,
    And keep her vigil there of holiest love;
To watch untiring by the lonely bed,
    Through the bright day, and in the solemn night,
'Til health ensues, or the loved form is laid
    To rest for ever. This is woman's right.

She is a flower that blossoms best, unseen,
    Sheltered within the precincts of her home;
There, should no dark'ning storm-cloud intervene,
    There, the loud-strife of worldlings never come.
Let her not scorn to act a *woman's* part,
    Nor strive to cope with manhood in its might,
But lay this maxim closely to her heart –
    That that which God ordains is surely right.

ADA (SARAH LOUISA FORTEN)
b. 1814

ADA was the pseudonym attached to a number of poems that abolitionist William Lloyd Garrison published in his weekly newspaper, *The Liberator*, between 1831 and 1837. Headnotes to the poems identify her as 'a young lady of color'; one adds that she and other members of her family had 'forced the respect even of those who would wish to crush the people of color to the earth'. Sarah Louisa Forten (b. 1814) has been identified as the author of most of these poems. One of eight children of a prosperous sail manufacturer and his wife, Forten was tutored at home. The Forten home was a gathering place for abolitionists, among them many distinguished writers and speakers. With her mother and sisters, Forten was a charter member of the biracial Philadelphia Female Anti-Slavery Society. She supported women's rights and belonged to the Female Literary Association of Philadelphia. She married Joseph Purvis in 1837 or '38 and moved to the country near Byberry, outside Philadelphia. Letters that she wrote to Elizabeth Whittier, sister of the poet John Greenleaf Whittier, and feminist abolitionist Angelina Grimké are included in *We Are Your Sisters: Black Women in the Nineteenth Century* (1984).

An Appeal to Women

Oh, woman, woman, in thy brightest hour
Of conscious worth, of pride, of conscious power
Oh, nobly dare to act a Christian's part,
That well befits a lovely woman's heart!
Dare to be good, as thou canst dare be great;
Despise the taunts of envy, scorn and hate;
Our 'skins may differ,' but from thee we claim
A sister's privilege, in a sister's name.

We are thy sisters, – God has truly said,
That of one blood, the nations he has made.
Oh, christian woman, in a christian land,
Canst thou unblushing read this great command?
Suffer the wrongs which wring our inmost heart
To draw one throb of pity on thy part;
Our 'skins may differ,' but from thee we claim
A sister's privilege, in a sister's name.

Oh, woman! – though upon thy fairer brow
The hues of roses and of lilies glow—
These soon must wither in their kindred earth,
From whence the fair and dark have equal birth.
Let a bright halo o'er thy virtues shed
A lustre, that shall live when thou art dead;
Let coming ages learn to bless thy name
Upon the altar of immortal fame.

The Scroll is Open

[From the Massachusetts Spy]

'We also respectfully announce our intention to present the same petition yearly before your honorable body, that it may, at least, be a memorial of us, that in the holy cause of human Freedom we have done what we could.'

The scroll is open – many a name is written—
    The ink is flowing from the lifted quill—
Say, is that lily hand with palsy smitten,
    That it should disobey the writer's will?

Her free consent already has been given,
    Why should she then thus hesitating stand?
Fears she the wrath of an offending Heaven,
    Its righteous judgments on a guilty land?

No! – but that anger – should female christians fear it,
    And from their holy purposes be swayed?

The world's dread laugh – they surely well may bear it,
    Tho' 'firm philosophers' may be dismayed.

What tho' they call us 'Female Politicians,'
    And many an ill-timed epithet bestow?
Shall they thus stem the tide of our petitions?
    And shall we steel our hearts to human woe?

To woman is assigned her proper station,
    To pluck life's thorn, and strew its path with flowers,
Exempted from the cares of legislation,
    No Amazonian prowess should be ours.

Yet 'moral courage' has been freely given,
    By Him whose wisdom never yet has erred,
And shall we trample on this gift of Heaven,
    For high and holy purposes conferred?

Ours be the 'Duty,' not the 'Rights of woman,'
    Knowing the strength of nature's dearest ties,
May we yet 'prove that ours are feelings human,'
    Holy affections, kindly sympathies.

Are we disheartened? Shall our footsteps, alter?
    Lonely and weeping are we seen to stand,
Like Israel's priests, between the porch and altar,
    Sad and dispirited, a fearful band?

No – perseverance yet may safely bear us
    O'er opposition's overwhelming tide;
We still will trust that they may deign to hear us,
    And our petitions may not be denied.

Oh! there is one tribunal, where we fear not,
    Humbly to bend the knee in fervent prayer,
And, tho' earth's magnates our petitions hear not,
    They shall ascend in blest acceptance there.

Then in each high and holy aspiration,
    With frequent intercession let us pray,
That those foul sins which stigmatise our nation,
    From her escutcheon may be washed away;

That Freedom's gift may yet to man be given,
    That he, disfranchised, yet may walk abroad—
Each shackle broken, every fetter riven—
    Erect and free, the image of his God.

CATHERINE ANA WARFIELD
1816–77

ELEANOR PERCY LEE
1820–49

CATHERINE ANA WARFIELD and ELEANOR PERCY LEE were sisters born in Mississippi. Their mother was institutionalised for insanity in 1820; their father, Nathaniel A. Ware, was a lawyer, political economist and naturalist who acquired considerable wealth through speculation in territorial lands. Catherine and Eleanor were educated together in private schools in Philadelphia, then moved to Cincinnati, Ohio. Catherine married Robert E. Warfield in 1833. They travelled in Europe and lived in Galveston, Texas, and Lexington and Louisville, Kentucky. Eleanor married Henry Lee, a native of Virginia. The two sisters collaborated on *The Wife of Leon, and Other Poems, by Two Sisters of the West* (1843), *The Indian Chamber and Other Poems* (1846) and several novels. Catherine wrote ten novels of her own and is considered one of the first important Southern women novelists.

The Sun-Struck Eagle

I saw an eagle sweep to the sky—
The Godlike! – seeking his place on high,
With a strong, and wild, and rapid wing—
A dark, and yet a dazzling thing;
And his arching neck, his bristling crest,
And the dark plumes quivering upon his breast;
And his eye, bent up to each beam of light,
Like a bright sword flash'd with a sword in fight.

I saw him rise o'er the forest trees;
I saw his pinion ride the breeze;
Beyond the clouds I watched him tower
On his path of pride – his flight of power.
I watched him wheeling, stern and lone,
Where the keenest ray of the sun was thrown;

Soaring, circling – bathed in light:
Such was that desert eagle's flight.

Suddenly, then, to my straining eye,
I saw the strong wing slack on high;
Falling, falling to earth once more;
The dark breast covered with foam and gore;
The dark eyes' glory dim with pain;
Sick to death with a sun-struck brain!
Reeling down from that height divine,
Eagle of heaven! such fall was thine!

Even so we see the sons of light,
Up to the day-beam steer their flight;
And the wing of genius cleaves the sky,
As the clouds rush on when the winds are high:
Then comes the hour of sudden dread—
Then is the blasting sunlight shed;
And *the gifted* fall in their agony,
Sun-struck eagle! to die like thee!

1844

Forests and Caverns

I have stood in forests, so old and vast,
They seemed a part of those ages past,
When the Eden freshness and youth of earth
Gave to her children a giant birth.
I have looked far up from the forest floor,
To the height of the oak, and the sycamore;
To the dark green maple, and graceful elm,
Monarchs all of that quiet realm—
Up through those branches far and dim,
To the dome, where many a giant limb,
Braced by the twisting and snake-like vine,
Shuts out the rains and the fair sunshine.

Gray leaden shadows forever brood
At the feet of that silent multitude;
And through the distant and dim arcades

The silent deer glance by like shades;
And sometimes the shout of the watching owl,
Or the wolf abroad in his midnight prowl,
Or the panther's cry o'er his feast of blood,
Startle the depths of the solitude.

But there are sounds of a wilder hour,
When the tempest weareth his robe of power!
When the rushing wind, with his battle shout,
And the storm and the driving rain are out!
Often the bolts of lightning fall,
Striking a king in his palace hall,
Scathing those branches whose lofty pride
Have the wrath of a thousand years defied,
And leaving a blacken'd and lonely stem,
Where once was a verdant diadem.

I have stood in caverns, where never came
A ray of light, save the torches' flame,
As they gleamed on the walls with their glittering spars,
And the arching roof with its mimic stars,
Yet leaving still a spell of gloom
Within each lofty and dreamlike room.
I have journey'd onwards, for darken'd miles,
Through slippery passways and narrow aisles;
And have heard the plash on the sullen stone,
Of the drops of damp, falling, one by one,
Down from the roof and the slimy walls
Of those deserted and mystic halls.

I have seen the bones that the sweeping waves
Flung in those caverns – eternal graves;
When the flood was loosed o'er the destined earth,
And the arc lay lone on a sea of dearth.
I have looked with wondering and awe-struck eyes
On the wrecks of departed centuries;
On giant limbs, which in memory seem
Disordered parts of a ghastly dream.
Ay! there they lie, in those chambers wan!
Creatures whose memory hath passed from man;
Whose very place in the chain of earth,
Hath been filled up by a newer birth.

1844

JULIA WARD HOWE
1819–1910

JULIA WARD HOWE was born in New York City, fourth of seven
children in a Wall Street banker's family. She was educated by govern-
esses and sent to a young ladies' school. In 1843 she married social
reformer Samuel Gridley Howe. They had six children. She published
her first collection of poems, *Passion Flowers* (1854), anonymously;
Words for the Hour (1857) followed. By the time her *Later Lyrics*
(1887) were published, she had established herself as a public figure.
Leonora (1857), a play about a woman who commits suicide after
failing to kill her unfaithful lover, was condemned as immoral and
closed after a week. Converted to abolitionism in the mid-1850s, she
became a lifelong campaigner for social reform despite her husband's
opposition to her public life. The 'Battle-Hymn of the Republic',
composed in 1862, became an anthem of Union troops during the
Civil War and one of the most frequently anthologised poems in
English. After Samuel Howe's death in 1876, her literary and reform
activities broadened and met with increasing success. She became
a leader of the American Woman Suffrage Association and the
women's club movement, founded the weekly *Woman's Journal* in
1870, preached in the Unitarian Church, campaigned for world peace,
and toured the West delivering lectures. Her memoirs, *Reminiscences,
1819–1899*, record links and conflicts among social change movements. She was the first woman elected to the American Academy of
Arts and Letters in 1908.

Battle-Hymn of the Republic

Mine eyes have seen the glory of the coming of the Lord:
He is trampling out the vintage where the grapes of wrath are stored;
He hath loosed the fateful lightning of his terrible swift sword:
    His truth is marching on.

I have seen Him in the watch-fires of a hundred circling camps;
They have builded Him an altar in the evening dews and damps;
I can read His righteous sentence by the dim and flaring lamps.
    His day is marching on.

I have read a fiery gospel, writ in burnished rows of steel:
'As ye deal with my contemners, so with you my grace shall deal;
Let the Hero, born of woman, crush the serpent with his heel,
    Since God is marching on.'

He has sounded forth the trumpet that shall never call retreat;
He is sifting out the hearts of men before his judgment-seat:
Oh! be swift, my soul, to answer Him! be jubilant, my feet!
    Our God is marching on.

In the beauty of the lilies Christ was born across the sea,
With a glory in his bosom that transfigures you and me:
As he died to make men holy, let us die to make men free,
    While God is marching on.

                      1862

from LYRICS OF THE STREET

The Lost Jewel

Cast on the turbid current of the street,
    My pearl doth swim;
Oh for the diver's cunning hands and feet
    To come to him!

No: I'll not seek the madness of thine eyes,
    Since, day by day,
Life brings its noiseless blessings from the skies;
    For which we pray.

While patient Duty, helped of heavenly Art,
    Her way pursues,
And holy loves re-edify the heart
    The passions use.

God's hand can bring unheard-of gifts to light
    From Fate's deep sea;
Has pearls enough to recompense the right,
    Only not thee.

Outside the Party

Thick throng the snow-flakes, the evening is dreary,
Glad rings the music in yonder gay hall;
On her who listens here, friendless and weary,
Heavier chill than the winter's doth fall.

At yon clear window, light-opened before me,
Glances the face I have worshipped so well:
There's the fine gentleman, grand in his glory;
There, the fair smile by whose sweetness I fell.

This is akin to him, shunned and forsaken,
That at my bosom sobs low, without bread;
Had not such pleading my marble heart shaken,
I had been quiet, long since, with the dead.

Oh! could I enter there, ghastly and squalid,
Stand in men's eyes with my spirit o'erborne,
Show them where roses bloomed, crushed now and pallid,
What he found innocent, leaving forlorn,—

How the fair ladies would fail from their dances,
Trembling, aghast at my horrible tale!
How would he shrink from my words and my glances!
How would they shrink from him, swooning and pale!

This is the hair that was soft to enchain him;
Snakelike, it snarls on my beautiless brow:
These are the hands that were fond to detain him
With a sense-magic then, powerless now!

No: could I come, like a ghost, to affright him,
How should that heal my wound, silence my pain?
Had I the wrath of God's lightning to smite him,
That could not bring me my lost peace again.

Ne'er let him grieve while good fortunes betide him,
Ne'er count again the poor game lost of old;
When he comes forth, with his young bride beside him,
Here shall they find us both, dead in the cold.

The Soul-Hunter

Who hunts so late 'neath evening skies,
A smouldering love-brand in his eyes?
His locks outshame the black of night,
Its stars are duller than his sight
    Who hunts so late, so dark.

A drooping mantle shrouds his form,
To shield him from the winter's storm?
Or is there something at his side,
That, with himself, he strives to hide,
    Who hunts so late, so dark?

He hath such promise, silver sweet,
Such silken hands, such fiery feet,
That, where his look has charmed the prey,
His swift-winged passion forces way,
    Who hunts so late, so dark.

Sure no one underneath the moon
Can whisper to so soft a tune:
The hours would flit from dusk to dawn
Lighter than dews upon the lawn
    With him, so late, so dark.

But, should there break a day of need,
Those hands will try no valorous deed:
No help is in that sable crest,
Nor manhood in that hollow breast
    That sighed so late, so dark.

O maiden! of the salt waves make
Thy sinless shroud, for God's dear sake;

Or to the flame commit thy bloom;
Or lock thee, living, in the tomb
　　So desolate and dark,—

Before thou list one stolen word
Of him who lures thee like a bird.
He wanders with the Devil's bait,
For human souls he lies in wait,
　　Who hunts so late, so dark.

Street Yarn

Roses caged in windows, heighten
　　Your faint blooms today;
Silks and sheeny satins, brighten;
　　He has passed this way!

Could ye keep his fleeting presence
　　Gone beyond recall,
But a little of his essence,
　　I would have you all.

Arabesque so quaint and shady,
　　That mightst catch his eye
To adorn a stately lady
　　Ere her hour went by,

Canst assure me that his glancing
　　Rested on thy fold?
Did that set your purples dancing?
　　Wake the sleepy gold?

Ye neglected apple-venders
　　Mouldering in the street,
Did he curse between your tenders,
　　Spurning with his feet?

Then must I an alms deliver
　　For his graceless pride;
Could I buy his sins forever,
　　I'd not be denied.

Paying patiently his ransom
 Never conscience-pricked;
Cheating Justice of her handsome
 Heartless derelict.

Did he view thee, ancient steeple,
 With thy weird clock-face,
Frowning down on sinful people
 Passing out of grace?

Nay, respond not to my question
 With thy prate of time:
Things to which my soul must hasten
 Lie beyond thy chime.

With no circumstance to screen us,
 We must meet again:
I shall bid God judge between us,
 Answering Amen.

1866

The House of Rest

I will build a house of rest,
Square the corners every one:
At each angle on his breast
Shall a cherub take the sun;
Rising, risen, sinking, down,
Weaving day's unequal crown.

In the chambers, light as air,
Shall responsive footsteps fall:
Brother, sister, art thou there?
Hush! we need not jar nor call;
Need not turn to seek the face
Shut in rapture's hiding-place.

Heavy load and mocking care
Shall from back and bosom part;
Thought shall reach the thrill of prayer,
Patience plan the dome of art.

None shall praise or merit claim,
Not a joy be called by name.

With a free, unmeasured tread
Shall we pace the cloisters through:
Rest, enfranchised, like the Dead;
Rest till Love be born anew.
Weary Thought shall take his time,
Free of task-work, loosed from rhyme.

No reproof shall grieve or chill;
Every sin doth stand confest;
None need murmur, 'This was ill':
Therefore do they grant us rest;
Contemplation making whole
Every ruin of the soul.

Pictures shall as softly look
As in distance shows delight;
Slowly shall each saintly book
Turn its pages in our sight;
Not the study's wealth confuse,
Urging zeal to pale abuse.

Children through the windows peep,
Not reproachful, though our own;
Hushed the parent passion deep,
And the household's eager tone.
One above, divine and true,
Makes us children like to you.

Measured bread shall build us up
At the hospitable board;
In Contentment's golden cup
Is the guileless liquor poured.
May the beggar pledge the king
In that spirit gathering.

Oh! my house is far away;
Yet it sometimes shuts me in.
Imperfection mars each day
While the perfect works begin.

In the house of labor best
Can I build the house of rest.

1866

ANN PLATO
b. ?1820

ANN PLATO was a member of the Colored Congregational Church of Hartford, Connecticut. With encouragement from her pastor, she published a volume of her writing, *Essays; Including Biographies and Miscellaneous Pieces, in Prose and Poetry* (1841; reprinted 1988), while a young woman. She was educated in schools and became a teacher of young children. Her essays reflect a knowledge of classical and modern history. A poem about her father indicates that he descended from Native Americans; other poems mourn the death of a brother.

Advice to Young Ladies

Day after day I sit and write,
   And thus the moments spend—
The thought that occupies my mind,—
   Compose to please my friend.

And then I think I will compose,
   And thus myself engage—
To try to please young ladies' minds,
   Which are about my age.

The greatest word that I can say,—
   I think to please, will be,
To try and get your learning young,
   And write it back to me.

But this is not the only thing
   That I can recommend;
Religion is most needful for
   To make in us a friend.

At thirteen years I found a hope,
   And did embrace the Lord;
And since, I've found a blessing great,
   Within his holy word.

Perchance that we may ne'er fulfill,
   The place of aged sires,
But may it with God's holy will,
   Be ever our desires.

The True Friend

Young persons, it is true, admire
The heart that burns with ardent fire—
   Where comes no sob or sigh,
They bear the summer's heat in measure,
If they enjoy it all with pleasure,
   Fatigue and trouble fly.

She is precisely like yourself—
In habits, principles, and wealth,
   In beauty's opening prime;
Her eyes and voice are of the same,
And like you is array'd in name,
   Useful alike in time.

Our dearest friends on earth do die,
We mourn disconsolate – and why!
   Their bodies are at rest!
But now the friend of whom I speak,
Is one whom all of you should seek,
   This friend is really best.

In language beautiful, might she
From Ruth and Time address thee;
   'With thee, I ever go,
Where thou diest, I will die,
Where thou art buried I will lie;
   Lord deal with me thus so.'

An introduction to this friend,
So surely ought you to attend,
　　Strive daily to improve;
Are you industrious, pious, good?
If true – the same is understood—
　　By friendship ne'er to move.

If you persist in wrongful deeds,
She has a way in which she heeds;
　　The heart has weight of stone:
'Tis said by some a punishment,
Severe to wrongful sentiment,
　　The feelings never won.

Be punctual to appointed time,
Frank to the questions that are mine,
　　Agree as I propose:
Set down at slumber, wait for me,
And answer what I say to thee,
　　And unto me disclose!

She, several questions you will ask,
Happy if you say yes, in task,
　　This Friend most true in heart;
That gold most pure, that rust cannot,
That thief nor robber, can't corrupt,
　　This Friend is ne'er to part.

ALICE CARY
1820–71

ALICE CARY and PHOEBE CARY (see pp. 104–7) were born on a farm near Cincinnati, Ohio, fourth and sixth of nine children. They had little education and few books but began writing early in their lives. Alice started publishing poetry in periodicals in 1838 and was praised by Edgar Allan Poe and John Greenleaf Whittier. Both sisters achieved national recognition when Rufus Griswold included them in *The Female Poets of America* (1849). Both were abolitionists. Following publication of *Poems of Alice and Phoebe Cary* (1850), the two sisters used their literary earnings to leave the farm and moved to New York City, where they set up housekeeping with Phoebe in the role of homemaker. Their Sunday evening receptions drew the New York literati. Alice became president of the first American women's club and filled a poetry column in the *New York Ledger*. Phoebe edited a book of hymns and worked briefly with Susan B. Anthony's suffrage paper, *The Revolution*. Luxury editions of their last poems (1873) and *The Poetical Works of Alice and Phoebe Cary with a Memorial of Their Lives* (1877) appeared posthumously.

The Window Just Over the Street

I sit in my sorrow a-weary, alone;
 I have nothing sweet to hope or remember,
For the spring o' th' year and of life has flown;
 'Tis the wildest night o' the wild December,
And dark in my spirit and dark in my chamber.

I sit and list to the steps in the street,
 Going and coming, and coming and going,
And the winds at my shutter they blow and beat;
 'Tis the middle of night and the clouds are snowing;
And the winds are bitterly beating and blowing.

I list to the steps as they come and go,
　And list to the winds that are beating and blowing,
And my heart sinks down so low, so low;
　　No step is stayed from me by the snowing,
　　Nor stayed by the wind so bitterly blowing.

I think of the ships that are out at sea,
　Of the wheels in th' cold, black waters turning;
Not one of the ships beareth news to me,
　　And my head is sick, and my heart is yearning,
　　As I think of the wheels in the black waters turning.

Of the mother I think, by her sick baby's bed,
　Away in her cabin as lonesome and dreary,
And little and low as the flax-breaker's shed;
　　Of her patience so sweet, and her silence so weary,
　　With cries of the hungry wolf hid in the prairie.

I think of all things in the world that are sad;
　Of children in homesick and comfortless places;
Of prisons, of dungeons, of men that are mad;
　　Of wicked, unwomanly light in the faces
　　Of women that fortune has wronged with disgraces.

I think of a dear little sun-lighted head,
　That came where no hand of us all could deliver;
And crazed with the cruelest pain went to bed
　　Where the sheets were the foam-fretted waves of the river;
　　Poor darling! may God in his mercy forgive her.

The footsteps grow faint and more faint in the snow;
　I put back the curtain in very despairing;
The masts creak and groan as th' winds come and go;
　　And the light in the light-house all weirdly is flaring;
　　But what glory is this, in the gloom of despairing!

I see at the window just over the street,
　A maid in the lamplight her love-letter reading.
Her red mouth is smiling, her news is so sweet;
　　And the heart in my bosom is cured of its bleeding,
　　As I look on the maiden her love-letter reading.

She has finished the letter, and folding it, kisses,
　And hides it – a secret too sacred to know;

And now in the hearth-light she softly undresses:
   A vision of grace in the roseate glow,
   I see her unbinding the braids of her tresses.

And now as she stoops to the ribbon that fastens
   Her slipper, they tumble o'er shoulder and face;
And now, as she patters in bare feet, she hastens
   To gather them up in a fillet of lace;
   And now she is gone, but in fancy I trace

The lavendered linen updrawn, the round arm
   Half sunk in the counterpane's broidered roses,
Revealing the exquisite outline of form;
   A willowy wonder of grace that reposes
   Beneath the white counterpane, fleecy with roses.

I see the small hand lying over the heart,
   Where the passionate dreams are so sweet in their sally;
The fair little fingers they tremble and part,
   As part to th' warm waves the leaves of the lily,
   And they play with her hand like the waves with the lily.

In white fleecy flowers, the queen o' the flowers!
   What to her is the world with its bad, bitter weather?
Wide she opens her arms – ah, her world is not ours!
   And now she has closed them and clasped them together—
   What to her is our world, with its clouds and rough weather?

Hark! midnight! the winds and the snows blow and beat;
   I drop down the curtain and say to my sorrow,
Thank God for the window just over the street;
   Thank God there is always a light whence to borrow
   When darkness is darkest, and sorrow most sorrow.

In Bonds

While shines the sun, the storm even then
   Has struck his bargain with the sea—
Oh, lives of women, lives of men,
   How pressed, how poor, how pinched ye be!

It is as if, having granted power
   Almost omnipotent to man,
Heaven grudged the splendor of the dower,
   And going back upon her plan,

Mortised his free feet in the ground,
   Closed him in walls of ignorance,
And all the soul within him bound
   In the dull hindrances of sense.

Hence, while he goads his will to rise,
   As one his fallen ox might urge,
The conflict of the impatient cries
   Within him wastes him like a scourge.

Even as dreams his days depart,
   His work no sure foundation forms,
Immortal yearnings in his heart,
   And empty shadows in his arms!

It is as if, being come to land,
   Some pestilence, with fingers black,
Loosed from the wheel the master hand
   And drove the homesick vessel back;

As if the nurslings of his care
   Chilled him to death with their embrace;
As if that she be held most fair
   Turned round and mocked him to his face.

And thus he stands, and ever stands,
   Tempted without and torn within;
Ashes of ashes in his hands,
   Famished and faint, and sick with sin.

Seeing the cross, and not the crown;
   The o'erwhelming flood, and not the ark;

Till gap by gap his faith throws down
   Its guards, and leaves him to the dark.

And when the last dear hope has fled,
   And all is weary, dreary pain,
That enemy, most darkly dread,
   Grows pitiful, and snaps the chain.

The West Country

Have you been in our wild west country? then
   You have often had to pass
Its cabins lying like birds' nests in
   The wild green prairie grass.

Have you seen the women forget their wheels
   As they sat at the door to spin—
Have you seen the darning fall away
   From their fingers worn and thin,

As they asked you news of the villages
   Where they were used to be,
Gay girls at work in the factories
   With their lovers gone to sea!

Ah, have you thought of the bravery
   That no loud praise provokes—
Of the tragedies acted in the lives
   Of poor, hard-working folks!

Of the little more, and the little more
   Of hardship which they press
Upon their own tired hands to make
   The toil for the children less:

And not in vain; for many a lad
   Born to rough work and ways,
Strips off his ragged coat, and makes
   Men clothe him with their praise.

Telling Fortunes

'Be not among wine-bibbers; among riotous eaters of
flesh; for the drunkard and the glutton shall come to
poverty; and drowsiness shall clothe a man with rags.'
Proverbs, 23: 20, 21

I'll tell you two fortunes, my fine little lad,
  For you to accept or refuse.
The one of them good, and the other one bad;
  Now hear them, and say which you choose!

I see by my gift, within reach of your hand,
  A fortune right fair to behold;
A house and a hundred good acres of land,
  With harvest fields yellow as gold.

I see a great orchard, the boughs hanging down
  With apples of russet and red;
I see droves of cattle, some white and brown,
  But all of them sleek and well-fed.

I see doves and swallows about the barn doors,
  See the fanning-mill whirling so fast,
See men that are threshing the wheat on the floors;
  And now the bright picture is past!

And I see, rising dismally up in the place
  Of the beautiful house and the land,
A man with a fire-red nose on his face,
  And a little brown jug in his hand!

Oh! if you beheld him, my lad, you would wish
  That he were less wretched to see;
For his boot-toes, they gape like the mouth of a fish,
  And his trousers are out at the knee!

In walking he staggers, now this way, now that,
  And his eyes they stand out like a bug's,
And he wears an old coat and a battered-in hat,
  And I think that the fault is the jug's!

For our text says the drunkard shall come to be poor,
  And drowsiness clothes men with rags;

And he doesn't look much like a man, I am sure,
    Who has honest hard cash in his bags.

Now which will you choose? to be thrifty and snug,
    And to be right side up with your dish;
Or to go with your eyes like the eyes of a bug,
    And your shoes like the mouth of a fish!

MARGARET JUNKIN PRESTON
1820–97

MARGARET JUNKIN PRESTON was born in Milton, Pennsylvania, oldest of eight children. Her father, a minister, taught her Latin, Greek and English literature. Her family moved frequently following her father's career, which included presidencies of three colleges. Margaret read avidly and began publishing in periodicals in 1849. Her first novel, *Silverwood* (1856), was published anonymously. She married John T. L. Preston, a professor of Latin, in 1857, acquiring several young stepchildren, and had two sons of her own. Despite her Northern origin, she supported the South during the Civil War. Her husband was an officer in the Confederate Army. *Beechenbrook: A Rhyme of the War* (1865), a long poem about the trials of white Southern women with husbands away at war, enjoyed wide popularity. Many of her poems in *Old Songs and New* (1870) and *Cartoons* (1875) animate biblical and classical characters in dramatic monologues, reflecting her admiration for Elizabeth Barrett Browning and Robert Browning. Her diary of the Civil War years, *The Life and Letters of Margaret Junkin Preston*, was published in 1903.

Erinna's Spinning

The Lesbian youths are all abroad today,
Filling the vales with mirth, and up and down
The festive streets, with roses garlanded,
Go hand in hand fair Mytilené's daughters.

Slaves follow, bearing baskets overheaped
With myrtle, ivy, lilies, hyacinths,
And all the world of sweets, wherewith to deck
The May-day altar of the flowery goddess.

And pranksome children, spilling on the paths
Acanthus-blossoms from their laden'd arms,
Come shouting after, mad with heyday glee,
Making fit ending to the gay procession.

Sweet goddess! frown not on me, though I bring
No odorous wreath to hang above thy shrine:
For, 'See, Erinna!' stern my mother saith,
'Thou gaddest not abroad with idle maidens.

'The buds will all unmask without thine aid,
The fruits round to their fullness, though no trains
Of dallying girls thus fray the noon-time hours
That wiser thrift should give to wheel and distaff.'

And so I bide at home the day-long hours,
A prisoner at my loom: but yet my heart
Steals after my companions, while I keep
Time to their dances with my droning spindle.

I hear Alcæus strike his lyric string,
I catch our Sappho's answering choric song
On some high festival, – and my stirr'd soul
Flutters to spring beyond the bars that cage it.

O for the April birth-right of the trees!
O for the Dryad's scope to sun my thoughts
Till they unfold in myriad leafiness,
As now the quickening earth unfolds her blossoms.

But like a frost the nipping voice grates harsh:
—'Hence with thy tablets, girl! The gods above
Made thee a woman, formed for household needs,
For wifely handicraft and ministration.

'Pluck out these climbing fancies from thy thought,
Poor, weedy things, that ape the fibrous strength
Of overshadowing man, – only to fail,
And failing so, to leave thee less a woman.

'Do what thou wilt, – gird up thy maiden-gear,—
Wrestle with athletes, – hurl the warlike dart,—
Spin forth the discus, – in the Isthmian games
Enroll thyself amid the sleek-limb'd runners;

'Or with the Delphian lyre, essay thy skill,—
Or measure dithyrambs with Æolian bards;
And for thy pains, – confess thyself outdone
Ever and always, gauged by manhood's stature.'

If I make answer, that chaste Artemis
Is wise as Pythius, or the Queen of Heaven
Is strong of purpose as Olympian Jove,—
She hastes to silence me with hot impatience:

'What man of men upon a woman's face
Hath pored to learn therefrom aught other lore
Than her one lesson, love?' I answer low,
—'A woman taught her art once to a hero!'

She chafes: – 'I am beholden for thy hint:
The stylus fits *thee*, sooth, as did the skein,
The hand of Hercules, who sat unsex'd
—Struck for his dulness by the queenly slipper!'

Whereat the taunt: 'What youth of Lesbos, stout,
Well-knit of limb, as ripe for peace as war,
In strophes versed by seer of Chios wrought,
Will think to choose *thee* for thy trick of singing?

'Nay – talk with him of soft Milesian wools—
Of Colchian linens, – rose or saffron dyes,—
Of broidery patterns for thy silken web,—
Of Cyprian wines; the youth is fond to listen.

' "This maiden," – (giving heed, he ponders thus,)
"Could order aptly housely offices,
Could rule discreetly the sweet realm of home,
Could rear, control and wisely guide my children." '

Herewith she ends: 'Erinna, have thou heed;
Let Lesbian virgins dance, let Sappho sing,
Improvident of wifehood's disciplines;
Thou, – rend thy scrolls, and keep thee to thy spinning.'

But what care I for wifehood? ... I, so young!
For matron dignities? – They clog and bind:
For petty talk – '*Are olives fine this year?*—'
'*Are figs full-formed?*' – Beshrew my mother's wisdom!

I would renounce them all for Sappho's bay,—
Forgo them all for room to chant out free
The silent rhythms I hum within my heart,
And so for ever leave my weary spinning!

1870

FRANCES JANE CROSBY VAN ALSTYNE
1820–1915

FRANCES JANE CROSBY VAN ALSTYNE was born in Southeast, New York. When she was six weeks old inappropriate treatment for an eye inflammation destroyed her sight except for dim perception of colour and light. At fifteen she entered the New York Institution for the Blind, where she became a star pupil, showing an unusual capacity for memorisation. She composed public addresses in verse and delivered them before legislatures to raise support for education of the blind. She taught English and history in the Institution from 1847 to 1858. She published verse in *The Blind Girl and Other Poems* (1844), *Monterey and Other Poems* (1851) and *Bells at Evening and Other Verses* (1897). Several of her poems became popular songs. In 1858 she married Alexander van Alstyne, a music teacher and church organist who had been one of her pupils. They lived in Brooklyn. Converted to evangelical Christianity in 1850 during a revival, Crosby began writing hymns in 1864. Working for several gospel music publishers, she wrote as many as seven hymns a day, totalling around nine thousand in her lifetime. She composed mentally at night and dictated new lyrics to a secretary or friend in the morning. Her publishers assigned her hymns nearly two hundred pseudonyms, but the name Fanny Crosby became a household word and the hymnist an icon of Protestant saintliness. Her most popular hymns spread worldwide through Sunday schools and evangelical missions, were translated into several languages, and remain in use today.

The Mandan Chief

The circumstance alluded to in the following lines, is that of the Mandan Chief, who, on the destruction of his tribe by the small pox, as the last survivor, rode to the prairies, where, after slaying his war-horse, destroyed himself.

He mounts his favorite steed of war,
  And o'er the prairie wild,
He speeds that fiery courser on—
  A lonely forest child.

His home is desolate and drear;
  His kindred, where are they?
That tribe, once powerful and brave,
  Disease hath swept away.

He yet survives; but what is life,
  When those we love are fled?
That Indian seeks a resting-place,
  Among the peaceful dead.

And now he halts; before him lies
  A vast expansive plain,
A moment, and that noble steed,
  By his own hand is slain.

Shade of my fathers! he exclaims,
  I come with you to rest;
He grasps the instrument of death,
  And plants it in his breast.

Fast streaming from the fatal wound,
  He sees the purple gore;
'Tis done! 'tis done! he faintly cries,
  Then falls, to rise no more.

Let Me Die on the Prairie

Let me die on the prairie! and o'er my rude grave,
In the soft breeze of summer the tall grass shall wave;
I would breathe my last sigh as the bright hues of even
Are melting away in the blue arch of Heaven.

Let me die on the prairie! unwept and unknown,
I would pass from this fair Earth forgotten, alone;—
Yet no! – there are hearts I have learned to revere,
And methinks there is bliss in affection's warm tear.

Oh, speak not to me of the green cypress shade;
I would sleep where the bones of the Indian are laid,
And the deer will bound o'er me with step light and free,
And the carol of birds will my requiem be.

Let me die on the prairie! I have wished for it long;
There floats in wild numbers the bold hunter's song;
'Tis the spot of all others the dearest to me,
And how sweet in its bosom my slumber will be!

On Hearing a Description of a Prairie

Oh! could I see as thou hast seen,
   The garden of the west,
When Spring in all her loveliness
   Fair nature's face has dressed.

The rolling prairie, vast and wild!
   It hath a charm for me—
Its tall grass waving to the breeze,
   Like billows on the sea.

Say, hast thou chased the bounding deer
   When smiled the rosy morn?
Or hast thou listened to the sound
   Of the merry hunter's horn?

Once could the noble red-man call
   That prairie wild his home;—
His cabin now in ruins laid,
   He must an exile roam,

And thou at twilight's pensive hour,
   Perchance hast seen him weep;—
Tread lightly o'er the hallowed spot,
   For there his kindred sleep.

I envy not the opulent
   His proud and lordly dome;
Far happier is the pioneer
   Who seeks a prairie home;—

Where no discordant notes are heard,
   But all is harmony;
Where soars aloft unfettered thought,
   And the heart beats light and free.

Thoughts in Midnight Hours

Pale Cynthia! lovely goddess of the night,
That o'er reposing nature sheds her light;—
And you, ye stars! that shine from pole to pole,
And round this dark terrestrial planet roll;

Fain would I to your distant regions soar,
And traverse worlds unseen, unknown before;—
My restless spirit would presume to scale
Those airy heights, and lift the future's veil.

Vain wish! aside that veil thou may'st not draw,
The present must be – ought to be, thy law;
Study what God reveals, and ask no more,
And where thou can'st not comprehend, adore.

He to those countless orbs has lustre given,
His hand directs them through the pathless heaven;
He, at a glance, the universe surveys;—
Deep and incomprehensible his ways.

But hark! another hour has passed away.
O time! thy rapid current who can stay?
And yet how unimproved thy moments fly;
Mortals forget that they are born to die.

Death comes when least expected – who can tell
For whom may next be tolled the funeral knell?
The greyhaired sire, the blooming and the brave,
The prince, the peasant, share one common grave.

We fondly gaze on those we love today,
The morrow dawns – and where, oh, where are they?
Lifeless and cold their cherished forms are laid
In solemn silence 'neath the grave's dark shade.

Religion! sacred treasure! but for thee
The world a solitary wild would be,
In darkest hour, thou, comforter, art nigh,
To wipe the gushing tear from sorrow's eye.

Who might not give a thousand worlds to know
The calm serenity thou dost bestow?
The richest gift to mortals ever given,
On earth our solace and foretaste of heaven.

But hush! what sounds are stealing on my ear?
'Tis but the sighing of the wind I hear—
And there is music in these plaintive notes—
How soft, yet mournful o'er my soul it floats.

How sweet at such an hour the parting sigh,
To heave upon a mother's breast and die;
When the triumphant soul shall wing its flight,
To hail in heaven a morn of holier light.

'Twere sad to languish in a distant land,
Our pillow smoothed but by a stranger's hand;
To pass the restless hours of night alone,
Without one heart congenial with our own.

No mother near in soothing tones to speak—
To bathe the aching head, the burning cheek;
Whence comes that shadowy form with noiseless tread?
From the dark mansions of the lonely dead?—

Why trembles thus my agitated frame?
'Tis but the phantom of a fevered brain;—
And see, it smiles benignant on me now,
A heavenly mildness sits upon that brow.

Speak, I conjure! inhabitant of bliss!
Say what has called thee to a world like this;
Dost bring some message from yon starry sphere?
Then deign thine accents to a mortal ear.

Frail child of earth, awake! delay no more!
Know thou the morn of life will soon be o'er;
Trust not the world, nor seek its smiles to gain,
False are its friendships, and its pleasures vain.

Farewell! I'll still thy faithful guardian be,
While floats thy bark o'er life's tempestuous sea;
And when its heavings and its storms shall cease,
Be thine the haven of eternal peace.

The vision speaks – then fading from my sight,
To heaven's celestial courts it wings its flight;
Night's dusky shadows quickly melt away,
And smiling nature hails the opening day.

We Are Going

We are going, we are going
   To a home beyond the skies,
Where the fields are robed in beauty,
   And the sunlight never dies;
Where the fount of joy is flowing
   In the valley green and fair,
We shall dwell in love together;
   There will be no parting there.

We are going, we are going,
   And the music we have heard
Like the echo of the woodland,
   Or the carol of a bird;
With the rosy light of morning,
   On the calm and fragrant air,
Still it murmurs, softly murmurs,
   There will be no parting there.

We are going, we are going,
   When the day of life is o'er,
To that pure and happy region
   Where our friends have gone before;
They are singing with the angels
   In that land so bright and fair;
We shall dwell with them forever;
   There will be no parting there.

1864

Blessed Assurance

Blessed assurance, Jesus is mine!
O what a foretaste of glory divine!
Heir of salvation, purchase of God,
Born of His Spirit, washed in His blood!

Chorus:
    This is my story, this is my song,
    Praising my Saviour all the day long.

Perfect submission, perfect delight,
Visions of rapture now burst on my sight;
Angels descending bring from above
Echoes of mercy, whispers of love.

Perfect submission, all is at rest,
I in my Saviour am happy and blest,—
Watching and waiting, looking above,
Filled with His goodness, lost in His love.

1873

I Am Thine, O Lord

I am Thine, O Lord, I have heard Thy voice,
    And it told Thy love to me;
But I long to rise in the arms of faith,
    And be closer drawn to Thee.

Chorus:
    Draw me nearer, nearer, blessed Lord,
        To the cross where Thou hast died;
    Draw me nearer, nearer, nearer, blessed Lord,
        To Thy precious bleeding side.

Consecrate me now to Thy service, Lord,
    By the power of grace divine;
Let my soul look up with a steadfast hope,
    And my will be lost in Thine.

O the pure delight of a single hour
   That before Thy throne I spend,
When I kneel in prayer, and with Thee, my God,
   I commune as friend with friend!

There are depths of love that I cannot know
   Till I cross the narrow sea,
There are heights of joy that I may not reach
   Till I rest in peace with Thee.

                                      1875

ELIZABETH DREW BARSTOW STODDARD
1823–1902

ELIZABETH DREW BARSTOW STODDARD was born in Mattapoisset, Massachusetts, daughter of a prosperous shipbuilder. She was educated at Wheaton Female Seminary. In 1851 she married poet Richard Stoddard, with whom she had three children; two died while young. The Stoddards' home in New York City became a meeting place for his circle of genteel minor poets. Elizabeth wrote poems, stories and sketches for periodicals, contributing the 'Lady Correspondent' column of the San Francisco *Alta* from 1854–8. She commented irreverently on the temperance movement, women writers, gender relations and other topics. Her early fiction, notably *The Morgesons* (1862), mixes literary modes while challenging repressive gender conventions. Neither her nor her husband's writing was commercially successful. Stoddard suppressed her unconventionality in later writings (*Two Men*, 1865; *Temple House*, 1867), still failing to capture a popular market and becoming increasingly bitter over the success of others whom she regarded as less talented. Like her fiction, her poems (collected in 1895) show the influence of such Gothic authors as Emily Brontë in depicting family tensions, incest and decaying households.

The House by the Sea

Tonight I do the bidding of a ghost,
　A ghost that knows my misery;
In the lone dark I hear his wailing boast,
　'Now shalt thou speak with me.'

Must I go back where all is desolate,
　Where reigns the terror of a curse,
To knock, a beggar, at my father's gate,
　That closed upon a hearse?

The old stone pier has crumbled in the sea;
    The tide flows through the garden wall;
Where grew the lily, and where hummed the bee,
    Black seaweeds rise and fall.

I see the empty nests beneath the eaves;
    No bird is near; the vines have died;
The orchard trees have lost the joy of leaves,
    The oaks their lordly pride.

Of what avail to set ajar the door
    Through which, when ruin fell, I fled?
If on the threshold I should stand once more,
    Shall I behold the dead?

Shall I behold, as on that fatal night,
    My mother from the window start,
When she was blasted by the evil sight,—
    The shame that broke her heart?

The yellow grass grows on my sister's grave;
    Her room is dark – she is not there;
I feel the rain, and hear the wild wind rave—
    My tears, and my despair.

A white-haired man is singing a sad song
    Amid the ashes on the hearth;
'Ashes to ashes, I have moaned so long
    I am alone on earth.'

No more! no more! I cannot bear this pain;
    Shut the foul annals of my race;
Accursed the hand that opens them again,
    My dowry of disgrace.

And so, farewell, thou bitter, bitter ghost!
    When morning comes the shadows fly;
Before we part, I give this merry toast,—
    The dead that do not die!

Nameless Pain

I should be happy with my lot:
A wife and mother – is it not
Enough for me to be content?
What other blessing could be sent?

A quiet house, and homely ways,
That make each day like other days;
I only see Time's shadow now
Darken the hair on baby's brow!

No world's work ever comes to me,
No beggar brings his misery;
I have no power, no healing art
With bruisèd soul or broken heart.

I read the poets of the age,
'Tis lotus-eating in a cage;
I study Art, but Art is dead
To one who clamors to be fed

With milk from Nature's rugged breast,
Who longs for Labor's lusty rest.
O foolish wish! I still should pine
If any other lot were mine.

The Wife Speaks

Husband, today could you and I behold
The sun that brought us to our bridal morn
Rising so splendid in the winter sky
(We thought fair spring returned), when we were wed;
Could the shades vanish from these fifteen years,
Which stand like columns guarding the approach
To that great temple of the double soul
That is as one – would you turn back, my dear,
And, for the sake of Love's mysterious dream,
As old as Adam and as sweet as Eve,
Take me, as I took you, and once more go

Towards that goal which none of us have reached?
Contesting battles which but prove a loss,
The victor vanquished by the wounded one;
Teaching each other sacrifice of self,
True immolation to the marriage bond;
Learning the joys of birth, the woe of death,
Leaving in chaos all the hopes of life—
Heart-broken, yet with courage pressing on
For fame and fortune, artists needing both?
Or, would you rather – I will acquiesce—
Since we must choose what is, and are grown gray,
Stay in life's desert, watch our setting sun,
Calm as those statues in Egyptian sands,
Hand clasping hand, with patience and with peace,
Wait for a future which contains no past?

'One morn I left him in his bed'

One morn I left him in his bed;
A moment after some one said,
'Your child is dying – he is dead.'

We made him ready for his rest,
Flowers in his hair, and on his breast
His little hands together prest.

We sailed by night across the sea;
So, floating from the world were we,
Apart from sympathy, we Three.

The wild sea moaned, the black clouds spread
Moving shadows on its bed,
But one of us lay midship dead.

I saw his coffin sliding down
The yellow sand in yonder town,
Where I put on my sorrow's crown.

And we returned; in this drear place
Never to see him face to face,
I thrust aside the living race.

Mothers, who mourn with me today,
Oh, understand me, when I say,
I cannot weep, I cannot pray;

I gaze upon a hidden store,
His books, his toys, the clothes he wore,
And cry, 'Once more, to me, *once* more!'

Then take, from me, this simple verse,
That you may know what I rehearse—
A grief – your and my Universe!

Before the Mirror

Now like the Lady of Shalott,
   I dwell within an empty room,
And through the day and through the night
   I sit before an ancient loom.

And like the Lady of Shalott
   I look into a mirror wide,
Where shadows come, and shadows go,
   And ply my shuttle as they glide.

Not as she wove the yellow wool,
   Ulysses' wife, Penelope;
By day a queen among her maids,
   But in the night a woman, she,

Who, creeping from her lonely couch,
   Unraveled all the slender woof;
Or, with a torch, she climbed the towers,
   To fire the fagots on the roof!

But weaving with a steady hand
   The shadows, whether false or true,
I put aside a doubt which asks
   'Among these phantoms what are you?'

For not with altar, tomb, or urn,
   Or long-haired Greek with hollow shield,

Or dark-prowed ship with banks of oars,
   Or banquet in the tented field;

Or Norman knight in armor clad,
   Waiting a foe where four roads meet;
Or hawk and hound in bosky dell,
   Where dame and page in secret greet;

Or rose and lily, bud and flower,
   My web is broidered. Nothing bright
Is woven here: the shadows grow
   Still darker in the mirror's light!

And as my web grows darker too,
   Accursed seems this empty room;
For still I must forever weave
   These phantoms by this ancient loom.

Above the Tree

Why should I tarry here, to be but one
To eke out doubt, and suffer with the rest?
Why should I labor to become a name,
And vaunt, as did Ulysses to his mates,
'I am a part of all that I have met.'
A wily seeker to suffice myself!
As when the oak's young leaves push off the old,
So from this tree of life man drops away,
And all the boughs are peopled quick by spring
Above the furrows of forgotten graves.
The one we thought had made the nation's creed,
Whose death would rive us like a thunderbolt,
Dropped down – a sudden rustling in the leaves,
A knowledge of the gap, and that was all!
The robin flitting on his frozen mound
Is more than he. Whoever dies, gives up
Unfinished work, which others, tempted, claim
And carry on. I would go free, and change
Into a star above the multitude,
To shine afar, and penetrate where those

Who in the darkling boughs are prisoned close,
But when they catch my rays, will borrow light,
Believing it their own, and it will serve.

PHOEBE CARY
1824–71

PHOEBE CARY (see biography p. 78).

Homes for All

Columbia, fairest nation of the world,
  Sitting in queenly beauty in the west,
With all thy banners round about thee furled,
  Nursing the cherub Peace upon thy breast;
Never did daughter of a kingly line
Look on a lovelier heritage than thine!

Thou hast deep forests stretching far away,
  The giant growth of the long centuries,
From whose dim shadows to the light of day
  Come forth the mighty rivers toward the seas,
To walk like happy lovers, hand in hand,
Down through the green vales of our pleasant land.

Thou hast broad prairies, where the lovely flowers
  Blossom and perish with the changing year;
Where harvests wave not through the summer hours,
  Nor with the autumn ripen in the ear;
And beautiful lakes that toss their milky spray
Where the strong ship hath never cleaved its way.

And yet with all thy broad and fertile land,
  Where hands sow not, nor gather in the grain,
Thy children come and round about thee stand,
  Asking the blessing of a home in vain,—
Still lingering, but with feet that long to press
Through the green windings of the wilderness.

In populous cities do men live and die,
    That never breathe the pure and liberal air;
Down where the damp and desolate rice-swamps lie,
    Wearying the ear of Heaven with constant prayer,
Are souls that never yet have learned to raise
Under God's equal sky the psalm of praise.

Turn not, Columbia! from their pleading eyes;
    Give to thy sons that ask of thee a home;
So shall they gather round thee, not with sighs,
    But as young children to their mother come;
And brightly to the centuries shall go down
The glory that thou wearest like a crown.

Harvest Gathering

The last days of the summer: bright and clear
    Shines the warm sun down on the quiet land,
Where corn-fields, thick and heavy in the ear,
    Are slowly ripening for the laborer's hand;
Seed-time and harvest – since the bow was set,
Not vainly has man hoped your coming yet!

To the quick rush of sickles, joyously
    The reapers in the yellow wheat-fields sung,
And bound the pale sheaves of the ripened rye,
    When the first tassels of the maize were hung;
That precious seed into the furrow cast
Earliest in spring-time, crowns the harvest last.

Ever, when summer's sun burns faint and dim,
    And rare and few the pleasant days are given,
When the sweet praise of our thanksgiving hymn
    Makes beautiful music in the ear of Heaven,
I think of other harvests whence the sound
Of singing comes not as the sheaves are bound.

Not where the rice-fields whiten in the sun,
    And the warm South casts down her yellow fruit,
Shout they the labors of the autumn done—

For there Oppression casts her deadly root,
And they, who sow and gather in that clime
Share not the treasures of the harvest-time.

God of the seasons! thou who didst ordain
    Bread for the eater who shall plant the soil,
How have they heard thee, who have forged the chain
    And built the dungeon for the sons of toil?
Burdening their hearts, not with the voice of prayer,
But the dull cries of almost dumb despair.

They who would see that growth of wickedness
    Planted where now the peaceful prairie waves,
And make the green paths of our wilderness
    Red with the torn and bleeding feet of slaves—
Forbid it, Heaven! and let the sharp axe be
Laid at the root of that most poison tree!

Let us behold its deadly leaves begin
    A fainter shadow o'er the world to cast,
And the long day that nursed its growth of sin
    Wane to a sunset that shall be its last;
So that the day-star, rising from the sea,
Shall light a land whose children will be free!

Shakespearian Readings

Oh, but to fade, and live we know not where,
To be a cold obstruction and to groan!
This sensible, warm woman to become
A prudish clod; and the delighted spirit
To live and die alone, or to reside
With married sisters, and to have the care
Of half a dozen children, not your own;
And driven, for no one wants you,
Round about the pendant world; or worse than worse
Of those that disappointment and pure spite
Have driven to madness: 'T is too horrible!
The weariest and most troubled married life
That age, ache, penury, or jealousy

Can lay on nature, is a paradise
To being an old maid.

That very time I saw, (but thou couldst not,)
Walking between the garden and the barn,
Reuben, all armed; a certain aim he took
At a young chicken, standing by a post,
And loosed his bullet smartly from his gun,
As he would kill a hundred thousand hens.
But I might see young Reuben's fiery shot
Lodged in the chaste board of the garden fence,
And the domesticated fowl passed on,
In henly meditation, bullet free.

My father had a daughter got a man,
As it might be, perhaps, were I good looking,
I should, your lordship.
And what's her residence?
A hut, my lord, she never owned a house,
But let her husband, like a graceless scamp,
Spend all her little means, – she thought she ought,—
And in a wretched chamber, on an alley,
She worked like masons on a monument,
Earning their bread. Was not this love indeed?

LUCY LARCOM
1824–93

LUCY LARCOM was born in Beverly, Massachusetts. An idyllic rural childhood ended when her sea-captain father died. His widow moved their ten children to Lowell, Massachusetts, where she ran a dormitory for young female millworkers. Lucy and her sisters went to work in the mills. Already a lover of poetry by age eleven, she made her bench into a library (books were forbidden in the factory) by papering it with poems clipped from newspapers. In 1846 she went to Illinois to teach. From 1849–52 she attended Monticello Seminary in Godfrey, Illinois. In 1854 she returned to Massachusetts to teach at Wheaton Seminary. Having refused a suitor who did not share her abolitionist views, Larcom embraced unmarried life. She edited the children's magazine *Our Young Folks* from 1865 to 1873, collaborated with John Greenleaf Whittier in compiling anthologies for children and frequently contributed poems to *St Nicholas* and other children's periodicals. She described her mill experiences in *An Idyl of Work* (1875) and *A New England Girlhood* (1889). Beginning in 1867 she published four volumes of her poetry. She also edited anthologies of verse and wrote a book of criticism, *Landscape in American Poetry* (1879).

A Little Cavalier

When I was very young indeed,—
　　Ages ago, my dear,—
I had, to stand by me at need,
　　A little cavalier;
The prettiest lad I ever met,
　　Black-eyed, red-cheeked, and fat:
His face I never can forget;
　　His name? Well – it was Nat.

I saw him first one pleasant day,
  Beside his mother's door;
His third year had not slipped away,
  And I was scarcely four.
Upon his arm a wooden gun
  He bore right soldierly;
I know not which it was first won
  My heart, that gun or he.

There never was a clumsier trap
  By child of mortal seen.
A button at its side went – snap!
  The gun was painted green.
But, shouldering it with martial tread,
  Proudest of girls was I;
While like a flag above his head
  Would my pink bonnet fly.

For Nat I gathered currants fine,
  And flowers that bloomed around;
Though only yellow celandine
  And blue gill-over-the-ground
Grew underneath the gray stone-wall,
  Still they retain their charm—
Those homely blossoms which recall
  That early sunshine warm.

I never tasted gingerbread,
  Or doughnuts crisp and new,
But in my mother's ear I said,
  'For little Nat some, too.'
The days were dull and dark when him
  To school I could not lead.
That love like ours at last grew dim
  A pity seems, indeed.

To me he brought no cake or toy;
  But then you know, my dear,
That he was nothing but a boy,
  And boys have ways so queer!
They do not stop to think of things
  That give us girls delight;

But take the best that fortune brings
    As if it were their right.

'T was no such trifle made us part:
    He loved my gifts to take,
And it was comfort to my heart
    To see him eat my cake.
It happened thus: One afternoon,
    As from the school we came,—
The day was sultry, late in June,
    Our faces both aflame,—

Beneath the blooming locust-trees
    We loitered, I and Nat;
His hair was lifted by the breeze;
    I firmly held his hat
By its long bridle-string of green,
    And lightly held his hand:
No happier tiny twain were seen
    Than we, in all the land.

A freckled girl was passing by,
    And down she gazed at me,
As if we children, Nat and I,
    Were something strange to see.
I looked at him and looked at her;
    Why did she scan us so?
The cruel words she uttered were,
    'I guess you've got a beau!'

'A beau! What! he?' At once I dropped
    The little hand and hat,
And home I ran, and never stopped
    Till I lost sight of Nat.
A beau! Some monstrous thing, no doubt,
    All tusks and fangs and claws;
The one they read to me about
    A *boa-constrictor* was.

None did I with my grief annoy,
    None should my terror know;
But, oh, I wondered if a boy
    Must always be a beau!

And so my happy days were done!
   That innocent-looking Nat,
The owner of that darling gun,
   How came *he* to be *that*?

Nat's doorstep nevermore I sought;
   No sign of woe gave he;
Much more of him I doubtless thought
   Than ever he of me.
Forgetting is not hard, for men
   As young as he, my dear,
And so I lost him there and then,—
   My little cavalier.

What the Train Ran Over

When the train came shrieking down,
   Did you see what it ran over?
I saw heads of golden brown,
   Little plump hands filled with clover.
Yes, I saw them, boys and girls,
   With no look or thought of flitting;
Not a tremble in their curls;—
   Where the track runs they were sitting.

From the windows of the train
   I could see what they were doing;
I could see their faces, plain:
   Some with dreamy eyes pursuing
Flight of passing cloud or bird;
   Others childish ditties flinging
On the air; I almost heard
   What the song was they were singing.

They were well-known faces, too;
   Do you marvel that I shiver
As I picture them to you
   Playing there beside the river?
With them I myself have played
   On that very spot: I wonder

Why I never was afraid
  Of the coming railway-thunder.

Little, sunburnt, barefoot boys
  In the shallow water wading,
Sea-birds scattering with your noise,
  Ragged hats your rogue-looks shading,
Will your sparkling eyes upon
  Yonder waves again flash never?
Is your heartsome laughter gone
  From the tired old world forever?

Dimpled Ruth, with brow of snow!
  Never thought I to outlive her,
While we watched the white boats go
  Up and down the small tide-river,
Past dark steeps of juniper,
  Ever widening, ever flowing
To the sea; I mourn for her,
  Gone so far beyond my knowing!

Well, the cruel train rolls on.
  What! your eyes with tears are filling
For my pretty playmates gone?
  Child, I am to blame for chilling
All your warm young fancies so:
  There are real troubles, plenty!
They lived – forty years ago;
  And the road has run here twenty.

And those children, – I was one,—
  Busy men and women, wander
Under life's midsummer sun.
  One or two have gone home yonder
Out of sight. But still I see
  Golden heads amid the clover
On the railway-track; to me
  This is what the train runs over.

FRANCES ELLEN WATKINS HARPER
1825–1911

FRANCES ELLEN WATKINS HARPER was born in Baltimore, Maryland, the only child of free black parents. Her mother died when she was three and she went to live with an aunt and uncle. Until age thirteen, she attended a school run by her uncle. After teaching for two years in Ohio and Pennsylvania, Watkins joined the Underground Railroad in 1854 and began travelling as a speaker for the Maine Anti-Slavery Society. A brilliant orator, she was also a prolific writer. She contributed to abolitionist newspapers such as *The Liberator* and her *Poems on Miscellaneous Subjects* (1854) ran to twenty printings. In 1860 she married Fenton Harper, a widower with three children. They had another child before he died in 1864. Harper supported the family as a travelling lecturer. After the emancipation of slaves, Harper's lectures focused on civil rights, education and economic opportunity for black men and women. She participated in the Women's Christian Temperance Union and the American Women's Suffrage Association, predominantly white organisations in which she faced racism. She served as director of the American Association of Colored Youth (starting 1893) and vice-president of the National Association of Colored Women (1896). The poems collected in *Sketches of Southern Life* (1872), many narrated by the character Aunt Chloe, reflect hope for a new age for African Americans and belief in a black feminism rooted in folk culture.

from AUNT CHLOE

The Deliverance

Master only left old Mistus
    One bright and handsome boy;
But she fairly doted on him,
    He was her pride and joy.

We all liked Mister Thomas,
    He was so kind at heart;
And when the young folkes got in scrapes,
    He always took their part.

He kept right on that very way
    Till he got big and tall,
And old Mistus used to chide him
    And say he'd spile us all.

But somehow the farm did prosper
    When he took things in hand;
And though all the servants liked him,
    He made them understand.

One evening Mister Thomas said,
    'Just bring my easy shoes;
I am going to sit by mother,
    And read her up the news.'

Soon I heard him tell old Mistus,
    'We're bound to have a fight;
But we'll whip the Yankees, mother,
    We'll whip them sure as night!'

Then I saw old Mistus tremble;
    She gasped and held her breath;
And she looked on Mister Thomas
    With a face as pale as death.

'They are firing on Fort Sumpter;
    Oh! I wish that I was there!—

Why, dear mother! what's the matter?
　　You're the picture of despair.'

'I was thinking, dearest Thomas,
　　'Twould break my very heart
If a fierce and dreadful battle
　　Should tear our lives apart.'

'None but cowards, dearest mother,
　　Would skulk unto the rear,
When the tyrant's hand is shaking
　　All the heart is holding dear.'

I felt sorry for old Mistus;
　　She got too full to speak;
But I saw the great big tear-drops
　　A running down her cheek.

Mister Thomas too was troubled
　　With choosing on that night,
Betwixt staying with his mother
　　And joining in the fight.

Soon down into the village came
　　A call for volunteers;
Mistus gave up Mister Thomas,
　　With many sighs and tears.

His uniform was real handsome;
　　He looked so brave and strong;
But somehow I couldn't help thinking
　　His fighting must be wrong.

Though the house was very lonesome,
　　I thought 'twould all come right,
For I felt somehow or other
　　We was mixed up in that fight.

And I said to Uncle Jacob,
　　'How old Mistus feels the sting,
For this parting with your children
　　Is a mighty dreadful thing.'

'Never mind,' said Uncle Jacob,
　　'Just wait and watch and pray,

For I feel right sure and certain,
　　Slavery's bound to pass away;

'Because I asked the Spirit,
　　If God is good and just,
How it happened that the masters
　　Did grind us to the dust.

'And something reasoned right inside,
　　Such should not always be;
And you could not beat it out my head,
　　The Spirit spoke to me.'

And his dear old eyes would brighten,
　　And his lips put on a smile,
Saying, 'Pick up faith and courage,
　　And just wait a little while.'

Mistus prayed up in the parlor,
　　That the Secesh all might win;
We were praying in the cabins,
　　Wanting freedom to begin.

Mister Thomas wrote to Mistus,
　　Telling 'bout the Bull's Run fight,
That his troops had whipped the Yankees
　　And put them all to flight.

Mistus' eyes did fairly glisten;
　　She laughed and praised the South,
But I thought some day she'd laugh
　　On tother side her mouth.

I used to watch old Mistus' face,
　　And when it looked quite long
I would say to Cousin Milly,
　　The battle's going wrong;

Not for us, but for the Rebels.—
　　My heart would fairly skip,
When Uncle Jacob used to say,
　　'The North is bound to whip.'

And let the fight go as it would—
　　Let North or South prevail—

He always kept his courage up,
   And never let it fail.

And he often used to tell us,
   'Children, don't forget to pray;
For the darkest time of morning
   Is just 'fore the break of day.'

Well, one morning bright and early
   We heard the fife and drum,
And the booming of the cannon—
   The Yankee troops had come.

When the word ran through the village,
   The colored folks are free—
In the kitchens and the cabins
   We held a jubilee.

When they told us Mister Lincoln
   Said that slavery was dead,
We just poured our prayers and blessings
   Upon his precious head.

We just laughed, and danced, and shouted
   And prayed, and sang, and cried,
And we thought dear Uncle Jacob
   Would fairly crack his side.

But when old Mistus heard it,
   She groaned and hardly spoke;
When she had to lose her servants,
   Her heart was almost broke.

'Twas a sight to see our people
   Going out, the troops to meet,
Almost dancing to the music,
   And marching down the street.

After years of pain and parting,
   Our chains was broke in two,
And we was so mighty happy,
   We didn't know what to do.

But we soon got used to freedom,
   Though the way at first was rough;

But we weathered through the tempest,
    For slavery made us tough.

But we had one awful sorrow,
    It almost turned my head,
When a mean and wicked cretur
    Shot Mister Lincoln dead.

'Twas a dreadful solemn morning,
    I just staggered on my feet;
And the women they were crying
    And screaming in the street.

But if many prayers and blessings
    Could bear him to the throne,
I should think when Mister Lincoln died,
    That heaven just got its own.

Then we had another President,—
    What do you call his name?
Well, if the colored folks forget him
    They wouldn't be much to blame.

We thought he'd be the Moses
    Of all the colored race;
But when the Rebels pressed us hard
    He never showed his face.

But something must have happened him,
    Right curi's I'll be bound,
'Cause I heard 'em talking 'bout a circle
    That he was swinging round.

But everything will pass away—
    He went like time and tide—
And when the next election came
    They let poor Andy slide.

But now we have a President,
    And if I was a man
I'd vote for him for breaking up
    The wicked Ku-Klux Klan.

And if any man should ask me
    If I would sell my vote,

I'd tell him I was not the one
   To change and turn my coat;

If freedom seem'd a little rough
   I'd weather through the gale;
And as to buying up my vote,
   I hadn't it for sale.

I do not think I'd ever be
   As slack as Jonas Handy;
Because I heard he sold his vote
   For just three sticks of candy.

But when John Thomas Reeder brought
   His wife some flour and meat,
And told he had sold his vote
   For something good to eat,

You ought to seen Aunt Kitty raise,
   And heard her blaze away;
She gave the meat and flour a toss,
   And said they should not stay.

And I should think he felt quite cheap
   For voting the wrong side;
And when Aunt Kitty scolded him,
   He just stood up and cried.

But the worst fooled man I ever saw,
   Was when poor David Rand
Sold out for flour and sugar;
   The sugar was mixed with sand.

I'll tell you how the thing got out;
   His wife had company,
And she thought the sand was sugar,
   And served it up for tea.

When David sipped and sipped the tea,
   Somehow it didn't taste right;
I guess when he found he was sipping sand
   He was mad enough to fight.

The sugar looked so nice and white—
   It was spread some inches deep—

But underneath was a lot of sand;
    Such sugar is mighty cheap.

You'd laughed to seen Lucinda Grange
    Upon her husband's track;
When he sold his vote for rations
    She made him take 'em back.

Day after day did Milly Green
    Just follow after Joe,
And told him if he voted wrong
    To take his rags and go.

I think that Samuel Johnson said
    His side had won the day,
Had not we women radicals
    Just got right in the way.

And yet I would not have you think
    That all our men are shabby;
But 'tis said in every flock of sheep
    There will be one that's scabby.

I've heard, before election came
    They tried to buy John Slade;
But he gave them all to understand
    That he wasn't in that trade.

And we've got lots of other men
    Who rally round the cause,
And go for holding up the hands
    That gave us equal laws,

Who know their freedom cost too much
    Of blood and pain and treasure,
For them to fool away their votes
    For profit or for pleasure.

                                        1872

ROSE TERRY COOKE
1827–92

ROSE TERRY COOKE was born on a farm near Hartford, Connecticut. Her father was a banker and congressman. She was educated at Hartford Female Seminary until reverses in the family's fortunes ended her education. She taught for three years, then devoted herself to writing and caring for the children of a deceased sister. She wrote realistic stories with regional settings and dialect, often featuring spinster heroines and exploring the politics of gender roles. She also published two collections of poems (1861, 1888) and a novel, *Steadfast* (1889). In 1873 she married Rollin H. Cooke, a widower with two daughters, who used up her savings. Needing the income, she wrote for leading periodicals, both adults' and children's, including *Atlantic*, *Harper's*, *Our Young Folks* and *St Nicholas*. Short story collections include *Rootbound* (1885), *Sphinx's Children and Other People* (1886), *Somebody's Neighbours* and *Huckleberries Gathered from New England Hills* (1891).

Schemhammphorasch

'This is the key which was given by the angel Michael
to Pali, and by Pali to Moses. If "thou canst read it,
then shalt thou understand the words of men, ... the
whistling of birds, the language of date-trees, the unity
of hearts, ... nay, even the thoughts of the rains."'
Gleanings after the Talmud

Ah! could I read Schemhammphorasch,
The wondrous keynote of the world,
What voices could I always hear
From tempests, with their black wings furled,
That on the sudden west winds steer,
And, muttering low their awful song,
Or pealing through the mountains strong,
Robe all the skies with sheeted fire;
That pour from heaven a rushing river,
That bid the hill-tops bow and quiver,
Mad with some fierce and wild desire.

The dreadful anthem of the wind,
That sweeps through forests as a plow,
That lays the greensward heaped below,
Would chant its meaning to my mind,
And I could tell the tale to man
In words that burn and glow with splendor;
Then should the whole wide sky surrender
Its hidden voice, its wondrous plan,
Asleep since earliest time began;
And all my soul, most like a blaze
That burns the branches whence it springeth,
Should flame to heaven in mightier lays
Than any mortal poet singeth,
If I could read Schemhammphorasch.

If I could read Schemhammphorasch,
When little birds are softly singing,
Or twitter from their greenwood nests,
Where safe and still the mother rests;
Or else, upon the glad wind springing,

Send up their tender morning song;
Then should I know their secret blisses,
The thrill of life and love they feel
When summer's sun their bright heads kisses,
Or summer's winds about them steal.
Or, listening to the early blossoms
That are so fleeting and so fair,
With perfume sighing from their bosoms
Its incense on the gracious air,
I think that I should hear a prayer
So sweet, so patient, and so lowly,
That mortal words most pure and rare
Would scarce unveil its meaning holy.
From forests whence the murmurous leaves
Breathe their content in rustling quiver,
Or droop when any rain-wind grieves,
Or where some broad and brimming river
O'erflowing to the mighty sea,
Sings the proud joy of destiny,
The glad acclaim of life and breath;
The courage of confronted death;
Ah! what a rapturous, glorious song
Should seize with bliss this earthly throng,
If I could read Schemhammphorasch!

If I could read Schemhammphorasch,
Then should I know the souls of men,
Too deep for any other ken;
I could translate the silent speech
Of glittering eye and knotted brow,
Though still the wily tongue might teach
A different script with voice and vow.
The blood that runs in traitorous veins;
The breath that gasps with hope or fear;
The stifled sigh, the hidden tear;
The death-pang of immortal pains,
That hide their mortal agony,
Would have their own low voice for me;
Their tale of hate and misery,
Their sob of passion and despair,
Their sacred love, their frantic prayer.

My soul would be the listening priest
To hear confession far and near,
And woe and want from first to least
Would shriek its utterance in my ear.
Ah, could I bear to live and hear
These cries that heaven itself might flee,
These terrors heaven alone may see,
If I could read Schemhammphorasch?

If I could read Schemhammphorasch,
My brain would burn with such a fire
As lights the awful cherubim;
My heart would burst with woe and ire,
My flesh would shrivel and expire;
Yea! God himself grow far and dim.
I cannot hold the boundless sea
In one small chalice lent to me;
I cannot grasp the starry sky
In one weak hand, and bid it lie
Where I would have a canopy;
I cannot hate and love together;
I cannot poise the heavy world,
Or hear its hiss through chaos hurled,
Or stay the falling of a feather.
No, not if Michael came once more,
Standing upon the sea and shore,
And held his right hand down to me,
That I that awful word might see,
And learn to read its lesson dread.
My soul in dust would bow her head,
Mine eyes would close, my lips would say,
'Oh, Master! take thy gift away:
Leave me to live my little day
In peace and trust while yet I may.
For could I live, or love, or pray,
If I could read Schemhammphorasch?'

'Che Sara Sara'

She walked in the garden
    And a rose hung on a tree,
Red as heart's blood,
    Fair to see.
'Ah, kind south-wind,
    Bend it to me!'
But the wind laughed softly,
    And blew to the sea.

High on the branches,
    Far above her head,
Like a king's cup
    Round, and red.
'I am comely,'
    The maiden said,
'I have gold like shore-sand,
    I wish I were dead!

'Blushes and rubies
    Are not like a rose,
Through its deep heart
    Love-life flows.
Ah, what splendors
    Can give me repose!
What is all the world worth?
    I cannot reach my rose.'

A Hospital Soliloquy

I swan! it's pleasant now we've beaten
    To think I staid an' seen it through.
I haint gin' in to no retreatin',
    And I've seen battles more'n two.

So now I'm finished and knocked under,
    For one leg's gone, an' t'other's lame;
I like to hear them cannon thunder,
    To tell the world we've got the game.

But better'n all the fire an flashin'
    Down on the Shenandoah route,
Where Phil's a swearin' and a dashin',
    Is see'n' them English folks back out.

I would ha gi'n a mint o'dollars
    Two years ago, to see 'em try
With Abr'am's hand gripped in their collars,
    How they liked eatin' humble-pie.

An' there they set, while we're a grinnin',
    And say 'twas all a darned mistake;
That old secesh done all the sinnin',
    And they have allers baked our cake.

I sot last night an' heerd the firin'
    An' see the rockets shoot the dark,
And heerd the others all inquirin'—
    'What's happened?' 'Who has hit the mark?'

The sick, and lame, and sore, an' sleepy,
    They gin a cheer! – 'twa'n't loud I know,
But then it made me kind o' creepy
    To hear their voices quaver so.

Thinks I, you're shot with English powder,
    An' hacked with English swords and guns;
They'll have to lie a little louder
    Afore they cheat us knowin' ones.

An' now the war's as good as over,
    And dead, and lame, an' mourners tell,
It wasn't livin' quite in clover,
    For them that lived or them that fell.

I kinder guess next time we do it,
    Them sassy English folks will find
When we get riled, an' buckle to it,
    They won't have time to change their mind!

1865

ACHSA W. SPRAGUE
c. 1828–62

ACHSA W. SPRAGUE was born on a farm in Plymouth Notch, Vermont, the sixth child in a family described by an acquaintance as intellectual but 'nervously unbalanced'. Her father was an alcoholic and the family was poor. She began teaching in a rural school at age twelve. In 1848 she was bedridden with joint disease, of which she was cured six years later by angelic powers. A stirring orator, she became a trance medium and travelled throughout the country lecturing on spiritualism, gathering a large following with her messages that the world of spiritual beings was immanent in the material world, that communication with this spirit world was possible, and that souls continued to progress eternally. Poetic inspiration through automatic writing and improvisation was one means of communication with the spirit world; others she experimented with were the paranormal phenomena of magnetism, hypnotism and the seance. Her social views were progressive; she opposed slavery, urged prison reform and condemned oppressive gender roles. She read widely; Elizabeth Barrett Browning's *Aurora Leigh* was especially important to her. Its influence is evident in her long dramatic poem, *The Poet*, drafted in seventy-two hours. Two books of poetry were published posthumously (*I Still Live, A Poem for the Times*, 1862; *The Poet and Other Poems*, 1864); other writings remain unpublished.

from THE POET

from Scene 3

Evening. A large public hall crowded with people of all
classes. Mr and Mrs Seymour, Ida and Bruce, seated
near the platform.

IDA

'Tis near the time. I'm glad 'tis getting late.
In such a place, how tedious 'tis to wait!

BRUCE

Yes, in such public gatherings every kind
Of influence meets, and every class of mind;
And with the busy tongues and moving feet,
'Tis seldom one finds comfort in his seat.—
I hope the entertainment will commence
Ere long, just to relieve thy heart's suspense.
Perhaps I set her gifts that night so high,
'Twill disappoint in the reality;
And yet I have no fear. Here lies the charm
Of every Improvisatrice, – in the calm
Or thrilling look of eye, and of the face,
The voice that catches some peculiar grace,
That sends the words home with such burning power,
They sway thee at their will, and charm the hour.
And then the thought that fresh from out the mint
Of mind, just newly coined, – though seen in print
It must lose half its charm, – when one can hear,
Strikes home with such a wild-bird's note upon the ear,
It seems as though the soul of one who sings,
Leaps sudden forth, and like a fountain springs
To meet thine own, and thou hadst caught the spray
Of real, living waves of song, the ray
Of golden sunlight over all outspread,
Wrapped like a glittering rainbow round thy head.
Here mind meets mind, fresh-gushing, young and new,

The soul stands half revealed, if true, or if untrue.
Catch up these words, and write them on a page,
They're like a wild-bird drooping in a cage;
His song rings not so sweet and strong and clear,
As when through forest-aisles it met the ear.
There every tree caught up the wild notes sung,
And back again in richer sweetness flung.
Now, but the voice is heard, and in such hour
His heart sings not; there lived his greatest power.—
She'll enter soon; then judge with eye and ear,
Whether 'she's stepped from woman's lofty sphere!'

IDA

I wonder where Kate is tonight? Suppose
At party, ball, or theatre – who knows?

BRUCE

Or Opera, – 'Don Giovanni's' sung,—
I think we'd surely find her there, among
The town's elite, who are not apt to trace
The trail of vice when 'tis disguised with grace.
I love the music, but detest each word.
Tomorrow night, 'tis 'Norma', – hast thou heard?

IDA

I have not, though I read it with delight.

BRUCE

We must be sure to go tomorrow night.
I'll ask thy parents now, – 'twill be so fine,—
If they'll consent to go, I know I've thine.

MR SEYMOUR

Bruce, Ida, hast thou heard those people there?
I think thy pet from them will get her share
Of vile abuse. Just list a moment, do!

STRANGER LADY

I don't believe a word! It is untrue
To think it comes impromptu, without thought:
With such transparent sham I'll not be caught!

YOUNG GENTLEMAN,
with white vest, jewelled rings, and mustache

Perhaps she's beautiful, – would show her face:
Her fair white hand perhaps she moves with grace.
Who knows but I may fall in love, first sight,
And failing to win hers, may go bedight?

YOUNG MISS,
with a simper

In love! I never thought thou hadst a heart.

YOUNG GENTLEMAN

In justice then thou ought to give me part
Of thine.—

STRANGER LADY

I think it is a real shame!
I feel, myself, as very much to blame
For coming here tonight. If Mrs Brown
Should know of this, she'd think us letting down
Our dignity, to mingle in this crowd.—
Such things as these ought not to be allowed.

MIDDLE-AGED GENTLEMAN,
with an air of careless indifference and mischievous look

I like to have the fun go on. I see
One and another look surprised at me,
And wonder much what motive brought me here.
But then I am not proud, like thee, my dear!

LADY

Proud! No indeed! And so I find it hard
To make the people our true sphere regard.
But come alone hereafter, if thou wilt!
I'm sure, I hold it hardly less than guilt
To countenance such things; she may be vile,
And use this new-born power as artful wile:
No woman with a pure, unsinful heart,
Would in a public place take such a part.

MIDDLE-AGED GENTLEMAN

Not quite so bad as that, perhaps, my dear!
There's so much said about a woman's sphere
Just now, perhaps she thinks she'll take a stand,
And make her woman's voice ring through the land.
Let's wait until we hear, and then decide,
Without regard to fashion, vanity or pride.

ELDERLY GENTLEMAN,
with white neckcloth

Sir, at the best I deem it real sin,
For her to stand such public place within.
You know that Paul says, sir, 'It is a shame
For woman publicly to speak.' I blame
Her very much; and then I have been told,
She teaches such pernicious doctrines, bold,
As if she had no fear of God or man;
But I'm determined to defeat this plan
Before 'tis older; and I came tonight
To hear her words myself, and just indite
The heads. Next Sunday, I intend to preach
A sermon, to denounce the whole, and teach
My congregation of this deadly sin,
Before she can commence their hearts to win.
I mean to warn my people, sir, to stay
Within the fold, and not be led away
By such strange women, teaching stranger things,
Though with deceitful, siren voice she sings.
I'll do my duty, though it is a cross
To come, – in Heaven I shall make up the loss!
                                        [*Sighs.*]

BRUCE,
to Mr Seymour, laughing

We have gone back to Pharisees again!
He thanks his God, he's not as other men.
No matter, truth will bide the test of all,
And by it let our poet stand or fall.
I hope he'll get a hit or two tonight.—
Ah, here she comes! They just turn on the light!

IMPROVISATRICE

[Enter Improvisatrice, preceded by an attendant bearing a harp. Intense silence in the audience. She leans over the harp a few moments, then raising her eyes toward heaven, touches the strings and commences singing.]

I seek no homage from the crowd,
   Though hushed in silence long;
I sing at last because my soul
   Will pour itself in song;
Because a fountain leaps within,
   Whose ever-dashing spray
Can catch the light, and bear it back,
   Like golden beams of day.

It matters not to me, the thought
   That others round me fling,
When on this altar now I lay
   My heart's best offering.
Far from the world I wrap me up
   In robes that none can see,
And find true joy in Thee, my God,
   If none shall smile on me.

I only care that other hearts
   Should feel this thrill of mine,—
A chord electric that would draw
   Each soul more close to Thine.
I only pray for power to break
   From every soul its chain,
A gift to win the tears that wash
   Away each guilty stain.

O human heart! that throbs and beats,
   So wrung with bitter grief,
Cast every sin from out thy midst,
   And thou shalt find relief!
When pure and clear as crystal shines
   The human soul shall be,
There is no place within its depths
   For such deep misery.

The light of heaven shall beam and burn
   Unto its depths below;
Through crystal walls it enters in,
   Like mist, dispersing woe.
And round its shrine for evermore
   The golden rays shall cling,
And through its aisles in thrilling strains,
   The angel, Peace, shall sing!
[*She pauses, leaning again upon her harp.*]

EMILY DICKINSON
1830–86

EMILY DICKINSON was born in Amherst, Massachusetts. The men of her family were attorneys active in politics and in the business affairs of Amherst College. Dickinson attended Amherst Academy and spent a year at Mount Holyoke Female Seminary, where she became notorious as the one student who would not publicly state that she had experienced evangelical Christian conversion. By the age of thirty, she stopped attending church and increasingly withdrew from other public functions, but she maintained a community through prolific correspondence. Among her friends were Helen Hunt Jackson, who urged her to publish her poems. She began writing poetry seriously around 1850 and, at the peak of her writing in 1862, wrote on average a poem a day. When she submitted poems to *Atlantic Monthly* in 1862, the editor, Thomas Wentworth Higginson, recommended changes in her diction and rhyme. Only seven of her poems were published during her lifetime. She did not reveal the extent of her writing. After her death, her sister Lavinia found over a thousand poems in a cabinet. Many were carefully copied with alternate wordings and stitched into manuscript books or fascicles. Higginson and Mabel Loomis Todd edited a selection of Dickinson's poems (altering punctuation and diction) in the 1890s; later selections were edited by Millicent Todd Bingham and Martha Dickinson Bianchi. Family disputes delayed publication of the complete poems until 1955, when Thomas Johnson produced an edition leaving her now famous dashes in the text. In 1981 R. W. Franklin published a facsimile edition, *The Manuscript Books of Emily Dickinson*.

from FASCICLE 34

Bereavement in their death to feel
Whom We have never seen,
A Vital Kinsmanship import
Our Soul and their's – between –

For Stranger – Strangers do not mourn –
There be Immortal friends
Whom Death see first – 'tis news of this
That paralyze Ourselves –

Who, vital only to Our Thought –
Such Presence bear away
In dying – 'tis as if Our Souls†   world/selves/Sun
Absconded – suddenly –

                                                        c. 1862

I think to Live – may be a Bliss†   life
To those who dare to try†   Allowed who dare to try –
Beyond my limit to conceive –
My lip – to testify –

I think the Heart I former wore
Could widen – till to me
The Other, like the little Bank
Appear – unto the Sea –

I think the Days – could every one
In Ordination stand –
And Majesty – be easier –
Than an inferior kind –

No numb alarm – lest Difference come –
No Goblin – on the Bloom –
No start† in Apprehension's Ear,   click
No Bankruptcy† – no Doom –   sepulchre/wilderness

But Certainties of Sun† –   Noon
Midsummer† – in the Mind –   Meridian
A steadfast South – upon the Soul –
Her Polar time† – behind –   Night

tangible/positive
true
truth

The Vision – pondered long –
So plausible[†] becomes
That I esteem the fiction – real[†] –
The Real[†] – fictitious seems –

been one
qualified

How bountiful the Dream –
What Plenty – it would be –
Had all my Life but been[†] Mistake
Just rectified[†] – in Thee

c. 1862

A little Road – not made of Man –
Enabled of the Eye –
Accessible to Thill of Bee –
Or Cart of Butterfly –

besides

sigh, vehicle

If Town it have – beyond[†] itself –
'Tis that – I cannot say –
I only know[†] – no Curricle[†] that rumble there
Bear Me –

c. 1862

too

Her Sweet turn to leave the Homestead
Came the Darker Way –
Carriages – Be sure – and Guests – true[†] –
But for Holiday

swelling

'Twas more pitiful Endeavor
Than did Loaded[†] Sea
O'er the Curls attempt to caper
It had cast away –

Never Bride had such Assembling –
Never kinsmen kneeled
To salute so fair a Forehead –
Garland be indeed –

Fitter for the Feet

Ever could endow

Fitter Feet[†] – of Her before us –
Than whatever Brow
Art of Snow – or Trick of Lily
Possibly bestow[†]

claim

Of her Father – Whoso ask[†] Her –
He shall seek as high

As the Palm – that serve the Desert –
To obtain the Sky –

Distance – be Her only Motion[†] –   signal
If 'tis Nay – or Yes –
Acquiescence – or Demurral –
Whosoever guess –

He[†] – must pass the Crystal Angle[†]   First, limit
That obscure[†] Her face –   divide
He – must have achieved in person
Equal Paradise –

             c. 1862

Pain – has an Element of Blank –
It cannot recollect
When it begun – or if there were
A time[†] when it was not –   day

It has no Future – but itself –
It's Infinite contain
It's Past – enlightened to perceive
New Periods – of Pain.

             c. 1862

So much Summer
Me for showing
Illegitimate –
Would a Smile's minute bestowing
Too exorbitant[†]   extravagant

To the Lady
With the Guinea[†]   importunate
Look – if She should know
Crumb of Mine
A Robin's Larder
Would[†] suffice to stow –   Could
             c. 1862

Promise This – When You be Dying –
Some[†] shall summon Me –   Some one
Mine belong Your latest Sighing –
Mine – to Belt Your Eye –

Not with Coins – though they be Minted
From an Emperor's Hand –
Be my lips – the only Buckle
Your low Eyes – demand –

Mine to stay – when all have wandered –
To devise once more
If the Life be too surrendered –
Life of Mine – restore –

best

surpass/excel in
More resembling you

Poured like this – My Whole[†] Libation –
Just that You should see
Bliss of Death – Life's Bliss extol thro[†]
Imitating You –[†]

Mine – to guard Your Narrow Precinct –
entice/persuade
Latest
Newest/Freshest

To seduce[†] the Sun
Longest[†] on Your South, to linger,
Largest[†] Dews of Morn

To demand, in Your low favor
Lest the Jealous Grass
Or later linger
Greener lean – Or fonder cluster[†]
Round some other face –

Mine to supplicate Madonna –
If Madonna be
regard so small/scarce
Could behold so far[†] a Creature –
Christ – omitted – Me –

Just to follow Your dear feature –
Ne'er so far behind –
For My Heaven –
Had I not been
Most enough – denied?

                                        c. 1862

I had no time to Hate –
Because
The Grave would hinder Me –
And Life was not so
Ample I
Could finish – Enmity –

Nor had I time to Love –
But since
Some Industry must be –
The little Toil of Love –
I thought
Be large enough for Me –

c. 1862

My Life had stood – a Loaded Gun –
In Corners – till a Day
The Owner passed – identified –
And carried Me away –

And now We roam in† Sovereign Woods –   the
And now We hunt the Doe –
And every time I speak for Him –
The Mountains straight – reply –

And do I smile, such cordial light
Upon the Valley glow –
It is as a Vesuvian face
Had let its pleasure through –

And when at Night – Our good Day done –
I guard My Master's Head –
'Tis better than the Eider-Duck's
Deep† Pillow – to have shared –   Low

To foe of His – I'm deadly foe –
None stir† the second time –   harm
On whom I lay a Yellow Eye –
Or an emphatic Thumb –

Though I than He – may longer live
He longer must – than I.
For I have but the power† to kill,   art
Without – the power to die –

c. 1863

The Sunrise runs for Both –
The East – Her Purple Troth
Keeps with the Hill –
The Noon unwinds Her Blue

Till One Breadth cover Two –
Remotest – still –

Nor does the Night forget
A Lamp for Each – to set –
Wicks wide away –
The North – Her blazing Sign
Erects in Iodine –
Till Both – can see –

The Midnight's Dusky Arms
Clasp Hemispheres, and Homes
And so
Upon Her Bosom – One –
And One upon Her Hem –
Both lie –

                                        c. 1863

No Bobolink – reverse His Singing
When the only Tree
Ever He minded occupying
By the Farmer be –

Core   Clove to the Root[†] –
                        His Spacious Future –
All Horizon – known –   Best Horizon – gone –[†]
                        Whose Music be His
                        Only Anodyne –
                        Brave Bobolink –

                                        c. 1863

One Blessing had I than the rest
So larger to my Eyes
That I stopped gauging – satisfied –
For this enchanted size –

It was the limit of my Dream –
The focus of my Prayer –
A perfect – paralysing Bliss –
Contented as Despair –

                        I knew no more of Want – or Cold –
Fictitious   Phantasms[†] both become

For this new Value[†] in the Soul –
Supremest Earthly Sum –

fortune/portion

The Heaven below the Heaven above –
Obscured with ruddier[†] Blue –
Life's Latitudes leant over – full –
The Judgment perished – too –

nearer/comelier

Why Bliss so scantily[†] disburse[†] –
Why Paradise defer[†] –
Why Floods be served to Us – in Bowls –
I speculate no more –

cautiously express/afford
demur

c. 1863

Victory comes late –
And is held low to freezing lips –
Too rapt with frost
To take it –
How sweet it would have tasted –
Just a Drop –
Was God so economical?
His Table's spread too high for Us –
Unless We dine on tiptoe –
Crumbs – fit such little mouths –
Cherries – suit Robins –
The Eagle's Golden Breakfast strangles – Them –
God keep His Oath to Sparrows –
Who of little Love – know how to starve –

c. 1863

The Mountains – grow unnoticed –
Their Purple figures rise
Without attempt – Exhaustion –
Assistance – or Applause –

In Their Eternal Faces
The Sun – with just[†] delight
Looks long – and last – and golden –
For fellowship[†] – at night –

broad

sympathy
c. 1863

Bar/Find

These – saw Visions –
Latch† them softly –
These – held Dimples –
Smooth them slow –
This – addressed departing accents –
Quick – Sweet Mouth – to miss thee so –

fondled in

This – We stroked –
Unnumbered – Satin –
These – we held among† our own –
Fingers of the Slim Aurora –
Not so arrogant – this Noon –

the

These – adjust – that ran to meet us –
Pearl – for† Stocking – Pearl for Shoe –
Paradise – the only Palace
Fit for Her reception – now –

                                        c. 1863

Strong Draughts of Their Refreshing Minds
To drink – enables Mine
Through Desert or the Wilderness
As bore it Sealed Wine –

To go elastic – Or as One
The Camel's trait–attained –
How powerful the Stimulus
Of an Hermetic Mind –

                                        c. 1863

Journey

impair/debar

We miss Her, not because We see –
The Absence† of an Eye –
Except its Mind accompany
Abridge† Society

scarcely, flights

As slightly† as the Routes† of Stars –
Ourselves – asleep below –
We know that their superior Eyes

Scan better – as they go –   Include Us – as they go –†
Convey us – as they go –

                                        c. 1865

Essential Oils – are wrung –
The Attar from the Rose

Be not expressed by Suns – alone –
It is the gift of Screws –

The General Rose – decay –
But this – in Lady's Drawer
Make Summer – When the Lady lie
In Ceaseless Rosemary –

c. 1863

HELEN HUNT JACKSON
1830–85

HELEN HUNT JACKSON was born in Amherst, Massachusetts, daughter of a professor. Her parents died when she was a child. She was raised thereafter by an aunt and educated at private schools. Her first husband, Lieutenant Edward Bissell Hunt, and her two sons all died within a short time and she began writing poetry to cope with these losses. Volumes of her poetry were published in 1870, 1873, 1886, 1892 and 1895. She wrote children's books, travel books, articles and book reviews for periodicals, using the pseudonyms 'H.H.', 'Saxe Holm' and 'Rip Van Winkle'. She contracted her second marriage to William Sharpless Jackson on the understanding that he would allow her complete freedom for self-development. Hearing Chief Standing Bear speak in 1879 on dispossession of the Plains Indians inspired her to begin pioneering work for Indian rights. *A Century of Dishonor* (1881), the first of Jackson's works published with her name, exposed the repeated violation of treaties and massacre of tribes. The book led to the founding of the Indian Rights Association. Appointed by the government to investigate the provision of land to Mission Indians in California, she transformed her investigative material to fiction in *Ramona* (1884), hoping to replicate the political effectiveness of *Uncle Tom's Cabin* by Harriet Beecher Stowe.

Solitude

'O Solitude,' I said, 'sweet Solitude!
I follow fast; I kneel to find thy trace;
I listen low in every secret place;
I lay rough hand on eager human lips;
I set aside all near companionships;
I know thou hast a subtler, rarer good.
O Priestess, how shalt thou be found and wooed?'

I tracked her where she passed in trackless fields;
I trod her path where footprint had not staid
In sunless woods; I stopped to hark where laid
Her very shadow its great bound of light
And gloom in lifeless arctic day and night;
And where, to tropic sun, mid-ocean yields
Its silent, windless waves, like mirror-shields;
But found her not. Great tribes roamed free
In every trackless field and wood. More plain
Than speech I heard their voice: in rain, the rain
Of endless chatter, and in sun, the sun
Of merry laughing noise, were never done.
All silence dinned with sound; and, jostling me,
In every place, went crowds I could not see.

In anger, then, at last I cried, 'Betray
Whomever thou canst cheat, O Solitude,
With promise of thy subtler, rarer good!
I seek my joy henceforth in haunts of men,
Forgetting thee, where thou hast never been!'
When, lo! that instant sounded close and sweet,
Above the rushing of the city street,
The voice of Solitude herself, to say,
'Ha, loving comrade, met at last! Which way?'

Distance

O subtile secret of the air,
Making the things that are not, fair
Beyond the things that we can reach
And name with names of clumsy speech;
By shadow-worlds of purple haze
The sunniest of sunny days
Outweighing in our hearts' delight;
Opening the eyes of blinded sight;
Holding an echo in such hold,
Bidding a hope such wings unfold,
That present sounds and sights between
Can come and go, unheard, unseen,—

O subtile secret of the air,
Heaven itself is heavenly fair
By help of thee! The saints' good days
Are good, because the good Lord lays
No bound of shore along the sea
Of beautiful Eternity.

My House Not Made with Hands

It is so old, the date is dim;
I hear the wise man vexing him
With effort vain to count and read,
But to his words I give small heed,
Except of pity that so late
He sitteth wrangling in the gate,
When he might come with me inside,
And in such peace and plenty bide.
The constant springs and summers thatch,
With leaves that interlock and match,
Such roof as keeps out fiercest sun
And gentle rain, but one by one
Lets in blue banner-gleams of sky
As pomp of days goes marching by
Under these roofs I lie whole days,
Watching the steady household ways:
Innumerable creatures come
And go, and are far more at home
Than I, who like dumb giant sit
Baffled by all their work and wit.
No smallest of them condescends
To notice me; their hidden ends
They follow, and above, below,
Across my bulky shape they go,
With swift, sure feet, and subtle eyes,
Too keen and cautious for surprise
In vain I try their love to reach;
Not one will give me trust or speech.
No second look the furry bee

Gives, as he bustles round, to me;
Before my eyes slim spiders take
Their silken ladders out and make
No halt, no secret, scaling where
They like, and weaving scaffolds there;
The beaded ants prick out and in,
Mysterious and dark and thin;
With glittering spears and gauzy mail
Legions of insects dart and sail,
Swift Bedouins of the pathless air,
Finding rich plunder everywhere;
Sweet birds, with motion more serene
Than stillest rest, soar up between
The fleecy clouds, then, sinking slow,
Light on my roof. I do not know
That they are there till fluttering
Low sounds, like the unravelling
Of tight-knit web, their soft wings make,
Unfurling farther flight to take.
All through my house is set out food,
Ready and plenty, safe and good,
In vessels made of cunning shapes,
Whose liquid spicy sweet escapes
By drops at brims of yellow bowls,
Or tips of trumpets red as coals,
Or cornucopias pink and white,
By millions set in circles tight;
Red wine turned jelly, and in moulds
Of pointed calyx laid on folds
Of velvet green; fruit-grains of brown,
Like dusty shower thickly strewn
On underside of fronds, and hid
Unless one lift the carven lid;
And many things which in my haste
And ignorance I reckon waste,
Unsightly and unclean, I find
Are but delicious food, designed
For travellers who come each day,
And eat, and drink, and go their way.
I am the only one who need
Go hungry where so many feed;

My birthright of protection lost,
Because of fathers' sins the cost
Is counted in the children's blood:
I starve where once I might have stood
Content and strong as bird or bee,
Feeding like them on flower or tree.
When I have hunger, I must rise
And seek the poisons I despise,
Leaving untouched on every hand
The sweet wild foods of air and land,
And leaving all my happier kin
Of beasts and birds behind to win
The great rewards which only they
Can win who Nature's laws obey.

Under these roofs of waving thatch,
Lying whole days to dream and watch,
I find myself grow more and more
Vassal of summer than before;
Allegiances I thought were sworn
For life I break with hate and scorn.
One thing alone I hope, desire:
To make my human life come nigher
The life these lead whose silent gaze
Reproaches me and all my ways;
To glide along as they all glide,
Submissive and unterrified,
Without a thought of loss or gain,
Without a jar of haste or pain,
And go, without one quickened breath,
Finding all realms of life, of death,
But summer hours in sunny lands,
To my next house not made with hands.

My Strawberry

O marvel, fruit of fruits, I pause
To reckon thee. I ask what cause
Set free so much of red from heats

At core of earth, and mixed such sweets
With sour and spice: what was that strength
Which out of darkness, length by length,
Spun all thy shining thread of vine,
Netting the fields in bond as thine.
I see thy tendrils drink by sips
From grass and clover's smiling lips;
I hear thy roots dig down for wells,
Tapping the meadow's hidden cells;
    Whole generations of green things,
Descended from long lines of springs,
I see make room for thee to bide
A quiet comrade by their side;
I see the creeping peoples go
Mysterious journeys to and fro,
Treading to right and left of thee,
Doing thee homage wonderingly.
I see the wild bees as they fare,
Thy cups of honey drink, but spare.
I mark thee bathe and bathe again
In sweet uncalendared spring rain.
I watch how all May has of sun
Makes haste to have thy ripeness done,
While all her nights let dews escape
To set and cool thy perfect shape.
Ah, fruit of fruits, no more I pause
To dream and seek thy hidden laws!
I stretch my hand and dare to taste,
In instant of delicious waste
On single feast, all things that went
To make the empire thou hast spent.

Emigravit

With sails full set, the ship her anchor weighs.
Strange names shine out beneath her figure head.
What glad farewells with eager eyes are said!
What cheer for him who goes, and him who stays!

Fair skies, rich lands, new homes, and untried days
Some go to seek; the rest but wait instead
Until the next stanch ship her flag doth raise.
Who knows what myriad colonies there are
Of fairest fields, and rich, undreamed-of gains
Thick planted in the distant shining plains
Which we call sky because they lie so far?
Oh, write of me, not 'Died in bitter pains,'
But 'Emigrated to another star!'

Opportunity

I do not know if, climbing some steep hill,
Through fragrant wooded pass, this glimpse I bought,
Or whether in some mid-day I was caught
To upper air, where visions of God's will
In pictures to our quickened sense fulfil
His word. But this I saw.
                              A path I sought
Through wall of rock. No human fingers wrought
The golden gates which opened sudden, still,
And wide. My fear was hushed by my delight.
Surpassing fair the lands; my path lay plain;
Alas, so spell-bound, feasting on the sight,
I paused, that I but reached the threshold bright,
When, swinging swift, the golden gates again
Were rocky wall, by which I wept in vain.

MARY MAPES DODGE
1831–1905

MARY MAPES DODGE was born in New York, daughter of a professor, and educated by tutors. She was married young to a lawyer and began writing to earn money for her two sons' education after her husband died. She achieved enduring popular success and won an award from the French Academy with *Hans Brinker; or The Silver Skates* (1865), a children's novel based on her reading of historian John Lothrop Motley's *The Rise of the Dutch Republic*. She edited the household and children's departments of the journal *House and Home* and contributed to *Harper's*, *Atlantic Monthly* and other periodicals. In 1873 she became the first editor of *St Nicholas*, which she named. *St Nicholas* became the premier magazine for children, richly illustrated and featuring works of eminent American and British writers, including Louisa May Alcott, Mark Twain, Rudyard Kipling, Frances Hodgson Burnett and Jean Ingelow. Dodge's children's verse is collected in *Rhymes and Jingles* (1874).

The Mayor of Scuttleton

The Mayor of Scuttleton burned his nose
Trying to warm his copper toes;
He lost his money and spoiled his will
By signing his name with an icicle-quill;
He went bare-headed, and held his breath,
And frightened his grandame most to death;
He loaded a shovel, and tried to shoot,
And killed the calf in the leg of his boot;
He melted a snow-bird, and formed the habit
Of dancing jigs with a sad Welsh rabbit;
He lived on taffy, and taxed the town;
And read his newspaper upside down;

Then he sighed, and hung his hat on a feather,
And bade the townspeople come together;
But the worst of it all was, nobody knew
What the Mayor of Scuttleton next would do.

'Fire in the window'

Fire in the window! flashes in the pane!
Fire on the roof-top! blazing weather-vane!
Turn about, weather-vane! put the fire out!
The sun's going down, sir, I haven't a doubt.

'Someone in the garden'

Someone in the garden murmurs all the day;
Someone in the garden moans the night away;
Deep in the pine-trees, hidden from our sight,
He murmurs all day, and moans all the night.

'The Moon came late'

The Moon came late to a lonesome bog,
And there sat Goggleky Gluck, the frog.
'My stars!' she cried, and veiled her face,
'What very grand people they have in this place!'

Shepherd John

Oh! Shepherd John is good and kind,
Oh! Shepherd John is brave;

He loves the weakest of his flock,
  His arm is quick to save.

But Shepherd John to little John
  Says: 'Learn, my laddie, learn!
In grassy nooks still read your books,
  And aye for knowledge burn.

Read while you tend the grazing flock:
  Had I but loved my book,
I'd not be still in shepherd's frock,
  Nor bearing shepherd's crook.

The world is wide, the world is fair,
  There's muckle work to do.
I'll rest content a shepherd still,
  But grander fields for you!'

'Early to bed'

Early to bed and early to rise:
If *that* would make me wealthy and wise
I'd rise at daybreak, cold or hot,
And go back to bed at once. Why not?

The Way To Do It

I'll tell you how I speak a piece:
  First, I make my bow;
Then I bring my words out clear
  And plain as I know how.

Next, I throw my hands up *so*!
  Then I lift my eyes—
That's to let my hearers know
  Something doth surprise.

Next, I grin and show my teeth,
  Nearly every one;

Shake my shoulders, hold my sides:
    That's the sign of fun.

Next I start and knit my brow,
    Hold my head erect:
Something's wrong, you see, and I
    Decidedly object.

Then I wabble at my knees,
    Clutch at shadows near,
Tremble well from top to toe:
    That's the sign of fear.

Now I start, and with a leap
    Seize an airy dagger.
'WRETCH!' I cry. That's tragedy,
    Every soul to stagger.

Then I let my voice grow faint,
    Gasp and hold my breath;
Tumble down and plunge about:
    That's a villain's death.

Quickly then I come to life,
    Perfectly restored;
With a bow my speech is done.
    Now you'll please applaud.

Poor Crow!

Give me something to eat,
    Good people, I pray;
I have really not had
    One mouthful today!

I am hungry and cold,
    And last night I dreamed
A scarecrow had caught me—
    Good land, how I screamed!

Of one little children
    And six ailing wives

(No, one wife and six children),
　Not one of them thrives.

So pity my case,
　Dear people, I pray;
I'm honest, and really
　I've come a long way.

The Wooden Horse

A real horse is good,
　But a horse made of wood
Is a much better horsey for me;
　For he need n't be tied,
　And he's steady beside,
And never gets lazy, you see.

When pulled, he will go;
　And he stops when you 'whoa!'
For he always is willing to please;
　And though you may stay
　By the water all day,
Not once for a drink will he tease.

Not a handful of feed,
　All his life, does he need;
And he never wants brushing or combing:
　And after a race
　All over the place,
He never stands panting and foaming.

He does n't heed flies,
　Though they light on his eyes;
Mosquitoes and gnats he won't mind:
　And he never will shy,
　Though a train whizzes by,
But always is gentle and kind.

A real horse, some day,
　Will be running away;
A donkey is so apt to kick;

A goat will upset you,
A doggie will fret you—
Your wooden horse has n't a trick!

No chance of a crash,
Or a runaway smash,
Though never so playful and free.
Oh! I like when I drive
To be brought home alive—
So a fine wooden horsey for me!

'Tinker, come bring your solder'

Tinker, come bring your solder,
   And mend this watch for me.
Haymaker, get some fodder,
   And give my cat his tea.
Cobbler, my horse is limping,
   He'll have to be shod anew;
While the smith brings forge and hammer,
   To make my daughter a shoe.
Bestir yourselves, my lazies!
   I give you all fair warning:
You must do your work 'twixt twelve at night,
   And an hour before one in the morning.

Taking Time to Grow

'Mamma! mamma!' two eaglets cried,
'To let us fly you've never tried.
We want to go outside and play;
We'll promise not to go away.'
The mother wisely shook her head:
'No, no, my dears. Not yet,' she said.

'But, mother dear,' they called again,
'We want to see those things called men,

And all the world so grand and gay,
Papa described the other day.
And – don't you know? – he told you then
About a little tiny wren,
That flew about so brave and bold,
When it was scarcely four weeks old?'

But still the mother shook her head;
'No, no, my dears, not yet,' she said.
'Before you see the world below,
Far bigger you will have to grow.
There's time enough to look for men;
And as for wrens – a wren's a wren.
What if your freedom does come late?
An eaglet can afford to wait.'

LOUISA MAY ALCOTT
1832–88

LOUISA MAY ALCOTT was born in Germantown, Pennsylvania, second of four daughters of transcendentalist philosopher Amos Bronson Alcott, who encouraged his daughters' intellectual and creative development. Their mother, Abigail May Alcott, was the family's stabilising centre as her husband's unsteady career kept the family poor. The family moved during Louisa's childhood to Boston, then to Concord, Massachusetts, where other leading transcendentalists were their neighbours. In her teens Alcott began teaching and writing to help support the family. Under pseudonyms, she wrote violent, suspenseful tales and juvenile stories for *The Liberator*, *Atlantic Monthly* and other periodicals, winning a prize in 1862. Letters she wrote while working as a Civil War nurse were compiled in *Hospital Sketches* (1863). In 1864 she became editor of a girls' magazine, *Merry's Museum*. Her favourite novel was her first, *Moods* (1864), but enduring popularity came with *Little Women* (1868), a novel based on her family's life. Sequels followed: *An Old-Fashioned Girl* (1870), *Little Men* (1871), *Jo's Boys* (1886). *Work* (1873), *Eight Cousins* (1875) and *Rose in Bloom* (1876) are novels dealing with social reform. Alcott was active in the temperance and suffrage movements.

The Lay of a Golden Goose

Long ago in a poultry yard
  One dull November morn,
Beneath a motherly soft wing
  A little goose was born.

Who straightway peeped out of the shell
  To view the world beyond,
Longing at once to sally forth
  And paddle in the pond.

'Oh! be not rash,' her father said,
　　A mild Socratic bird;
Her mother begged her not to stray
　　With many a warning word.

But little goosey was perverse,
　　And eagerly did cry,
'I've got a lovely pair of wings,
　　Of course I ought to fly.'

In vain parental cacklings,
　　In vain the cold sky's frown,
Ambitious goosey tried to soar,
　　But always tumbled down.

The farm-yard jeered at her attempts,
　　The peacocks screamed, 'Oh fie!
You're only a domestic goose,
　　So don't pretend to fly.'

Great cock-a-doodle from his perch
　　Crowed daily loud and clear,
'Stay in the puddle, foolish bird,
　　That is your proper sphere.'

The ducks and hens said, one and all,
　　In gossip by the pool,
'Our children never play such pranks;
　　My dear, that fowl's a fool.'

The owls came out and flew about,
　　Hooting above the rest,
'No useful egg was ever hatched
　　From transcendental nest.'

Good little goslings at their play
　　And well-conducted chicks
Were taught to think poor goosey's flights
　　Were naughty, ill-bred tricks.

They were content to swim and scratch,
　　And not at all inclined
For any wild-goose chase in search
　　Of something undefined.

Hard times she had as one may guess,
  That young aspiring bird,
Who still from every fall arose
  Saddened but undeterred.

She knew she was no nightingale,
  Yet spite of much abuse,
She longed to help and cheer the world,
  Although a plain gray goose.

She could not sing, she could not fly,
  Nor even walk with grace,
And all the farm-yard had declared
  A puddle was her place.

But something stronger than herself
  Would cry, 'Go on, go on!
Remember, though an humble fowl,
  You're cousin to a swan.'

So up and down poor goosey went,
  A busy, hopeful bird.
Searched many wide unfruitful fields,
  And many waters stirred.

At length she came unto a stream
  Most fertile of all *Niles*,
Where tuneful birds might soar and sing
  Among the leafy isles.

Here did she build a little nest
  Beside the waters still,
Where the parental goose could rest
  Unvexed by any *bill*.

And here she paused to smooth her plumes,
  Ruffled by many plagues;
When suddenly arose the cry,
  'This goose lays golden eggs.'

At once the farm-yard was agog;
  The ducks began to quack;
Prim Guinea fowls relenting called,
  'Come back, come back, come back.'

Great chanticleer was pleased to give
   A patronizing crow,
And the contemptuous biddies clucked,
   'I wish my chicks did so.'

The peacocks spread their shining tails,
   And cried in accents soft,
'We want to know you, gifted one,
   Come up and sit aloft.'

Wise owls awoke and gravely said,
   With proudly swelling breasts,
'Rare birds have always been evoked
   From transcendental nests!'

News-hunting turkeys from afar
   Now ran with all thin legs
To gobble facts and fictions of
   The goose with golden eggs.

But best of all the little fowls
   Still playing on the shore,
Soft downy chicks and goslings gay,
   Chirped out, 'Dear Goose, lay more.'

But goosey all these weary years
   Had toiled like any ant,
And wearied out she now replied,
   'My little dears, I can't.

'When I was starving, half this corn
   Had been of vital use,
Now I am surfeited with food
   Like any Strasbourg goose.'

So to escape too many friends,
   Without uncivil strife,
She ran to the Atlantic pond
   And paddled for her life.

Soon up among the grand old Alps
   She found two blessed things,
The health she had so nearly lost,
   And rest for weary limbs.

But still across the briny deep
  Couched in most friendly words,
Came prayers for letters, tales, or verse,
  From literary birds.

Whereat the renovated fowl
  With grateful thanks profuse,
Took from her wing a quill and wrote
  This lay of a Golden Goose.

                                    1870

ELIZABETH AKERS ALLEN
1832–1911

ELIZABETH AKERS ALLEN was born in Strong, Maine, second of three daughters. Her mother died when she was four. Raised by a stepmother, she suffered repeated physical abuse until sent to boarding school. As an adult, she advocated equal rights and morals for women and men, and campaigned to end violence against women and cruelty to animals. In 1851 she married Marshall Taylor, whom she later divorced. Her first book of poems, *Forest Buds, from the Woods of Maine* (1856), appeared under the pseudonym Florence Percy, as did 'Rock Me to Sleep' (*Saturday Evening Post*, 1860), which circulated widely, sung around campfires during the Civil War and recited by generations of schoolchildren. In 1860 she married Benjamin Akers; he died a few months later. During the Civil War she worked as a government clerk in Washington and tended wounded soldiers. In 1864 she married Elijah Allen. Later verse was collected in *Silver Bridge* (1886), *The High Top Sweeting* (1891) and *The Sunset Song* (1902).

Street Music

Methought a sweet sound from the street uprose,—
   And as I pause, and strive again to hear,
'St Patrick's Day' draws softly to its close,
   And 'Jordan's' waves flow sweetly to my ear,
What though from humble source the chorus floats?
   Music is music, and I listen still;
I have 'an ear', – ay, *two*! – Even jews-harp notes
   Pass current with me, hear them where I will,
A slight Italian boy, with jetty hair
   Shading dark eyes, grinds out the melody,
Pulverized music! – In his garb and air

I read of sunnier lands beyond the sea,
And, dreaming, wander to a fairer clime,
Recalled, too suddenly, by – *'If you please, a dime!'*

1856

Rock Me to Sleep

Backward, turn backward, O Time, in your flight,
Make me a child again just for tonight!
Mother, come back from the echoless shore,
Take me again to your heart as of yore;
Kiss from my forehead the furrows of care,
Smooth the few silver threads out of my hair;
Over my slumbers your loving watch keep;—
Rock me to sleep, mother, – rock me to sleep!

Backward, flow backward, O tide of the years!
I am so weary of toil and of tears,—
Toil without recompense, tears all in vain,—
Take them, and give me my childhood again!
I have grown weary of dust and decay,—
Weary of flinging my soul-wealth away;
Weary of sowing for others to reap;—
Rock me to sleep, mother – rock me to sleep!

Tired of the hollow, the base, the untrue,
Mother, O mother, my heart calls for you!
Many a summer the grass has grown green,
Blossomed and faded, our faces between:
Yet, with strong yearning and passionate pain,
Long I tonight for your presence again.
Come from the silence so long and so deep;—
Rock me to sleep, mother, – rock me to sleep!

Over my heart, in the days that are flown,
No love like mother-love ever has shone;
No other worship abides and endures,—
Faithful, unselfish, and patient like yours:
None like a mother can charm away pain
From the sick soul and the world-weary brain.

Slumber's soft calms o'er my heavy lids creep;—
Rock me to sleep, mother, – rock me to sleep!

Come, let your brown hair, just lighted with gold,
Fall on your shoulders again as of old;
Let it drop over my forehead tonight,
Shading my faint eyes away from the light;
For with its sunny-edged shadows once more
Haply will throng the sweet visions of yore;
Lovingly, softly, its bright billows sweep;—
Rock me to sleep, mother, – rock me to sleep!

Mother, dear mother, the years have been long
Since I last listened your lullaby song:
Sing, then, and unto my soul it shall seem
Womanhood's years have been only a dream.
Clasped to your heart in a loving embrace,
With your light lashes just sweeping my face,
Never hereafter to wake or to weep;—
Rock me to sleep, mother, – rock me to sleep!

1860

In the Defences

Along the ramparts which surround the town
   I walk with evening, marking all the while
How night and autumn, closing softly down,
   Leave on the land a blessing and a smile.

In the broad streets the sounds of tumult cease,
   The gorgeous sunset reddens roof and spire,
The city sinks to quietude and peace,
   Sleeping, like Saturn, in a ring of fire;

Circled with forts, whose grim and threatening walls
   Frown black with cannon, whose abated breath
Waits the command to send the fatal balls
   Upon their errands of dismay and death.

And see, directing, guiding, silently
   Flash from afar the mystic signal lights,

As gleamed the fiery pillar in the sky
  Leading by night the wandering Israelites.

The earthworks, draped with summer weeds and vines,
  The rifle-pits, half hid with tangled briers,
But wait their time; for see, along the lines
  Rise the faint smokes of lonesome picket-fires,

Where sturdy sentinels on silent beat
  Cheat the long hours of wakeful loneliness
With thoughts of home, and faces dear and sweet,
  And, on the edge of danger, dream of bliss.

Yet at a word, how wild and fierce a change
  Would rend and startle all the earth and skies
With blinding glare, and noises dread and strange,
  And shrieks, and shouts, and deathly agonies.

The wide-mouthed guns would roar, and hissing shells
  Would pierce the shuddering sky with fiery thrills,
The battle rage and roll in thunderous swells,
  And war's fierce anguish shake the solid hills.

But now how tranquilly the golden gloom
  Creeps up the gorgeous forest-slopes, and flows
Down valleys blue with fringy aster-bloom,—
  An atmosphere of safety and repose.

Against the sunset lie the darkening hills,
  Mushroomed with tents, the sudden growth of war;
The frosty autumn air, that blights and chills,
  Yet brings its own full recompense therefor;

Rich colors light the leafy solitudes,
  And far and near the gazer's eyes behold
The oak's deep scarlet, warming all the woods,
  And spendthrift maples scattering their gold.

The pale beech shivers with prophetic woe,
  The towering chestnut ranks stand blanched and thinned,
Yet still the fearless sumac dares the foe,
  And waves its bloody guidons in the wind.

Where mellow haze the hill's sharp outline dims,
  Bare elms, like sentinels, watch silently,

The delicate tracery of their slender limbs
   Pencilled in purple on the saffron sky.

Content and quietude and plenty seem
   Blessing the place, and sanctifying all;
And hark! how pleasantly a hidden stream
   Sweetens the silence with its silver fall!

The failing grasshopper chirps faint and shrill,
   The cricket calls, in mossy covert hid,
Cheery and loud, as stoutly answering still
   The soft persistence of the katydid.

With dead moths tangled in its blighted bloom,
   The golden-rod swings lonesome on its throne,
Forgot of bees; and in the thicket's gloom,
   The last belated peewee cries alone.

The hum of voices, and the careless laugh
   Of cheerful talkers, fall upon the ear;
The flag flaps listlessly adown its staff;
   And still the katydid pipes loud and near.

And now from far the bugle's mellow throat
   Pours out, in rippling flow, its silver tide,
And up the listening hills the echoes float
   Faint and more faint, and sweetly multiplied.

Peace reigns; not now a soft-eyed nymph that sleeps
   Unvexed by dreams of strife or conqueror,
But Power, that, open-eyed and watchful, keeps
   Unwearied vigil on the brink of war.

Night falls; in silence sleep the patriot bands;
   The tireless cricket yet repeats its tune,
And the still figure of the sentry stands
   In black relief against the low full moon.

MARY ABIGAIL DODGE (GAIL HAMILTON)
1833–96

MARY ABIGAIL DODGE, 'Gail Hamilton', was born in Hamilton, Massachusetts, daughter of a schoolteacher and a farmer. She attended the village school and completed her education at Ipswich Female Seminary in 1850. She taught physical education at Ipswich, Hartford Female Seminary and Hartford High School. In 1858 she moved to Washington where she began her writing career while serving as a governess. Early writings appeared in the abolitionist journal *The National Era*. She co-edited *Our Young Folks* with Lucy Larcom (1865–7) and in 1870 managed *Wood's Household Magazine*. Viewing authorship as a means to autonomy, she urged women to write. Through articles in periodicals, her pseudonym became a guarantee of witty and aggressive criticism applied to a broad variety of topics. Her books consist largely of collections of her writings for periodicals. She wrote on women's issues, *Woman's Wrongs, a Counter Irritant* (1868) and *Woman's Worth and Worthlessness* (1872) and on authors' rights, *A Battle of the Books* (1870), in addition to children's books, books on religion, a novel, *First Love Is Best* (1877) and a travel book, *Wool Gathering* (1867). Her poems were posthumously collected by her sister, H. Augusta Dodge, in *Chips, Fragments and Vestiges* (1902). Dodge is said to have proposed to John Greenleaf Whittier, who turned her down but remained a loyal friend despite her making enemies elsewhere in the literary world.

Note

In a presentation copy of 'New Atmosphere' (1866) Mr Whittier wrote on the fly-leaf:

'It may be that she wields a pen
Too sharply nibbed for thin-skinned men,

That her keen arrows search and try
The armor joints of dignity,
And, though alone for error meant,
Sing through the air irreverent.

'Heaven mend her faults! I will not pause
To weigh and doubt and peck at flaws,
Or waste my pity when some fool
Provokes her measureless ridicule.'

The next volume of his poetry contained the whole
poem under the title 'Lines on a Fly-leaf', which called
out the following repartee:

Oh! My!
A little fly
Folding her wings
On a fly-leaf
Brief,
Suddenly sings
Exclamation-points and things
To see a poet
Painting her picture so that all the world will know it
And receive it—
But won't more than half believe it;
For the beauty dear is all in your eyes
And doesn't belong to flies
Of my size!

Paint a bee in your bonnet,
Paint a wasp alighting on it;
Paint a devil's darning needle:
And don't wheedle
All the good folk into spying
And trying
To find where I am lying
Underneath the glory
Of your story,
Whereas before a drawing
Of a hornet with a sting,
They would say with quick ha-ha-ing
'On my word, 'tis just the thing!'

'Heaven mend her faults' – Oh!
The wicked little Quaker,
To go and make her
Break her
Heart, talking about faults
When thee know I haven't any—
Or not many—
Nothing to hurt you,
Only just enough to keep
Me from dissolving into a tasteless pap of virtue—
Or to be loved with holy fervor
By the *New York Observer*,
And the apostles of that shoddy
Sort of gospel now springing up from Oregon to Passamaquoddy,
Which teaches with a din,
Very pleasant to the din – ner
Not to save the world from sin,
But to fill the world with sinners!

Come now in good sooth,
Little friend, speak the truth—
Thy love for me such is
Thee put in those touches
Of rebuke and restriction
To quiet thy conscience, not speak thy conviction,
For thee know, heart and hand
I'm as good as thee can stand!
Am I not as sweet as maple molasses
When thee scold me for fingering thy brasses?*
And did not the poet say of yore,
Angels could no more?

* Imagine Whittier and me sitting together one whole day and two evenings, talking
all the time. One of the brass knobs on the Franklin stove was loose and came off in
my hand. I turned it over and remarked upon its brightness. He said, 'Now doesn't
thee know that thee is making work?' 'How?' I asked. 'Why, destroying the brightness
by handling it.' I rubbed it with my handkerchief and asked the housekeeper if I had
made her any work. 'Oh,' she said, 'you make me no work. Mr Whittier takes care
of the brasses himself.' ... The little balls of the trimming of my dress kept coming
off and were lying around on the floor. I picked up one just as I was coming away
and said, 'There, I will give thee that as a keepsake.' He laughed, and said he had
two in his pocket already! He told some company in the evening that I had talked
so much it made him hoarse. (*Extract from Letter.*)

Ah, would not angels pity her
To be scolded by the 'Saintly Whittier'?
That's Mrs Hannaford—
And cannot a man afford
When pulpits preach him
And the women screech him
Up for a saint,
Not to throw stones at them that – aint?

Ah, dear poet, and dear friend,
One whole sheet of paper has come to an end,
And the saucy fly with her jests and jeers
Shall stop her buzzing about my ears.
She folds her wings, she droops her eyes
And feels with an innermost glad surprise
The amber glory in which she lies—
The joy and beauty and wonder wrought
In the golden glow of a poet's thought.

SARAH C. WOOLSEY (SUSAN COOLIDGE)
1835–1905

SARAH C. WOOLSEY, 'Susan Coolidge', was born in Cleveland, Ohio, oldest of five children. She attended private schools. The family moved to New Haven, Connecticut, when she was twenty. She worked in hospitals during the Civil War. After her father's death in 1870, the family moved to Newport, Rhode Island, near the home of Woolsey's friend Helen Hunt Jackson. She began writing that year while on vacation with Jackson. Her first publication was a collection of stories for children, *The New Year's Bargain* (1871). Her most popular books followed the adventures of a tomboy, Katy Carr, from childhood to adulthood, beginning with *What Katy Did* (1872). Woolsey's *Verses* were published in 1880.

A Home

What is a home? A guarded space,
   Wherein a few, unfairly blest,
Shall sit together, face to face,
   And bask and purr and be at rest?

Where cushioned walls rise up between
   Its inmates and the common air,
The common pain, and pad and screen
   From blows of fate or winds of care?

Where Art may blossom strong and free,
   And Pleasure furl her silken wing,
And every laden moment be
   A precious and peculiar thing?

And Past and Future, softly veiled
   In hiding mists, shall float and lie

Forgotten half, and unassailed
    By either hope or memory,

While the luxurious Present weaves
    Her perfumed spells untried, untrue,
Broiders her garments, heaps her sheaves,
    All for the pleasure of a few?

Can it be this, the longed-for thing
    Which wanderers on the restless foam,
Unsheltered beggars, birds on wing,
    Aspire to, dream of, christen 'Home'?

No. Art may bloom, and peace and bliss;
    Grief may refrain and Death forget;
But if there be no more than this,
    The soul of home is wanting yet.

Dim image from far glory caught,
    Fair type of fairer things to be,
The true home rises in our thought,
    A beacon set for men to see.

Its lamps burn freely in the night,
    Its fire-glows unchidden shed
Their cheering and abounding light
    On homeless folk uncomforted.

Each sweet and secret thing within
    Gives out a fragrance on the air,—
A thankful breath, sent forth to win
    A little smile from others' care.

The few, they bask in closer heat;
    The many catch the further ray.
Life higher seems, the world more sweet,
    And hope and Heaven less far away.

So the old miracle anew
    Is wrought on earth and provéd good,
And crumbs apportioned for a few,
    God-blessed, suffice a multitude.

My Rights

Yes, God has made me a woman,
    And I am content to be
Just what He meant, not reaching out
    For other things, since He
Who knows me best and loves me most has ordered this for me.

A woman, to live my life out
    In quiet womanly ways,
Hearing the far-off battle,
    Seeing as through a haze
The crowding, struggling world of men fight through their busy
    days.

I am not strong or valiant,
    I would not join the fight
Or jostle with crowds in the highways
    To sully my garments white;
But I have rights as a woman, and here I claim my right.

The right of a rose to bloom
    In its own sweet, separate way,
With none to question the perfumed pink
    And none to utter a nay
If it reaches a root or points a thorn, as even a rose-tree may.

The right of the lady-birch to grow,
    To grow as the Lord shall please,
By never a sturdy oak rebuked,
    Denied nor sun nor breeze,
For all its pliant slenderness, kin to the stronger trees.

The right to a life of my own,—
    Not merely a casual bit
Of somebody else's life, flung out
    That, taking hold of it,
I may stand as a cipher does after a numeral writ.

The right to gather and glean
    What food I need and can
From the garnered store of knowledge

Which man has heaped for man,
Taking with free hands freely and after an ordered plan.

The right – ah, best and sweetest!—
To stand all undismayed
Whenever sorrow or want or sin
Call for a woman's aid,
With none to cavil or question, by never a look gainsaid.

I do not ask for a ballot;
Though very life were at stake,
I would beg for the nobler justice
That men for manhood's sake
Should give ungrudgingly, nor withhold till I must fight and take.

The fleet foot and the feeble foot
Both seek the self-same goal,
The weakest soldier's name is writ
On the great army-roll,
And God, who made man's body strong, made too the woman's
soul.

HARRIET PRESCOTT SPOFFORD
1835–1921

HARRIET PRESCOTT SPOFFORD was born in Calais, Maine. Her father was a lawyer and lumber merchant. She began writing for Boston newspapers in her twenties to support her invalid parents. In 1858 she sent Thomas Wentworth Higginson, editor of *Atlantic Monthly*, a story that so impressed him he suspected it was plagiarised. Thereafter Spofford achieved critical and popular success with short stories and gothic romances (*Sir Rohan's Ghost*, 1860; *The Amber Gods*, 1863; *Azarian*, 1864). In 1865 she married lawyer Richard Spofford, who was also a poet. They moved to Washington, DC, then returned to Newburyport, Massachusetts, in 1874. Their home became a gathering place for literary friends (e.g. Rose Terry Cooke), the topic of Spofford's *A Little Book of Friends* (1916). In her fiction Spofford championed sexual freedom for women ('An Ideal' in *Scarlet Poppy*, 1894; 'Wages of Sin' in *Old Madame and Other Tragedies*, 1900) and treated domestic culture as a scene of sisterhood (*Three Heroines of New England Romance*, 1894; *A Master Spirit*, 1896; and *An Inheritance*, 1897). Her poems are collected in *Titian's Garden* (1897).

Magdalen

If any woman of us all,
   If any woman of the street,
Before the Lord should pause and fall,
   And with her long hair wipe his feet;

He, whom with yearning hearts we love,
   And fain would see with human eyes
Around our living pathway move,
   And underneath our daily skies;

The Maker of the heavens and earth,
  The Lord of life, the Lord of death,
In whom the universe had birth
  But breathing of our breath one breath!—

If any woman of the street
  Should kneel, and with the lifted mesh
Of her long tresses wipe his feet,
  And with her kisses kiss their flesh,—

How round that woman would we throng!
  How willingly would clasp her hands,
Fresh from that touch divine, and long
  To gather up the twice-blest strands!

How eagerly with her would change
  Our trivial innocence, nor heed
Her shameful memories and strange,
  Could we but also claim that deed!

The Tryst

Out of the darks and deeps of space,
  Where worlds in awful shadow swim,
I came to meet the ancient sun,
  Obeying all my bond with him.

Wrapped in the glimmer of my scarf,
  My wefts of silver brede and lace,
Woven of stars and winds, I pressed,
  And felt his glory on my face.

When, lo, along my hurrying way
  A shining fillet he had lost,
Or, sooth, another sphere, a star
  That into being he had tost.

A ball of swirling fire, fierce waves
  Of molten jewels leaping fast
And shattering crests of flame and jets
  Of kindling spume, I saw and passed.

Æons of ages, and again
　　On my parabolas I swept
Where, lapped in opalescent films,
　　The fire-ball rolled and, dreaming, slept.

And yet new ages, and I saw
　　In green of vasty forest shade
That sphere enfolded, and in seas
　　Where nameless monsters plunged and played.

Once more from darks and deeps of space
　　To meet my mighty love I sprung:
Lo, the blue sky, the fleecy cloud;
　　Mooned with soft light the planet swung.

And there were temples on the heights,
　　And homes beneath the fruited trees,
And never had I seen before
　　Beings so beautiful as these.

They blushed, they smiled, they laughed, they loved;—
　　Fain would I pause before I pass.
What songs they sang! But then what tears
　　They wept! And there were graves, alas!

Born of that whorl of fire-mist, now
　　A little less than gods, they sought
In vain the secret of the stars,
　　The mystery of their own thought.

Away, away! Tremendous whiles
　　Shall lapse; but one day, seamed and charred,
I find this soft and gleaming world
　　A shrunken ball, a lifeless shard.

And when at last, perchance, I come,
　　The elemental force withdrawn,
Of light, of heat, of motion, life,
　　In that place Nothingness shall yawn.

Away! My master and my lord,
　　Still drawn by thy almighty will,
Though worlds be born in purple depths,
　　Though worlds shall fail, I seek thee still.

What shudder sways me? ah, what chill
  Shakes all my splendor as I flee?
Can loss like that be ours? Oh, love,
  Can that fate fall on such as we?

SARAH M. B. PIATT
1836–1919

SARAH M. B. PIATT was born in Lexington, Kentucky. Her mother died when she was seven. She was shuttled among relatives for the remainder of her childhood. She attended Henry Female College in New Castle, Kentucky. Her earliest poems, influenced by the British Romantics, were published in newspapers. Later she contributed frequently to national journals such as *Atlantic Monthly, Harper's* and *St Nicholas*. In 1861 she married John James Piatt, a government employee who also wrote poetry. They had seven children, two of whom died while small. They lived in Washington, DC until 1867, then moved to North Bend, Ohio. They lived in Ireland from 1882–93 where he was US Consul. Piatt's poems thereafter were published by both British and American presses and periodicals. She published seventeen volumes of poetry, many for children but with adult interest (among them *A Voyage to the Fortunate Isles*, 1874; *That New World*, 1876; *The Witch in the Glass and Other Poems*, 1889; *An Irish Wildflower*, 1891).

The Palace-Burner

(Paris, 1871)
A PICTURE IN A NEWSPAPER

She has been burning palaces. 'To see
   The sparks look pretty in the wind?' Well, yes—
And something more. But women brave as she
   Leave much for cowards, such as I, to guess.

But this is old, so old that everything
   Is ashes here – the woman and the rest.
Two years are – oh! so long. Now you may bring
   Some newer pictures. – You like this one best?

You wish that you had lived in Paris then?
   You would have loved to burn a palace, too?
But they had guns in France, and Christian men
   Shot wicked little Communists like you.

You would have burned the palace? – Just because
   You did not live in it yourself! Oh! why
Have I not taught you to respect the laws?
   You would have burned the palace – would not *I*?

Would I? ... Go to your play ... Would I, indeed?
   I? Does the boy not know my soul to be
Languid and worldly, with a dainty need
   For light and music? Yet he questions me.

Can he have seen my soul more near than I?
   Ah! in the dusk and distance sweet she seems,
With lips to kiss away a baby's cry,
   Hands fit for flowers, and eyes for tears and dreams.

Can he have seen my soul? And could she wear
   Such utter life upon a dying face:
Such unappealing, beautiful despair:
   Such garments – soon to be a shroud – with grace?

Would *I* burn palaces? The child has seen
   In this fierce creature of the Commune here,
So bright with bitterness and so serene,
   A being finer than my soul, I fear.

                      1886

The Witch in the Glass

'My mother says I must not pass
   Too near that glass;
She is afraid that I will see
A little witch that looks like me,
With a red, red mouth to whisper low
The very thing I should not know!'

'Alack for all your mother's care!
A bird of the air,
A wistful wind, or (I suppose
Sent by some hapless boy) a rose,
With breath too sweet, will whisper low
The very thing you should not know!'

1889

A Child's Party

(In Kentucky, AD 185–)

Before my cheeks were fairly dry,
    I heard my dusky playmate say:
'Well, now your mother's in the sky,
    And you can always have your way.

'Old Mistress has to stay, you know,
    And read the Bible in her room.
—Let's have a party! Will you, though?'
    Ah, well, the whole world was in bloom.

'A party would be fine, and yet—
    There's no one here I can invite.'
'Me and the children.' 'You forget—'
    'Oh, please, pretend that I am white.'

I said, and think of it with shame,
    'Well, when it's over, you'll go back
There to the cabin all the same,
    And just remember you are black.

'I'll be the lady, for, you see,
    I'm pretty,' I serenely said.
'The black folk say that you would be
    If – if your hair just wasn't red.'

'I'm pretty anyhow, you know.
    I saw this morning that I was.'
'Old Mistress says it's wicked, though,
    To keep on looking in the glass.'

Our quarrel ended. At our feet
  A faint-green blossoming carpet lay,
By some strange chance, divinely sweet,
  Just shaken on that gracious day.

Into the lonesome parlour we
  Glided, and from the shuddering wall
Bore, in its antique majesty,
  The gilded mirror dim and tall.

And then a woman, painted by
  Ignotus, doubtless, tired and fair,
From her unhappy place on high,
  Went with us – just to take the air!

Next the quaint candlesticks we took:
  Their waxen tapers every one
We lighted, to see how they'd look;—
  A strange sight, surely, in the sun!

Then, with misgiving, we undid
  The secret closet by the stair;—
There, with patrician dust half-hid,
  My ancestors, in china, were.

(Hush, child, this splendid tale is true!)
  Were one of these on earth today,
You'd know right well my blood was *blue*;—
  You'd own I was not common clay!

There too, long hid from eyes of men,
  A shining sight we two did see.
Oh, there was solid silver then
  In this poor hollow world – ah me!

We spread the carpet. By a great
  Grey tree we let the mirror stare,
While graven spoon and pictured plate
  Were wildly scattered here and there.

And then our table: thereon gleamed,
  Adorned with many an apple-bud,
Foam-frosted, dainty things that seemed—
  Not made of most delicious mud!

Next came our dressing. As to that,
   I had the fairiest shoes (on each
Were four gold buttons!), and a hat
   And plume like blushes of the peach.

But there was my dark, elfish guest
   Still standing shabby in her place;—
How could I use her to show best
   My own transcendent bloom and grace?

'You'll be my grandmama,' I sighed,
   After much thought, somewhat in fear.
She, joyous, to her sisters cried:
   'Call me Old Mistress! – do you hear?'

About that little slave's weird face
   And rude, round form I fastened all
My grandmama's most awful lace,
   And grandmama's most sacred shawl.

Then one last sorrow came to me:
   'I didn't think of it before,
But at a party there should be
   One gentleman, I think, or more.'

'There's Uncle Sam, you might ask him.'
   I looked, and, in an ancient chair,
Sat a bronze grey-beard, still and grim
   On Sundays called Old Brother Blair.

Above a book his brows were bent;
   It was his pride, as I had heard,
To study the New Testament
   (In which he could not spell one word).

'Oh, he is not a gentleman,'
   I said with my Caucasian scorn.
'He is,' replied the African:
   'He is. He's quit-a-ploughin' corn.

'He got so old they set him free.
   He preaches now, you ought to know.
I tell you we are proud when he
   Eats dinner at our cabin, though.'

'Well – ask him!' Lo, he raised his head.
　　His voice was shaken and severe:
'Here, Sisters in the Church,' he said,
　　'Here – for old Satan's sake, come here!

'That white child's done put on her best
　　Silk bonnet. (It looks like a rose!)
And this black little imp is dressed
　　In all Old Mistress' finest clothes.

'Come, look! They've got the parlour glass,
　　And all the silver, too. Come, look!
(Such plates as these here on the grass!)'
　　And Uncle Sam shut up his book.

The priestess of the eternal flame
　　That warmed our Southern kitchen hearth
Rushed out. The housemaid with her came
　　Who swept the cobwebs from the earth.

Then there was one bent to the ground;—
　　Her hair, than lilies not less white,
With a bright handkerchief was crowned;
　　Her lovely face was weird as night.

I felt the flush of sudden pride;—
　　The others soon grew still with awe,
For, standing bravely at my side,
　　My mother's nurse and mine they saw.

'Who blamed my child?' she said. 'It makes
　　My heart ache when they trouble you.
—Here's a whole basketful of cakes,
　　And I'll come to the party too!' ...

Tears made of dew were in my eyes
　　(These after-tears are made of brine):
No sweeter soul is in the skies
　　Than hers, my mother's nurse and mine.

　　　　　　　　　　　　　　　　1895

MARY ELIZA PERINE TUCKER LAMBERT
1838–?

MARY ELIZA PERINE TUCKER LAMBERT was born in Cahawba, Alabama. She attended boarding school in New York and, after graduating, married John M. Tucker and moved to Georgia. Her father and husband both having lost their property in the Civil War, she returned to New York to sell her poems and look for work as a journalist. She succeeded at both, becoming a regular contributor to New York newspapers. In 1871 she married a Philadelphia journalist, Colonel James H. Lambert and moved to his city where she became a journal editor. Her *Poems* (dedicated to Governor Charles J. Jenkins of Georgia, a notorious anti-Reconstructionist, and his wife) and *Loew's Bridge: A Broadway Idyl* were both published in 1867; in 1868 she published *Life of Mark M. Pomeroy*, the biography of a New York newspaper publisher.

from LOEW'S BRIDGE:
A BROADWAY IDYL

Men swell the current, – many of them wear
Upon their brows the cruel badge of care.
The magic Greenback, like some rolling ball,
Gathers the man-moss, hurls them into 'Wall'.
Each eager face in passing seems to say—
'Chasing a dollar, comrades, clear the way!
I am ambitious, and I fain would win:
Would gain the dollar even if I sin.'
And oft, alas, in raging lust for gold,
Life's cup is broken, and a soul is sold!
Some push along with satisfaction's air,
While others wear the visage of despair.

Some, looking forward, in perspective see
When their one dollar shall ten thousand be.
Some glancing upward, building in the sky
Bright airy castles soon to fade and die:
While sad-faced men look backward and pass on
Cursing the day that ever they were born.
For empty pockets begets woes untold,
And friends and comfort vanish with our gold.
Then should we wonder that the trash is sought,
With which e'en friendship is oft sold and bought?
There, mark the difference in the prosperous man,
And one who gains existence as he can—
One with his head erect, the other bowed,
The poor are humble, but the rich are proud.

Hark! surely there is music in the air!
    'Tis 'Dixie' floating on this Northern breeze.
Thrilling each Southern heart with thoughts
    Of a lost Nation's hope, and her despair.
This world is strange, 'tis an anomaly!
For glancing downward now I see
A one-armed soldier, in a coat of blue—
And, by-the-by, his legs are missing too,
    Grinding with his one hand the 'Dixie' song.
Perchance, who knows, that very tune was played,
When in the midst of some mad martial raid
    The missile came along
Which left of noble manhood but the wreck.

    Now, standing by his side, is one
I know, a warrior, brave for Southern rights:
    All strife is ended, and all warring done.
And the blue-clad soldier's eyes seem dancing lights,
    As in his hand the Southern warrior places
His mite; true, 'tis a small donation,
But it betrays the great appreciation
    Of a brave soul, for spirit kindred born.

Now 'Yankee Doodle' falls upon my ear,
Then 'Erin's Wearing of the Green' I hear;
And as the human current moves along,
I read their Nation as each hears the song—

For faces speak, and eyes will tell the truth:
When Memory, with swift electric string,
Draws Past to Present, on sweet music's wing.
A tear in manhood's eye is no disgrace,
And pity lends a charm to every face.
Statesmen, the satellites of Fame,
    Are mingling with the throng,
Some heart sore with a Nation's blame,
    Some charmed by the Siren song
        Of present popularity.
Ah me! how changes tide with time,
    Public opinion is as vacillating
As seasons are, forever on the change.
Warm, temperate, cold, in changing only true,
Or like some serpent, with its roseate hue,
Of commendation, luring on its victim
E'en to death; who, wounded by the sting
Of misconception, like the poor snail,
Shrinks in his shell, and starving for fame,
    Dies in obscurity. [...]

'Tis marvellous how mortals can invent
The ways and means to increase worldly stores.
Scorn not beginnings, and each small thing prize,
From e'en a cord, sometimes large fortunes rise.
Yon apple-woman, vender of small wares,
Stale lozenges, fruit, candy, and vile cakes,
Who sells to urchins pennies' worth of aches,
Has now the gold safe hoarded in the bank,
With which to buy high place in fashion's rank.
Merit is nothing, money rules the day
Right royally, with rare despotic sway.

Something familiar comes before me now,
A picture of the Southern cotton-plant.
Broadway today, with its white glittering shield,
Is not as pure as Southern cotton field;
    With flakes of snow bursting from bolls of green,
Like some imprisoned genius scorning to be
Confined by laws, which bind society,
And breaking bonds is wafted on the breeze
Of public favor, or gathered by the slaves

Of Fashion, whose vile hands
    Pollute its purity.
True, fragments now and then
Are gently taken to the hearts of men—
White flowers of fancy oftimes sink to rest
Deep in the wells of some fair maiden's breast:
Pure in themselves, they yet become more fair
By contact with the holy thoughts in there.

Cotton and slaves, 'twas thus we counted gold,
The slaves are free, the free in bondage sold;
And now some man with rare prolific brains,
Genius inventive, by the name of Gaines,
Has made a bitters of the cotton plant;
Polluting thus the hitherto white name
By clothing it in the vile badge of shame.

White, glaring white, is all the earth below,
And Broadway seems a 'universe of snow'.
Or like the Ocean's silver-crested waves,
Upon whose breasts thousands of barks are tossed;
Some brave the storm, – by cautious pilots mann'd,
Some strike on breakers, ere they reach the land,
    And are forever lost. [...]

Well, times have changed, the galling chain
    That made the black man bow
Subservient to a master's mighty will,
    Is broken for Eternity;
And with that chain the cord that bound
Our Southern souls in idleness to earth,
Wealth earned by others, strown with lavish hand,
With but one power, the power to command,
    Is loosed,
And on Ambition's wings our eager soul
Can reach the mount, Ambition's much-prized goal,
And grasping to our hearts the spectre Fame,
We faint to find the goddess but a name.

Dreaming again! Ah, how the memory clings
To the dead past; a touch but opes the door
Of the dim vista of departed years,
And phantoms of our hopes and fears,

In dreamy indistinct array,
Seem flitting up and down this snowy way.
A loaded wagon now, has ope'd the door—
'Wilcox and Gibbs'' machine – and nothing more.

Now, I am in the sunny land of flowers,
And smell the perfume from the jasmine bowers;
By opened window sit I half my days,
Sewing the while, but stopping oft to gaze
At two bright fairies, who with sable friends
    Hide, like the pixies,
Underneath the petals of some bright flower,
Whose clear celestial hue
My darlings shame, with their bright eyes of blue.

They crown each other with the garlands fair,
The 'grey-beard' mingles with their silken hair
    Like cords of silver, with the jet and gold,
Soft tiny hands are resting on my brow,
    I too am crowned:
'I would have made your wreath of white,'
The eldest says, 'you are so good,
But, mother, sister said that you were true,
And so we added all these violets blue.'
My good machine partaking of my pride
Sang one sweet song, and made the stitches fine,
Making the children hers as well as mine. [...]

The seasons change, opinions change,
    And even senses change with time;
In age we see not with the eyes
    We looked from in our youth's full prime.
Couleur de rose is turned to sober grey,
Which grows more sombre every hour and day;
    And Fashion too, like all things here below,
Is ever changing, as the sunset cloud;
First a vast mountain, then a fleecy shroud,
A mass of darkness, now of crimson hue,
Soft, silver-tinted, then a violet blue,
    Then blending all the shades in the rainbow.

Now Fashion's minions, in the last new style,
Pass and repass, disdaining the slight smile
    That curls the lip of ever scornful man,
Whose brains inventive all new styles design,
    From fancy gaiters to arranging hair.
I've studied Nature, and I've studied Art,
Can at a glance detect, in smallest part
Of a grand toilet, whose great Artist's skill,
Moulded the madam to her august will,
If from the fashion-plates of Harper's good
'Bazar', 'Die Modenwelt' or 'Magazine
Of Madam Demorest', the robes were made.
If the rival artists of the present day,
Which hold in Fashion's world the sway
    Of reigning queens,
Their wondrous genius used to create
The airy, fairy figures slight,
Which make this city full of light.

I know, if from our 'Merchant Prince' was bought
The fabric rare, made in a foreign land,
Upon whose very surface seems inwrought
A sightless eye, a wasted, helpless hand
Of some poor wretch, who e'en his senses gave
To deck the garment over which we rave.
Those tasty habits, costly, plain, and neat,
Disclosing 'neath their folds two tiny feet,
Snugly encased in leather-shoes thick soled,
Are snares which catch the unwary heart of man;
Those costly jewels, too, from 'Browne and Spaulding's'
    bought—
Are many a lesson to the wedded taught,
That Fanchon bonnet, ribbon and a flower,
Speak to man's pocket with all potent power.
But Fashion, although charming for a while,
Has not the lasting power of a smile. [...]

Men robed in later styles the dark halls fill,
Hold eager consultation; then a thrill
Of indignation seems to move the mass,
And to the office of the Surrogate they throng,
In a chill current, like the whirlwind strong—

And eagerly they seek, in each small nook to find
Some traces of the WILL they left behind.
Some smiling faces look upon me now,
But many glance, with a dark lowering brow,
Upon the fragments of a broken will.

In deep sepulchral tones, amid the ghostly din,
A stern voice utters, 'Bring the culprit in.'
    And the last Surrogate
Is ushered in, and takes his chair of state;
Grim Death is standing by his head,
And o'er him spirits of the happy dead
    Are keeping watch.
Orphans and widows, with all patience wait
To hear the verdict of the Surrogate.
He tears the *will*, declares 'tis LAW's command,
And in a moment all the ghostly band
Have vanished, save the solemn clerk
Who writes until earth's pall of night
Is changed for robes of glorious light.

1867

QUEEN LILI'UOKALANI
(LYDIA KAMAKAEHA)
1838–1917

QUEEN LILI'UOKALANI ('lily of the heavens'), Lydia Kamakaeha, was born in Honolulu, Hawaii, third of four children of the royal couple. From age four she was educated by Euro-American missionaries in the Royal School. She was a member of the Congregational Church and an active participant in the Hawaiian royal court. In 1862 she married John Owen Dominis, son of a sea captain, who became governor of Oahu and Maui. Her brother David Kalakaua became monarch in 1874 and designated her as his heir. In 1881 she served as regent while her brother toured the world on diplomatic and trade missions. Succeeding to the throne in 1891, she sought to restore to her office powers that American officials had wrested from her brother. When she tried to proclaim a new constitution in 1893, American business interests, with the support of the Navy, organised to overthrow her. In 1894 she spent eight months under house arrest, charged with treason against the United States. In 1896 she travelled to Washington, DC pursuing restoration of the throne. While there she published *Hawaii's Story by Hawaii's Queen* and assembled a song book. Despite her efforts, the United States annexed Hawaii in 1898. She was given an annual pension and treated as a valued relic. She kept extensive diaries in English mixed with Hawaiian, both recording her thoughts and experiences for history and concealing them from readers uninitiated in Hawaiian poetic allusiveness. She wrote over four hundred *mele* (songs or poems) in her lifetime, many composed for competitions held by singing clubs of the Hawaiian court.

Aloha'oe

(FAREWELL TO THEE)

Proudly swept the rain by the cliffs
As on it glided through the trees
Still following ever the *liko*

The *Ahihi lehua* of the vale.

> *Chorus:*
> Farewell to thee, farewell to thee
> Thou charming one who dwells in shaded bowers
> One fond embrace ere I depart
> Until we meet again.

Thus sweet memories come back to me
Bringing fresh remembrance of the past
Dearest one, yes, thou art mine own
From thee, true love shall ne'er depart.

I have seen and watched thy loveliness,
Thou sweet Rose of Maunawili
And 'tis there the birds oft love to dwell
And sip the honey from thy lips.

1877

Sanoe

Listen, Sanoe
Dewy *lehua* bud
Here I am
Waiting for your voice.

The answer comes
I am satisfied
Softly, sweetheart
You excite my whole being.

My body is waiting
Waiting there in yearning belief
How are we to fulfill
The desire of our thoughts?

Calling to you, my water lily
Budding for the two of us
Here close by is a compliment
The *manu** comes to deliver.

* *manu*: bird

The Queen is listening
The aroma of the scents comes together
Mixes and rises upward
So similar, so alike.

c. 1892

Ku'u Pua I Paoakalani

(MY FLOWER AT PAOAKALANI)

O ye gentle breeze which wafts to me
Sweet cherished memories of thee,
Of that sweet never-fading flower
That blooms in the fields of Paoakalani.

> *Chorus:*
> Though I've often seen those beauteous flowers
> That grew at Uluhaimalama
> But none of those could be compared
> To my flower which blooms in the fields of Paoakalani.

Her face is fair to behold
With softest eyes as black as jet,
Pink cheeks so delicate of hue,
That grew in the fields of Paoakalani.

Now name to me the one I love,
Ye gentle breezes passing by,
And bring to me that blossom fair
That blooms in the fields of Paoakalani.

1895

Ka Waiapo Lani

(HEAVENLY SHOWERS)

As if the flow of the waters
From the triple streams of heavenly showers

So the sacred Ao* of the eighth heavens
Whose flames have scorched the land.

> *Chorus:*
> Should our hearts' love be restored
> And our rights be ours once more
> Then will our sacred beloved shoals of Kane
> Be the firm foundation of the land.

The heavens expand and bestow
Her beauteous crownlets free
Its life to her people for offerings given
And from loyal hearts ascended prayers.

Cold words and looks reprove
Oh, turn not thus away
Give kindly greetings, words of love
And a heart which beats within.

1896

* Ao: spout

ADAH ISAACS MENKEN
?1839–68

ADAH ISAACS MENKEN was probably the daughter of a free mulatto father and Creole mother, born in New Orleans, though her biographers admit not to know for certain. She married at least four times, had and lost two children and had affairs with Alexander Dumas *père* and Charles Algernon Swinburne. At fifteen, she gave Shakespeare readings in Texas and married her first husband, Alexander Isaac Menken, a Jewish businessman. She studied Judaism and wrote acclaimed poems and articles for the *Israelite*. Beginning her acting career in New Orleans in 1856, she became famous in the United States, England and France, with press coverage of her scandalous private life packing theatres. Her consummate role was as the lead in *Mazeppa* (a play based on Byron's poem of that name) which she played in a body stocking, riding across the stage chained to the back of a horse. She wrote prose for newspapers and journals and championed Walt Whitman's poetry. Among her friends were literary men of San Francisco and New York, as well as the French novelist George Sand. In 1867, her health and career failing, she prepared *Infelicia*, a collection of thirty-one free-verse poems showing the influence of Whitman and of her scriptural studies, centring on Jewish and women's themes. She died in Paris a week before the book's publication.

Judith

'Repent, or I will come unto thee quickly, and will fight
thee with the sword of my mouth.' Revelation, 2:16

I

Ashkelon is not cut off with the remnant of a valley.
  Baldness dwells not upon Gaza.
  The field of the valley is mine, and it is clothed in verdure.

The steepness of Baal-perazim is mine;
And the Philistines spread themselves in the valley of Rephaim.
They shall yet be delivered into my hands.
For the God of Battles has gone before me!
The sword of the mouth shall smite them to dust.
I have slept in the darkness—
But the seventh angel woke me, and giving me a sword of flame,
points to the blood-ribbed cloud, that lifts his reeking head above
the mountain.
Thus am I the prophet.
I see the dawn that heralds to my waiting soul the advent of
power.

> Power that will unseal the thunders!
> Power that will give voice to graves!
> Graves of the living;
> Graves of the dying;
> Graves of the sinning;
> Graves of the loving;
> Graves of the despairing;

And oh! graves of the deserted!
These shall speak, each as their voices shall be loosed.
And the day is dawning.

2

Stand back, ye Philistines!
Practice what ye preach to me;
I heed ye not, for I know ye all.
Ye are living burning lies, and profanation to the garments which
with stately steps ye sweep your marble palaces.
Your palaces of Sin, around which the damning evidence of guilt
hangs like a reeking vapor.
Stand back!
I would pass up the golden road of the world.
A place in the ranks awaits me.
I know that ye are hedged on the borders of my path.
Lie and tremble, for ye well know that I hold with iron grasp the
battle axe.
Creep back to your dark tents in the valley.
Slouch back to your haunts of crime.
Ye do not know me, neither do ye see me.

But the sword of the mouth is unsealed, and ye coil yourselves in slime and bitterness at my feet.

I mix your jeweled heads, and your gleaming eyes, and your hissing tongues with the dust.

My garments shall bear no mark of ye.

When I shall return this sword to the angel, your foul blood will not stain its edge.

It will glimmer with the light of truth, and the strong arm shall rest.

3

Stand back!

I am no Magdalene waiting to kiss the hem of your garment.

It is mid-day.

See ye not what is written on my forehead?

I am Judith!

I wait for the head of my Holofernes!

Ere the last tremble of the conscious death-agony shall have shuddered, I will show it to ye with the long black hair clinging to the glazed eyes, and the great mouth opened in search of voice, and the strong throat all hot and reeking with blood, that will thrill me with wild unspeakable joy as it courses down my bare body and dabbles my cold feet!

My sensuous soul will quake with the burden of so much bliss.

Oh, what wild passionate kisses will I draw up from that bleeding mouth!

I will strangle this pallid throat of mine on the sweet blood!

I will revel in my passion.

At midnight I will feast on it in the darkness.

For it was that which thrilled its crimson tides of reckless passion through the blue veins of my life, and made them leap up in the wild sweetness of Love and agony of Revenge!

I am starving for this feast.

Oh forget not that I am Judith!

And I know where sleeps Holofernes.

1873

OWL WOMAN (JUANA MANWELL [PAPAGO])
fl. ?1880

OWL WOMAN, known also by the Spanish name Juana Manwell, was an elderly woman when ethnomusicologist Frances Densmore recorded her songs in 1920. She lived in San Xavier, a Papago village near Tucson, Arizona. About forty years earlier, when Owl Woman was grieving the deaths of her husband and other relatives, spirits appeared to her and took her to view the spirit land, where she found relatives happily living in old ways, 'on the ground' rather than in houses. The spirits decided to give Owl Woman songs for the cure of sickness. Newly dead Papagos were appointed as messengers delivering one or two songs at a time. She began using the songs when her grandson appeared to be dying. He recovered after treatment with songs and owl feathers. Over time she received hundreds of songs. A treatment lasted all night. Between songs she stroked the patient's body with owl feathers sprinkled with ashes. She led up to twenty other singers who played gourd rattles.

SONGS FOR THE FOUR PARTS OF THE NIGHT
———————

Brown owls come here in the blue evening,
They are hooting about,
They are shaking their wings and hooting.

How shall I begin my song
In the blue night that is settling?
I will sit here and begin my song.

The owl feather is rolling in this direction and beginning to sing.
The people listen and come to hear the owl feather
Rolling in this direction and beginning to sing.

Early in the evening they come hooting about,

Some have small voices and some have large voices,
Some have voices of medium strength, hooting about.

I can not make out what I see.
In the dark I enter.
I can not make out what I see.

Poor old sister, you have cared for this man and you want to see
him again, but now his heart is almost covered with night. There
is just a little left.

Ahead of me some owl feathers are lying,
I hear something running toward me,
They pass by me, and farther ahead
I see spirit-tufts of downy white feathers.

Yonder lies the spirit land.
Yonder the spirit land I see.
Farther ahead, in front of me,
I see a spirit stand.

Sadly I was treated, sadly I was treated,
Through the night I was carried around,
Sadly was I treated.

A railroad running west,
He travels westward.
When he gets a certain distance
He flaps his wings four times and turns back.

Yonder are spirits laughing and talking as though drunk.
They do the same things that we do.
Now we will join them.

I pity you, my feathers,
I pity you, my feathers, that they make fun of,
They must mean what they say,
Or perhaps they are crazy in their hearts.

On the west side people are singing as though drunk. The women
are singing as though they were drunk.

On the west side they are singing, the women hear it.

In the great night my heart will go out,
Toward me the darkness comes rattling,

In the great night my heart will go out.
I am going far to see the land,
I am running far to see the land,
While back in my house the songs are intermingling.

Ashes Hill Mountain, toward it I am running,
I see the Ashes Hill come out clearer.

They brought me to the waters of the spirits.
In these waters the songs seem to be stringing out.

The spirit person, the spirit person is going around, around me.

A low range of mountains, toward them I am running.
From the top of these mountains I will see the dawn.

I am not sure whether I am running west or east but I run on and
    on.
I find that I am running east.

I am dead here, I die and lie here,
I am dead here, I die and lie here,
Over on top of *Vihuhput* I had my dawn.

Black Butte is far. Below it I had my dawn.
I could see the daylight coming back of me.

I am afraid it will be daylight before I reach the place to see.
I feel that the rays of the sun are striking me.

The owl feather is likely to find the daylight.
He is looking for it.
He is looking to see the dawn shine red in the east.

The morning star is up.
I cross the mountains into the light of the sea.

I think I have found out.
I think I have found out.
With the owl songs I have found out and I will return home.

Translated from Papago by Frances Densmore; recorded 1920

CONSTANCE FENIMORE WOOLSON
1840–94

CONSTANCE FENIMORE WOOLSON, grand-niece of novelist James Fenimore Cooper, grew up in Cleveland, Ohio. She was educated at private girls' schools. After her father's death in 1869, she travelled with her mother through the eastern and southern states writing travel sketches for leading periodicals. When her mother died in 1879, she moved to Europe with her sister. She met novelist Henry James in 1880 and began a lifelong friendship. Woolson published a children's novel, essays, poetry including the innovative verse narrative *Two Women* (1877), a novel for adults, *Anne* (1880) and collections of short fiction before leaving the United States. Her later publications include *Dorothy and Other Italian Stories* (1895), *The Front Yard and Other Italian Stories* (1896), a novella *For the Major* (1883) and three novels *East Angels* (1886), *Jupiter Lights* (1889) and *Horace Chase* (1894). She died from what may have been a suicidal fall from her apartment window in Venice. A book of collected travel writing, *Mentone, Cairo, and Corfu* (1896), was published posthumously.

from TWO WOMEN

One

Through miles of green cornfields that lusty
    And strong face the sun and rejoice
In his heat, where the brown bees go dusty
    With pollen from flowers of their choice,
'Mong myriads down by the river
    Who offer their honey, the train

Flies south with a whir and a shiver,
Flies south through the lowlands that quiver
    With ripening grain—

Fair wheat, like a lady for fancies,
    Who bends to the breeze, while the corn
Held stiff all his stubborn green lances
    The moment his curled leaf was born;
And grapes, where the vineyards are sweeping
    The shores of the river whose tide—
Slow moving, brown tide – holds the keeping
Of War and of Peace that lie sleeping,
    Couched lions, each side.

Hair curlless, and hid, and smooth-banded,
    Blue innocent maidenly eyes,
That gaze at the lawless rough-handed
    Young soldiers with grieving surprise
At oaths on their lips, the deriding
    And jestings that load every breath,
While on with dread swiftness are gliding
Their moments, and o'er them is biding
    The shadow of death!

Face clear-cut and pearly, a slender
    Small maiden with calm, home-bred air;
No deep-tinted hues you might lend her
    Could touch the faint gold of her hair,
The blue of her eyes, or the neatness
    Of quaint little gown, smoothly spun
From threads of soft gray, whose completeness
Doth fit her withdrawn gentle sweetness—
    A lily turned nun.

Ohio shines on to her border,
    Ohio all golden with grain;
The river comes up at her order,
    And curves toward the incoming train;
'The river! The river! O borrow
    A speed that is swifter – Afar
Kentucky! Haste, haste, thou Tomorrow!'
Poor lads, dreaming not of the sorrow,
    The anguish of war.

The Other

West from the Capital's crowded throng
The fiery engine rushed along,
Over the road where danger lay
On each bridge and curve of the midnight way,
Shooting across the rivers' laps,
Up the mountains, into the gaps,
Through West Virginia like the wind,
Fire and sword coming on behind,
Whistling defiance that echoed back
To mountain guerrillas burning the track,
'Do the worst, ye rebels, that ye can do
To the train that follows, but *I* go through!'

A motley crowd – the city thief;
The man of God; the polished chief
Of a band of gamblers; the traitor spy;
The correspondent with quick, sharp eye;
The speculator who boldly made
His fifty per cent in a driving trade
At the edge of the war; the clean lank clerk
Sent West for sanitary work;
The bounty-jumper; the lordling born
Viewing the country with wondering scorn—
A strange assemblage filled the car
That dared the midnight border-band,
Where life and death went hand-in-hand
Those strange and breathless days of war.

The conductor's lantern moves along,
Slowly lighting the motley throng
Face by face; what sudden gleam
Flashes back in the lantern's beam
Through shadows down at the rearward door?
The conductor pauses; all eyes explore
The darkened corner: a woman's face
Thrown back asleep – the shimmer of lace,
The sheen of silk, the yellow of gold,
The flash of jewels, the careless fold
Of an India shawl that half concealed

The curves superb which the light revealed;
A sweep of shoulder, a rounded arm,
A perfect hand that lay soft and warm
On the dingy seat; all the outlines rare
Of a Milo Venus slumbered there
'Neath the costly silk whose heaviest fold
Subordinate seemed – unnoticed mould
For the form beneath.
                              The sumptuous grace
Of the careless pose, the sleeping face,
Transfixed all eyes, and together drew
One and all for a nearer view:
The lank clerk hasted, the gambler trod
On the heels of the gazing man of God;
The correspondent took out his book,
Sharpened his pencil with eager look;
The soldiers fought as to who should pass
The first; the lord peered through his glass,
But no sooner saw the sleeping face
Than he too hasted and left his place
To join the crowd.
                              Then, ere any spoke,
But all eager gazed, the lady woke.

Dark-brown, sleepy, velvet eyes,
Lifted up in soft surprise,
A wealth of hair of auburn red,
Falling in braids from the regal head
Whose little hat with waving plume
Lay on the floor – while a faint perfume,
The roses, crushed in sleep, betrayed,
Tangled within the loosened braid;
Bold features, Nubian lips, a skin
Creamy pallid, the red within
Mixed with brown where the shadow lies
Dark beneath the lustrous eyes.
She smiles; all hearts are at her feet.
She turns; each hastens to his seat.
The car is changed to a sacred place
Lighted by one fair woman's face;
In sudden silence on they ride,

The lord and the gambler, side by side,
The traitor spy, the priest as well,
Bound for the time by a common spell,
And each might be in thought and mien
A loyal knight escorting his queen,
So instant and so measureless
Is the power of a perfect loveliness.

1862

INA COOLBRITH
1842–1928

INA COOLBRITH was born Josephine Smith in Nauvoo, Illinois, a niece of Joseph Smith, founder of the Mormon Church. Her father died when she was an infant; her mother remarried and renounced Mormonism. In 1849 her stepfather moved the family to California in search of gold. Ina attended Los Angeles schools and studied her only two books, Shakespeare and Byron. Her poems were first published in local newspapers when she was in her teens. In 1859 she married an ironworks owner; she divorced him in 1861 because of his violence. Their only child died an infant. In 1865 she took her mother's maiden name, Coolbrith, and moved to San Francisco. She became the only female member of the Bohemian Club, held weekly salons for travelling artists and writers, and was co-editor with Bret Harte of *Overland Monthly*. In 1874 she took in three foster children. A librarian from 1874 to 1906, she guided the reading of young Jack London and Isadora Duncan. When the 1906 earthquake destroyed her home and possessions, friends raised money for her. She became California's first poet laureate in 1915. Her poetry is collected in *A Perfect Day* (1881), *The Singer by the Sea* (1894), *Songs from the Golden Gate* (1895) and *Wings of Sunset* (1929), which includes 'Concha', a long first-person narrative poem, mixing Spanish with English, about a young Chicana's struggle with orthodox religion and prescribed gender roles.

Longing

O foolish wisdom sought in books!
O aimless fret of household tasks!
O chains that bind the hand and mind—
A fuller life my spirit asks!

For there the grand hills, summer-crowned,
   Slope greenly downward to the seas;
One hour of rest upon their breast
   Were worth a year of days like these.

Their cool, soft green to ease the pain
   Of eyes that ache o'er printed words;
This weary noise – the city's voice,
   Lulled in the sound of bees and birds.

For Eden's life within me stirs,
   And scorns the shackles that I wear;
The man-life grand – pure soul, strong hand,
   The limb of steel, the heart of air!

And I could kiss, with longing wild,
   Earth's dear brown bosom, loved so much,
A grass-blade fanned across my hand,
   Would thrill me like a lover's touch.

The trees would talk with me; the flowers
   Their hidden meanings each make known—
The olden lore revived once more,
   When man's and nature's heart were one!

And as the pardoned pair might come
   Back to the garden God first framed,
And hear Him call at even-fall,
   And answer, 'Here am I,' unshamed—

So I, from out these toils, wherein
   The Eden-faith grows stained and dim,
Would walk, a child, through nature's wild,
   And hear His voice and answer Him.

My 'Cloth of Gold'

O but the wind is keen,
   And the sky is dull as lead!
If only leaves were brown,
   Were only withered and dead,

Perhaps I might not frown,
   However the storm might beat;
But to see their delicate green
   Tossing in wind and rain,
   Whirling in lane and street,
Trampled in mud and dirt—
   Alive to the winter pain,
To the sting and the hurt!

I wish they all were hid
In a fleecy coverlid;
I wish I could bury the rose
Under the northern snows,
And make the land take off
The purple and red and buff,
   And flamy tints that please
Her tropical Spanish taste,
   And mantle her shapeliness,
   Just once, in the delicate dress
Of her sisters, fairer faced,
   Over the seas.

If but for a single day
   This vivid, incessant green
Might vanish quite away,
   And never a leaf be seen;
And woods be brown and sere,
And flowers disappear:
If only I might not see
Forever the fruit on the tree,
   The rose on its stem!
For spring is sweet, and summer
Ever a blithe new-comer—
   But one tires even of them!

You were pleasant to behold,
   When days were warm and bland,
My beautiful 'Cloth of Gold',
   My rose of roses, nursed
   With careful, patient hand;
   So sunny and content,
With butterflies about you,

And bees that came and went,
And could not do without you:
    But better to die at first,
With the earliest blossom born,
Than to live so crumpled and torn,
So dripping and forlorn.

Better that you should be
    Safe housëd and asleep
        Under the tough brown bark,
Like your kindred over the sea;
    Nor know if the day be drear,
        Nor heed if the sky be dark,
If it rain or snow.
    But ah! to be captive here,
    The live-long, dragging year,
    To the skies that smile and weep;
    The skies that thrill and woo you,
    That torture and undo you,
That lure and hold you so—
And will not let you go!

Ownership

In a garden that I know,
Only palest blossoms blow.

There the lily, purest nun,
Hides her white face from the sun,

And the maiden rose-bud stirs
In a garment fair as hers.

One shy bird, with folded wings
Sits within the leaves and sings;

Sits and sings the daylight long,
Just a patient, plaintive song.

Other gardens greet the spring
With a blaze of blossoming;

Other song-birds, piping clear,
Chorus from the branches near;

But my blossoms, palest known,
Bloom for me and me alone,

And my bird, though sad and lonely,
Sings for me, and for me only.

Lines

On Hearing Kelley's Music to 'Macbeth'

O melody, what children strange are these
   From thy most vast, illimitable realm?
   These sounds that seize upon and overwhelm
   The soul with shuddering ecstasy! Lo! here
   The night is, and the deeds that make night fear;
Wild winds and waters, and the sough of trees
   Tossed in the tempest; wail of spirits banned,
   Wandering, unhoused of clay, in the dim land;
The incantation of the Sisters Three,
   Nameless of deed and name – the mystic chords
   Weird repetitions of the mystic words;
   The mad, remorseful terrors of the Thane,
   And bloody hands – which bloody must remain.
   Last, the wild march; the battle hand to hand
Of clashing arms, in awful harmony,
   Sublimely grand, and terrible as grand!
The clan-cries; the barbaric trumpetry;
   And the one fateful note, that, throughout all,
   Leads, follows, calls, compels, and holds in thrall.

EMMA LAZARUS
1849–87

EMMA LAZARUS was born in New York City, fourth daughter of a wealthy businessman, and educated by tutors. Her family were Sephardic Jews whose roots in America dated to the seventeenth century. She published her first book of poems privately in 1866. Other early works include *Admetus, and Other Poems* (1871), a novel, *Alide: An Episode of Goethe's Life* (1874), translations of medieval Hebrew poetry and of Heinrich Heine's poems and a tragedy, *The Spagnoletto* (1876). In the late 1870s she became acquainted with Ralph Waldo Emerson and, travelling in Europe, met such literary figures as Robert Browning and Henry James. Later works, such as *By the Waters of Babylon* (1887), a collection of short prose-poems, show inspiration from activism against the persecution of European Jews. She became an advocate for the working classes, women and immigrants, engaging in charity work and supporting socialist economic change. In journal articles in 1882 and 1883 she urged establishment of a Jewish homeland in Palestine and education for Russian Jewish immigrants. She helped found the New York Hebrew Technical Institute. She wrote her famous sonnet 'The New Colossus' to raise funds for the Statue of Liberty's pedestal.

How Long?

How long, and yet how long,
Our leaders will we hail from over seas,
Masters and kings from feudal monarchies,
    And mock their ancient song
With echoes weak of foreign melodies?

That distant isle mist-wreathed,
Mantled in unimaginable green,
Too long hath been our mistress and our queen.

Our fathers have bequeathed
Too deep a love for her, our hearts within.

She made the whole world ring
With the brave exploits of her children strong,
And with the matchless music of her song.
    Too late, too late we cling
To alien legends, and their strains prolong.

This fresh young world I see,
With heroes, cities, legends of her own;
With a new race of men, and overblown
    By winds from sea to sea,
Decked with the majesty of every zone.

I see the glittering tops
Of snow-peaked mounts, the wid'ning vale's expanse,
Large prairies where free herds of horses prance,
    Exhaustless wealth of crops,
In vast, magnificent extravagance.

These grand, exuberant plains,
These stately rivers, each with many a mouth,
The exquisite beauty of the soft-aired south,
    The boundless seas of grains,
Luxuriant forests' lush and splendid growth.

The distant siren-song
Of the green island in the eastern sea,
Is not the lay for this new chivalry.
    It is not free and strong
To chant on prairies 'neath this brilliant sky.

The echo faints and fails;
It suiteth not, upon this western plain,
Our voice or spirit; we should stir again
    The wilderness, and make the vales
Resound unto a yet unheard-of strain.

Success

Oft have I brooded on defeat and pain,
The pathos of the stupid, stumbling throng.
These I ignore today and only long
To pour my soul forth in one trumpet strain,
One clear, grief-shattering, triumphant song,
For all the victories of man's high endeavor,
Palm-bearing, laureled deeds that live forever,
The splendor clothing him whose will is strong.
Hast thou beheld the deep, glad eyes of one
Who has persisted and achieved? Rejoice!
On naught diviner shines the all-seeing sun.
Salute him with free heart and choral voice,
'Midst flippant, feeble crowds of spectres wan,
The bold, significant, successful man.

The New Colossus *

Not like the brazen giant of Greek fame,
With conquering limbs astride from land to land;
Here at our sea-washed, sunset gates shall stand
A mighty woman with a torch, whose flame
Is the imprisoned lightning, and her name
Mother of Exiles. From her beacon-hand
Glows world-wide welcome; her mild eyes command
The air-bridged harbor that twin cities frame.
'Keep, ancient lands, your storied pomp!' cries she
With silent lips. 'Give me your tired, your poor,
Your huddled masses yearning to breathe free,
The wretched refuse of your teeming shore.
Send these, the homeless, tempest-tost to me,
I lift my lamp beside the golden door!'

1883

* Written in aid of Bartholdi Pedestal Fund, 1883.

Long Island Sound

I see it as it looked one afternoon
In August, – by a fresh soft breeze o'erblown.
The swiftness of the tide, the light thereon,
A far-off sail, white as a crescent moon.
The shining waters with pale currents strewn,
The quiet fishing-smacks, the Eastern cove,
The semi-circle of its dark, green grove.
The luminous grasses, and the merry sun
In the grave sky; the sparkle far and wide,
Laughter of unseen children, cheerful chirp
Of crickets, and low lisp of rippling tide,
Light summer clouds fantastical as sleep
Changing unnoted while I gazed thereon.
All these fair sounds and sights I made my own.

City Visions

I

As the blind Milton's memory of light,
The deaf Beethoven's phantasy of tone,
Wrought joys for them surpassing all things known
In our restricted sphere of sound and sight,—
So while the glaring streets of brick and stone
Vex with heat, noise, and dust from morn till night,
I will give rein to Fancy, taking flight
From dismal now and here, and dwell alone
With new-enfranchised senses. All day long,
Think ye 't is I, who sit 'twixt darkened walls,
While ye chase beauty over land and sea?
Uplift on wings of some rare poet's song,
Where the wide billow laughs and leaps and falls,
I soar cloud-high, free as the winds are free.

2

Who grasps the substance? who 'mid shadows strays?
He who within some dark-bright wood reclines,

'Twixt sleep and waking, where the needled pines
Have cushioned all his couch with soft brown sprays?
He notes not how the living water shines,
Trembling along the cliff, a flickering haze,
Brimming a wine-bright pool, nor lifts his gaze
To read the ancient wonders and the signs.
Does he possess the actual, or do I,
Who paint on air more than his sense receives,
The glittering pine-tufts with closed eyes behold,
Breathe the strong resinous perfume, see the sky
Quiver like azure flame between the leaves,
And open unseen gates with key of gold?

1883

1492

Thou two-faced year, Mother of Change and Fate,
Didst weep when Spain cast forth with flaming sword,
The children of the prophets of the Lord,
Prince, priest, and people, spurned by zealot hate.
Hounded from sea to sea, from state to state,
The West refused them, and the East abhorred.
No anchorage the known world could afford,
Close-locked was every port, barred every gate.
Then smiling, thou unveil'dst, O two-faced year,
A virgin world where doors of sunset part,
Saying, 'Ho, all who weary, enter here!
There falls each ancient barrier that the art
Of race or creed or rank devised, to rear
Grim bulwarked hatred between heart and heart!'

1883

from ON THE VOYAGE
TO JERUSALEM

(translation from Hebrew poet Abul Hassan Judah Ben Ha-Levi, born
between 1080 and 1090)

A watery waste the sinful world has grown,
With no dry spot whereon the eye can rest,
No man, no beast, no bird to gaze upon,
Can all be dead, with silent sleep possessed?
Oh, how I long the hills and vales to see,
To find myself on barren steppes were bliss.
I peer about, but nothing greeteth me,
Naught save the ship, the clouds, the waves' abyss,
The crocodile which rushes from the deeps;
The flood foams gray; the whirling waters reel,
Now like its prey whereon at last it sweeps,
The ocean swallows up the vessel's keel.
The billows rage – exult, oh soul of mine,
Soon shalt thou enter the Lord's sacred shrine!

1867

HENRIETTA CORDELIA RAY
1849–1917

HENRIETTA CORDELIA RAY was born in New York, one of three sisters. All were educated beyond college, one becoming the first black woman lawyer in Washington, DC. H. Cordelia Ray (her preferred name) and her sister Florence earned masters in pedagogy degrees, remained unmarried and lived together throughout their lives. They collaborated on *Sketch of the Life of the Rev. Charles B. Ray* (1887), a biography of their father, a distinguished Congregationalist pastor and social activist. Ray taught in New York schools, tutored in music, mathematics and languages, and taught literature classes to teachers. Her debut as a poet occurred at the dedication of the Freedmen's Monument, a sculpture unveiled by President Grant in 1876, when a reading of her ode 'Lincoln' was part of the ceremony. Her poetry appeared in periodicals and was collected in *Sonnets* (1893) and *Poems* (1910).

Self-Mastery

To catch the spirit in its wayward flight
Through mazes manifold, what task supreme!
For when to floods has grown the quiet stream,
Much human skill must aid its rage to fight;
And when wild winds invade the solemn night,
Seems not man's vaunted power but a dream?
And still more futile, ay, we e'en must deem
This quest to tame the soul, and guide aright
Its restless wanderings, – to lure it back
To shoals of calm. Full many a moan and sigh
Attend the strife; till, effort merged in prayer,
Oft uttered, clung to – when of strength the lack

Seems direst – brings the answer to our cry:
A gift from Him who lifts our ev'ry care.

1893

The Quest of the Ideal

Fair Hope with lucent light in her glad eyes,
Fleet as Diana, through the meadow speeds;
Nor dewy rose nor asphodel she heeds,
For lo! unwonted radiance in the skies
Bids her not pause. The silv'ry shimmer lies
'Mid blooming vistas, whence the pathway leads
To heights aerial. The glow recedes
As panting Hope toils on, while awed surprise
Fills her sweet glances; will the vision fade
Ere she can reach it? Nay, 'tis lovelier far,
Rarer perspectives open to her gaze;
Then hasten on, expectantly, glad maid!
The splendor still will tremble there afar;
Yet count this quest the holiest of thy days.

1893

An Ocean Musing

Far, far out lie the white sails all at rest;
Like spectral arms they seem to touch and cling
Unto the wide horizon. Not a wing
Of truant bird glides down the purpling west;
No breeze dares to intrude, e'en on a quest
To fan a lover's brow; the waves to sing
Have quite forgotten till the deep shall fling
A bow across its vibrant chords. Then, lest
One moment of the sea's repose we lose,
Nor furnish Fancy with a thousand themes
Of unimagined sweetness, let us gaze
On this serenity, for as we muse,

Lo! all is restless motion: life's best dreams
Give changing moods to even halcyon days.

1893

The Tireless Sculptor

E'en as the sculptor chisels patiently
The marble's jagged edges, day by day,
Striving to smooth all blemishes away,
Till – when from ev'ry flaw the stone is free,
And naught save perfect contours does he see—
Embodied harmony and beauty may
Atone for all the weary hours' delay,—
So Life, the sculptor, moulds unceasingly
The soul of man. How often in recoil
The spirit shrinks, nor can through prescience know
Of coming grace and majesty. 'Tis willed
The scars should deeper be, until the toil
And chiseling are adequate; when lo!
God's all-unfathomed plan is quite fulfilled.

Toussaint L'Ouverture

To those fair isles where crimson sunsets burn,
We send a backward glance to gaze on thee,
Brave Toussaint! thou wast surely born to be
A hero; thy proud spirit could but spurn
Each outrage on thy race. Couldst thou unlearn
The lessons taught by instinct? Nay! and we
Who share the zeal that would make all men free,
Must e'en with pride unto thy life-work turn.
Soul-dignity was thine and purest aim;
And ah! how sad that thou wast left to mourn
In chains 'neath alien skies. On him, shame! shame!
That mighty conqueror who dared to claim
The right to bind thee. Him we heap with scorn,
And noble patriot! guard with love thy name.

ELLA WHEELER WILCOX
1850–1919

ELLA WHEELER WILCOX was born in Johnstown Center, Wisconsin, youngest of four children in a farming family. Her mother encouraged her to read. She attended public schools and the University of Wisconsin. She wrote her first novel at age nine and published her first essay at fifteen. By eighteen she was earning money as a writer. Her first book, *Drops of Water* (1872), was a collection of temperance verse. By 1880 she was part of Milwaukee's literary circle. Her *Poems of Passion* (1883) was initially rejected by a publisher because of their erotic content but, when accepted by another publisher, sold 60,000 copies in two years. Though a pioneering and influential advocate for women's sexual pleasure, she held rather conventional views on gender roles. She married Robert Marius Wilcox, a silversmith, in 1884 and moved to Meriden, Connecticut. Their only child died in infancy. They travelled widely in Europe and Asia and became involved with theosophy and paranormal exploration. She was a prolific poet, for a time writing daily poems for a newspaper syndicate. She published forty-six books and sustained wide popularity through the 1920s. Near the end of her life she suffered a nervous breakdown after touring World War I camps reciting poems and lecturing on sexually transmitted diseases. Other books include *Maurine* (1876), *Perdita and Other Stories* (1886), *Poems of Pleasure* (1888), *Custer and Other Poems* (1896), *Men, Women, and Emotions* (1896), *Collected Poems* (1924).

Communism

When my blood flows calm as a purling river,
When my heart is asleep and my brain has sway,
It is then that I vow we must part forever,
That I will forget you, and put you away

Out of my life, as a dream is banished
Out of the mind when the dreamer awakes;
That I know it will be when the spell has vanished,
Better for both of our sakes.

When the court of the mind is ruled by Reason,
I know it is wiser for us to part;
But Love is a spy who is plotting treason,
In league with that warm, red rebel, the Heart.
They whisper to me that the King is cruel,
That his reign is wicked, his law a sin,
And every word they utter is fuel
To the flame that smolders within.

And on nights like this, when my blood runs riot
With the fever of youth and its made desires,
When my brain in vain bids my heart be quiet,
When my breast seems the center of lava-fires,
Oh, then is the time when most I miss you,
And I swear by the stars and my soul and say
That I will have you, and hold you, and kiss you,
Though the whole world stands in the way.

And like Communists, as mad, as disloyal,
My fierce emotions roam out of their lair;
They hate King Reason for being royal—
They would fire his castle, and burn him there.
O Love! they would clasp you, and crush you and kill you,
In the insurrection of uncontrol.
Across the miles, does this wild war thrill you
That is raging in my soul?

1883

Solitude

Laugh, and the world laughs with you;
   Weep, and you weep alone,
For the sad old earth must borrow its mirth,
   But has trouble enough of its own.
Sing, and the hills will answer;

Sigh, it is lost on the air,
The echoes bound to a joyful sound,
But shrink from voicing care.

Rejoice, and men will seek you;
Grieve, and they turn and go.
They want full measure of all your pleasure,
But they do not need your woe.
Be glad, and your friends are many;
Be sad, and you lose them all,—
There are none to decline your nectar'd wine,
But alone you must drink life's gall.

Feast, and your halls are crowded;
Fast, and the world goes by.
Succeed and give, and it helps you live,
But no man can help you die.
There is room in the halls of pleasure
For a large and lordly train,
But one by one we must all file on
Through the narrow aisles of pain.

1883

Burdened

'Genius, a man's weapon, a woman's burden.' *Lamartine*

Dear God! there is no sadder fate in life,
    Than to be burdened so that you can not
    Sit down contented with the common lot
Of happy mother and devoted wife.
To feel your brain wild and your bosom rife
    With all the sea's commotion; to be fraught
    With fires and frenzies which you have not sought,
And weighed down with the wide world's weary strife.

To feel a fever alway in your breast,
    To lean and hear half in affright, half shame,
    A loud-voiced public boldly mouth your name,
To reap your hard-sown harvest in unrest,

And know, however great your meed of fame,
You are but a weak woman at the best.

1888

In the Night

Sometimes at night, when I sit and write,
  I hear the strangest things,—
As my brain grows hot with burning thought,
  That struggles for form and wings,
I can hear the beat of my swift blood's feet,
  As it speeds with a rush and a whir
From heart to brain and back again,
  Like a race-horse under the spur.

With my soul's fine ear I listen and hear
  The tender Silence speak,
As it leans on the breast of Night to rest,
  And presses his dusky cheek.
And the darkness turns in its sleep, and yearns
  For something that is kin;
And I hear the hiss of a scorching kiss,
  As it folds and fondles Sin.

In its hurrying race through leagues of space,
  I can hear the Earth catch breath,
As it heaves and moans, and shudders and groans,
  And longs for the rest of Death.
And high and far, from a distant star,
  Whose name is unknown to me,
I hear a voice that says, 'Rejoice,
  For I keep ward o'er thee!'

Oh, sweet and strange are the sounds that range
  Through the chambers of the night;
And the watcher who waits by the dim, dark gates,
  May hear, if he lists aright.

1888

No Classes!

No classes here! Why, that is idle talk.
  The village beau sneers at the country boor;
The importuning mendicants who walk
  Our cities' streets despise the parish poor.

The daily toiler at some noisy loom
  Holds back her garments from the kitchen aid.
Meanwhile the latter leans upon her broom,
  Unconscious of the bow the laundress made.

The grocer's daughter eyes the farmer's lass
  With haughty glances; and the lawyer's wife
Would pay no visits to the trading class,
  If policy were not her creed in life.

The merchant's son nods coldly at the clerk;
  The proud possessor of a pedigree
Ignores the youth whose father rose by work;
  The title-seeking maiden scorns all three.

The aristocracy of blood looks down
  Upon the 'nouveau riche'; and in disdain,
The lovers of the intellectual frown
  On both, and worship at the shrine of brain.

'No classes here,' the clergyman has said;
  'We are one family.' Yet see his rage
And horror when his favorite son would wed
  Some pure and pretty player on the stage.

It is the vain but natural human way
  Of vaunting our weak selves, our pride, our worth!
Not till the long-delayed millennial day
  Shall we behold 'no classes' on God's earth.

1892

Woman

Give us that grand word 'woman' once again,
And let's have done with 'lady': one's a term
Full of fine force, strong, beautiful, and firm,
Fit for the noblest use of tongue or pen;
And one's a word for lackeys. One suggests
The Mother, Wife, and Sister! One the dame
Whose costly robe, mayhap, gives her the name.
One word upon its own strength leans and rests;
The other minces tiptoe. Who would be
The perfect woman must grow brave of heart
And broad of soul to play her troubled part
Well in life's drama. While each day we see
The 'perfect lady' skilled in what to do
And what to say, grace in each tone and act
('Tis taught in schools, but needs some native tact),
Yet narrow in her mind as in her shoe.
Give the first place then to the nobler phrase,
And leave the lesser word for lesser praise.

1892

My Grave

If, when I die, I must be buried, let
No cemetery engulph me – no lone grot,
Where the great palpitating world comes not,
Save when, with heart bowed down and eyelids wet,
It pays its last sad melancholy debt
To some outjourneying pilgrim. May my lot
Be rather to lie in some much-used spot,
Where human life, with all its noise and fret,
Throbs on about me. Let the roll of wheels,
With all earth's sounds of pleasure, commerce, love,
And rush of hurrying feet surge o'er my head.
Even in my grave I shall be one who feels

Close kinship with the pulsing world above;
And too deep silence would distress me, dead.

1892

ROSE HARTWICK THORPE
1850–1939

ROSE HARTWICK THORPE was born in Mishawaka, Indiana. Her family moved to Kansas and then to Litchfield, Michigan, in 1860, where she attended public schools. She wrote 'Curfew Must Not Ring Tonight' when she was twenty. Later published in a Detroit newspaper, it achieved widespread popularity and an illustrated edition was published in 1882. She married Edmund C. Thorpe, a carriage-maker who wrote German dialect verse, in 1871. They had two daughters. When her husband's business failed in 1881, she provided income by editing Sunday school publications in Chicago. They moved to San Antonio, Texas, and later to Pacific Beach, California. Thorpe published regularly in children's periodicals such as *St Nicholas*. Her verse was collected in *The Yule Log* (1881), *Temperance Poems* (1887), *Ringing Ballads* (1887) and *The Poetical Works of Rose Hartwick Thorpe* (1912); she also published several children's books. After her husband's death in 1916, she worked for women's suffrage and with the YWCA and San Diego Women's Club.

Curfew Must Not Ring Tonight

England's sun was slowly setting o'er the hill-tops far away,
Filling all the land with beauty at the close of one sad day;
And its last rays kissed the forehead of a man and maiden fair,—
He with steps so slow and weary, she with sunny, floating hair;
He with bowed head, sad and thoughtful; she with lips so cold
   and white,
Struggled to keep back the murmur, 'Curfew must not ring
   tonight!'

'Sexton,' Bessie's white lips faltered, pointing to the prison old,
With its walls so tall and gloomy, – moss-grown walls dark, damp,
   and cold—

'I've a lover in that prison, doomed this very night to die
At the ringing of the curfew, and no earthly help is nigh.
Cromwell will not come till sunset'; and her lips grew strangely
    white
As she spoke in husky whispers, 'Curfew must not ring tonight!'

'Bessie,' calmly spoke the sexton (every word pierced her young
    heart
Like a gleaming death-winged arrow, like a deadly poisoned dart),
'Long, long years I've rung the curfew from that gloomy,
    shadowed tower;
Every evening, just at sunset, it has tolled the twilight hour.
I have done my duty ever, tried to do it just and right;
Now I'm old I will not miss it: Curfew bell must ring tonight!'

Wild her eyes and pale her features, stern and white her thoughtful
    brow,
And within her heart's deep centre Bessie made a solemn vow.
She had listened while the judges read, without a tear or sigh,
'At the ringing of the curfew Basil Underwood *must die.*'
And her breath came fast and faster, and her eyes grew large and
    bright;
One low murmur, faintly spoken, 'Curfew *must not* ring tonight!'

She with quick step bounded forward, sprang within the old
    church door,
Left the old man coming, slowly, paths he'd trod so oft before.
Not one moment paused the maiden, but, with cheek and brow
    aglow,
Staggered up the gloomy tower where the bell swung to and fro;
As she climbed the slimy ladder, on which fell no ray of light,
Upward still, her pale lips saying, 'Curfew *shall not* ring tonight!'

She has reached the topmost ladder; o'er her hangs the great, dark
    bell;
Awful is the gloom beneath her, like the pathway down to hell.
See, the ponderous tongue is swinging! 't is the hour of curfew
    now!
And the sight has chilled her bosom, stopped her breath and paled
    her brow.
Shall she let it ring? No, never! Her eyes flash with sudden light,
As she springs and grasps it firmly: 'Curfew *shall not* ring tonight!'

Out she swung, far out; the city seemed a speck of light below,
There 'twixt heaven and earth suspended, as the bell swung to
     and fro.
And the sexton at the bell-rope, old and deaf, heard not the bell;
Sadly thought that twilight curfew rang young Basil's funeral
     knell.
Still the maiden, clinging firmly, quivering lip and fair face white,
Stilled her frightened heart's wild beating: '*Curfew shall not ring
     tonight!*'

It was o'er! – the bell ceased swaying, and the maiden stepped
     once more
Firmly on the damp old ladder, where, for hundred years before,
Human foot had not been planted. The brave deed that she had
     done
Should be told long ages after. As the rays of setting sun
Light the sky with golden beauty, aged sires, with heads of white,
Tell the children why the curfew did not ring that one sad night.

O'er the distant hills comes Cromwell. Bessie sees him, and her
     brow,
Lately white with sickening horror, has no anxious traces now.
At his feet she tells her story, shows her hands, all bruised and
     torn;
And her sweet young face, still haggard with the anguish it had
     worn,
Touched his heart with sudden pity, lit his eyes with misty light.
'Go! your lover lives,' cried Cromwell. 'Curfew shall not ring
     tonight!'

Wide they flung the massive portals, led the prisoner forth to die,
All his bright young life before him, 'neath the darkening English
     sky.
Bessie came, with flying footsteps, eyes aglow with lovelight sweet,
Kneeling on the turf beside him, laid his pardon at his feet.
In his brave, strong arms he clasped her, kissed the face upturned
     and white,
Whispered, 'Darling, you have saved me! Curfew will not ring
     tonight.'

MOLLIE E. MOORE DAVIS
1852–1909

MOLLIE E. MOORE DAVIS was born in Talladega, Alabama, and grew up on a Texas plantation until the Civil War. She learned to ride, shoot and swim with her brother and was educated at home by her parents. Her first book of verse, *Minding the Gap* (1867), went through five editions. In 1874 she married Thomas E. Davis, formerly a Confederate Major, then editor of a New Orleans periodical. In 1880 they moved to New Orleans, where their home became a centre of social and intellectual life. Davis presided over a literary circle called the Geographics and a literary club called Quarante. Her poems and sketches were published in *Harper's* and other periodicals. Her stories on postbellum Southern life led a craze among white readers for 'negro dialect' tales. Davis's poetry is collected in *Poems* (1872) and *Selected Poems* (1927).

Going Out and Coming In

Going out to fame and triumph,
    Going out to love and light;
Coming in to pain and sorrow,
    Coming in to gloom and night.
Going out with joy and gladness,
    Coming in with woe and sin;
Ceaseless stream of restless pilgrims
    Going out and coming in!

Through the portals of the homestead,
    From beneath the blooming vine;
To the trumpet-tones of glory,
    Where the bays and laurels twine;
From the loving home-caresses
    To the chill voice of the world—

Going out with gallant canvas
   To the summer breeze unfurled.

Through the gateway, down the footpath,
   Through the lilacs by the way;
Through the clover by the meadow,
   Where the gentle home-lights stray;
To the wide world of ambition,
   Up the toilsome hill of fame,
Winning oft a mighty triumph,
   Winning oft a noble name.

Coming back all worn and weary,
   Weary with the world's cold breath;
Coming to the dear old homestead,
   Coming in to age and death.
Weary of its empty flattery,
   Weary of its ceaseless din,
Weary of its heartless sneering,
   Coming from the bleak world in.

Going out with hopes of glory,
   Coming in with sorrows dark;
Going out with sails all flying,
   Coming in with mastless barque.
Restless stream of pilgrims, striving
   Wreaths of fame and love to win,
From the doorways of the homestead
   Going out and coming in!

Cry of a People

Why are your lilies so tall and pure,
   Oh, land of the South, and why
Breathes your rose such a passionate tenderness
   When your morning breezes sigh?
Why should your forests be grand and broad,
   Or your rivers full and free?
Or why should your birds entrance the soul
   With wonderful melody?

Why is there a glory about your nights,
    And a golden glimmering haze
Steeping like floods of amber wine
    Your full-blown, splendid days?
Ill fits the sunshine with broken hearts,
    Or roses with sorrow and death:
—Leaden should be your skies above,
    And barren your fields beneath!

EDITH M. THOMAS
1854–1925

EDITH M. THOMAS was born on a farm in Ohio. Her parents encouraged her early literary interests. She attended Geneva Normal School and enrolled for one semester at Oberlin College, leaving to earn a living. Visiting New York, she met Helen Hunt Jackson, who read and praised her poems. Attracted to city life, in 1887 she moved to New York, where she became part of the literary scene. She worked as an editor on *Century Dictionary* and *Harper's*. Her poems, some well regarded by modernist poets such as Sara Teasdale, appeared in both adults' and children's periodicals, including *Atlantic* and *St Nicholas*, and in *Lyrics and Sonnets* (1887), *The Inverted Torch* (1890), *Fair Shadow Land* (1893), *A Winter Swallow* (1896), *The Flower from the Ashes* (1915) and *Selected Poems* (1926).

Cries of the Newsboy

(NEWS! SUN! OR WORLD!)

I

Cruel the roar of the city ways,
   Where life on a myriad errands whirled;
But suddenly up from the jarring maze,
   Like a rocket thrown high, went a ringing cry:
'New-Sunny-World! New-Sunny-World!'

There wasn't a glimpse of the sun anywhere;
   Up through the streets the sea fog curled;
Grim was the light and leaden the air;
   The world looked old, yet that voice rang bold:
'New-Sunny-World! New-Sunny-World!'

The brisk little crier I could not see,
   But I treasured the rocket cry he hurled,

And thought, 'This is wonderful news to me!
 Heigh-ho! is it true? Is it so to you?
  A New Sunny World?'

2

Up from the city's murky streets forlorn,
There comes a ringing cry at early morn,
That lets my fancy pass these stony bounds,
By hinting of sweet country sights and sounds.

Down there a little Mercury of the press,
Bright-eyed, shock-haired, and ragged, as I guess,
Cries the damp roll of 'Tribunes' 'neath his arm;
The listening walls give back the shrill alarm.

'T is *Morning piapers! Morning piapers!* still—
Like some quaint bird with but one call or trill;
'T is *Morning piapers! Morning piapers!*—aye,
There is an old-world accent in the cry.

Unknown this cuckoo fledgeling of the street
Beguiles my lingering sleep with service sweet
Of morning pipers, piping blithe and clear
From some imagined sward or thicket near.

LIZETTE WOODWORTH REESE
1856–1935

LIZETTE WOODWORTH REESE was born in Waverly, Maryland, and educated in Baltimore public schools. She taught English from 1873 to 1921, four of those years at a segregated black high school. She was a founder of the Women's Literary Club in Baltimore and in 1931 was named poet laureate of Maryland. Her first book of poems, *A Branch of May* (1887), published by subscription, was a critical success and was followed by eight further volumes of poems as well as prose reminiscences, *A Victorian Village* (1929) and *The York Road* (1931), narrative poems, *Little Henrietta* (1927) and *The Old House in the Country* (1936) and an autobiographical novel, *Worleys*, published posthumously. Her spare style, using common diction in traditional poetic forms, influenced a younger generation of women poets, including Edna St Vincent Millay and Louise Bogan, and some anthologists have considered her a modern poet.

Mid-March

It is too early for white boughs, too late
For snows. From out the hedge the wind lets fall
A few last flakes, ragged and delicate.
Down the stripped roads the maples start their small,
Soft, 'wildering fires. Stained are the meadow stalks
A rich and deepening red. The willow tree
Is woolly. In deserted garden-walks
The lean bush crouching hints old royalty,
Feels some June stir in the sharp air and knows
Soon 'twill leap up and show the world a rose.

The days go out with shouting; nights are loud;
Wild, warring shapes the wood lifts in the cold;
The moon's a sword of keen, barbaric gold,
Plunged to the hilt into a pitch black cloud.

Telling the Bees

A Colonial Custom

Bathsheba came out to the sun,
Out to our wallèd cherry-trees;
The tears adown her cheek did run,
Bathsheba standing in the sun,
Telling the bees.

My mother had that moment died;
Unknowing, sped I to the trees,
And plucked Bathsheba's hand aside;
Then caught the name that there she cried
Telling the bees.

Her look I never can forget,
I that held sobbing to her knees;
The cherry-boughs above us met;
I think I see Bathsheba yet
Telling the bees.

Indian Summer

Cast on this shore at end of year,
Survivors of the wreck and storm,
We build our fire of driftwood here,
Somewhat to gain of the old cheer,
And spread our stiffened hands to warm.
Nor gold nor any spice have we;
From West or East no carvèd things;
But ever to us keeps and clings
The stinging odor of the sea!

A Street Scene

The east is a clear violet mass
Behind the houses high;
The laborers with their kettles pass;
The carts are creaking by.

Carved out against the tender sky,
The convent gables lift;
Half way below the old boughs lie
Heaped in a great white drift.

They tremble in the passionate air;
They part, and clean and sweet
The cherry flakes fall here, fall there;
A handful stirs the street.

The workmen look up as they go;
And one, remembering plain
How white the Irish orchards blow,
Turns back, and looks again.

An Old Belle

A daughter of the Cavaliers
(A phrase a little dulled with years),
But something sweeter than them all,
Serene she sits at evenfall.

Tall tulips crowd the window-sill,
Vague ghosts of those that blew at will—
Ere she was old and time so fleet—
In one walled space down Camden street.

And straight – she and her lover there—
In that town garden take the air;
Tall tulips lift in scarlet tire,
Brimming the April dusk with fire.

Without, the white of harbored ships;
The road that to the water slips;

The tang of salt; the scent of sea;
Within, her only love and she!

Back to the new she comes once more,
To roofs ungabled, ways that roar;
To the sole April left her still,
That potted scarlet on the sill.

Dust are those pleasant garden walls;
Her only love in green Saint Paul's;
Serene she sits at her day's close;
Last of her kin, but still a rose!

The Day Before Spring

There is a faltering crimson by the wall,
  Now on a vine, and now on brier thinned,
    As though one bearing lantern through the wind,
Here hides his light, but yonder lets it fall.
And we remember and remember; all
  Ancestral stirrings point unto this fate,—
  That we shall come unto our old estate,
Defrauding days unloose their iron thrall.
Without, the trees seem crowding to the street,
  Like simple folk that breathless here and there
    Crowd toward a haunted space, to verify
Some dim report of ghost or vision fleet;
  And lo, at dusk, across the silent square,
    As in a whirl of bloom, a Shape goes by!

Trust

I am thy grass, O Lord!
  I grow up sweet and tall
But for a day; beneath Thy sword
  To lie at evenfall.

Yet have I not enough
  In that brief day of mine?

The wind, the bees, the wholesome stuff
   The sun pours out like wine.

Behold, this is my crown;
   Love will not let me be;
Love holds me here; Love cuts me down;
   And it is well with me.

Lord, Love, keep it but so;
   Thy purpose is full plain;
I die that after I may grow
   As tall, as sweet again.

Mystery

Elude me still, keep ever just before,
A cloudy thing, a shape with wingèd feet.
I shall pursue, but be you strict and fleet,
Unreachable as gusts that pass the door.
Better than doubting eye that eye of yore
Which set tall robbers stalking through the night;
Or of the wind, lane's hollow, briars white,
Made for the April-tide one ghost the more.
For safe am I that have you still in sight;
See you down each new road, upon you come
In crocus days; under the stripped tree find;
In creed and song, in harvest as in blight;
My chiefest joy till I grow cold and dumb;
Till my years fail, and you are left behind!

Reserve

Keep back the one word more,
Nor give of your whole store;
For, it may be, in Art's sole hour of need,
   Lacking that word, you shall be poor indeed.

ZARAGOZA CLUBS
fl. 1860

The ZARAGOZA CLUBS were women's poetry clubs in Los Angeles organised to promote the composition of poetry in solidarity with soldiers fighting against the French invasion of Mexico. They were named for General Ignacio Zaragoza, leader of the Mexican victory at the Battle of Puebla, 5 May 1862, the event commemorated today on Cinco de Mayo. The poems included here are selected from those published in the Spanish-language newspaper *El Nuevo Mundo* of San Francisco in 1865.

from HÉROES DEL CINCO DE MAYO

Merced J. de Gonzáles

Méjico libre ha de ser
Pese al francés insolente.
Esto mi instinto presente
Si sabemos sostener
Nuestro digno presidente.
Con heroísmo defended
Donde quiera que te hallares
De nuestra patria los lores;
Y en su entusiasmo Merced
Brinda por Benito Juárez.

My heart tells me
Mexico will be free
Despite the arrogant French,
If we know how to assist
Our worthy president.

With heroism we should defend
The leaders of our country
Wherever we might be;
And Merced in her enthusiasm
Gives a Hail! to Benito Juárez.

Andrea Belarde

¿Qué hombre será el más villano?
            Maximiliano.
¿Y cuál será el más bribón?
            Napoleón.
Dios con una maldición
Los confunda á los abismos,
Y allí con los diablos mismos
Propongan en intervención,
Brindo por su destrucción.

Which man is the greatest villain?
            Maximilian.
And who is the most evil one?
            Napoleon.
But God has redeemed our nation
And sent them both to damnation,
And this, their eternal perdition,
Is their reward for intervention
They brought for our destruction.

Bell Warner

A todo el Norte quiero ver
Libre, fuerte, independiente;
Quiero verlo prepotente,
Y con gusto placentero
Brindo por el presidente.

I long to see all the North
Free, strong, and independent;
I long to see a mighty power
Full of happiness and joy;
I give a Hail! to our President.

Arcadia Alvarado

Yo no quiero monarquía,
Yo no quiero aristocracia;
Ni del traidor la palacia,
Quiero ver la patria mía
Libre de toda desgracia.

I reject their monarchy,
I reject aristocracy;
I reject a traitor's palace;
I accept this and nothing less:
My country free from all disgrace.

Refujio Díaz

El tonto Maximiliano
Y su consorte Carlota
Al buen sentido derrota
Por que el hombre es un marrano
    Y su mujer una idiota.
De conformidad ese dúo
Goviernan à los traidores,
A frailes y aduladores,
Sin más talento que un buho.

That stupid Maximilian
And his consort Carlota
Have shattered all true reason
Because the man is a pig
    And his woman is an idiot.
In a union of peers those two
May govern the traitors,
Friars, and adulators,
With no more talent than an owl.

Francisca García

¡Méjico! tú que en tus Campos
El sol de mi vida ví,
Cuna do yo me mecí
De juveniles encantos.

Tú que en el bosque moviente
De tus perfumadas brisas
Gocé las dulces delicias
De su divino ambiente.
Quisiera hacer con mi vida
     Tu ventura.
Con cuánto amor y ternura
La diera, patria querida
Y que fueras grande y fuerte
     En el mundo
Y que el universo inerte
Te admirara absorto, mudo.

Mexico! You in whose countryside
I saw the first light of my life,
The cradle where I was lulled
In my youthful enchantments.
You in whose forests swaying
With your perfumed breezes
I rejoiced in sweet delights
Of your divine environs.
I long to weave my life
     Into your fortune.
With such love and tenderness
I give my life to you, dear country,
I long to see you great and strong
     Throughout the world,
And may the inert universe
Gaze upon you silent and amazed.

Refujia Díaz

Mis amigos una copa,
En honor de los valientes
Que cubriendo están sus frentes
Con laureles de victoria.
Por que la pelea no en vano,
Sea tan tenaz tan terrible
Que à su frente estruendo, horrible
¡Se muera Maximiliano!

My friends, I give a toast
In honor of the valiant ones
Whose heads are wreathed
In laurels of sweet victory.
Know your struggle is not in vain,
Be it ever so cruel and fierce,
For we will resound together,
'Maximilian soon will die!'

Pub. 29 March 1865

from HOMENAJES DE GRATITUD

Isabel Warner

Cuando el infame francés
En San Pedro combatió
En el momento encontró
De la fortuna un revés
Y su fama se acabó.
Doy mi amor al que defiende
De su patria los umbrales;
Por el valiente Rosales
Mi pecho en fuego se enciende.
¡Que vivan los liberales!

When the French, to their shame,
In San Pedro came to war,
In one moment they did deplore
How their glory came to blame,
And their fame was gone for evermore.
I give my love to him who did defend
His country in its time of need;
To valiant Rosales for his noble deed
My bosom's fire to him I send;
May our liberators always succeed!

Teresa Morales

¿Por qué, Méjico hermoso,
Mi relicario amado,
La planta del malvado
Te pisa presuroso?
Mas detengan su carrera
De su jefe los esclavos,
Pues todavía tenemos bravos
Como el capitán Herrera;
Brindo por que nunca muera.

Tell me, lovely Mexico,
My reliquary of love,
Why does that malicious one
In arrogance tread on you?
Though slaves have helped
The cause of their master Maximilian,
We do not lack for noble soldiers,
Like Herrera, our noble Captain;
I Hail! that his fame may never die.

Refugio Arce de Silva

En medio de la tarde
Parace que cruzaba
Un ángel que cantaba;
¡O muerte o libertad!
Mas esto es realidad;
Y la reunión entera
Lo contemplara en Rivera.

In the middle of the evening
I thought I saw an angel
Crossing past and singing:
'Either Death or Liberty.'
But that was not a vision;
The entire congregation
Had gazed upon Rivera.

Filomeno Ibarra

En la antigua Roma había
De Vesta, templo formado,
Do por mujeres cuidado,
Perenne se mantenía
Constante el fuego sagrado.
   Las socias de 'Zaragoza'
A las de Vesta imitando,
El fuego patrio atizando,
Con inquietud afanosa
La lámpara están cuidando.

In ancient Rome there stood
A temple built to Vesta,
Tended all by women, and
Its constant sacred flame
Was kept perpetually burning.
   Now the members of 'Zaragoza'
Following the rules of Vesta
Keep our country's fire bright
And with painstaking pride
Take constant care of our lamp.

Pub. 21 July 1865
Translations by Luis A. Torres, 1994

CHARLOTTE PERKINS STETSON GILMAN
1860–1935

CHARLOTTE PERKINS STETSON GILMAN was born in Hartford, Connecticut, a niece of novelist Harriet Beecher Stowe. Her father abandoned the family soon after her birth. With her mother and older brother, she moved frequently throughout her childhood. At an early age she defied gender conventions by espousing dress reform and physical fitness training for women. She attended the Rhode Island School of Design and taught art and designed greeting cards for a living. In 1882 she married Charles Walter Stetson, whom she divorced in 1894. She became severely depressed after the birth of their daughter in 1885 and was prescribed a rest cure, an experience fictionalised in her now famous story *The Yellow Wall Paper* (1892). In 1888 she moved to California and became a leading figure in the utopian socialist movement. She toured as a lecturer on labour and women's issues. In 1900 she married a cousin, George Houghton Gilman. Her poems are collected in *In This Our World* (1893), which ran to five editions over a decade. Her major work, *Women and Economics* (1898), brought her international recognition as a thinker of the women's movement. Thereafter she published prolifically both non-fiction and fiction. In 1909 she founded *Forerunner*, a periodical on social issues, through which she published her novels: *What Diantha Did* (1910); the feminist utopian novel *Herland* (1915) and *With Her in Ourland* (1916). Suffering breast cancer, she committed suicide in 1935, leaving an autobiography, *The Living of Charlotte Perkins Gilman*.

Homes

A SESTINA

We are the smiling comfortable homes
With happy families enthroned therein,

Where baby souls are brought to meet the world,
Where women end their duties and desires,
For which men labor as the goal of life,
That people worship now instead of God.

Do we not teach the child to worship God?—
Whose soul's young range is bounded by the homes
Of those he loves, and where he learns that life
Is all constrained to serve the wants therein,
Domestic needs and personal desires,—
These are the early limits of his world.

And are we not the woman's perfect world,
Prescribed by nature and ordained of God,
Beyond which she can have no right desires,
No need for service other than in homes?
For doth she not bring up her young therein?
And is not rearing young the end of life?

And man? What other need hath he in life
Than to go forth and labor in the world,
And struggle sore with other men therein?
Not to serve other men, nor yet his God,
But to maintain these comfortable homes,—
The end of all a normal man's desires.

Shall not the soul's most measureless desires
Learn that the very flower and fruit of life
Lies all attained in comfortable homes,
With which life's purpose is to dot the world
And consummate the utmost will of God,
By sitting down to eat and drink therein.

Yea, in the processes that work therein—
Fulfilment of our natural desires—
Surely man finds the proof that mighty God
For to maintain and reproduce his life
Created him and set him in the world;
And this high end is best attained in homes.

Are we not homes? And is not all therein?
Wring dry the world to meet our wide desires!
We crown all life! We are the aim of God!

The Anti-Suffragists

Fashionable women in luxurious homes,
With men to feed them, clothe them, pay their bills,
Bow, doff the hat, and fetch the handkerchief;
Hostess or guest, and always so supplied
With graceful deference and courtesy;
Surrounded by their servants, horses, dogs,—
These tell us they have all the rights they want.

Successful women who have won their way
Alone, with strength of their unaided arm,
Or helped by friends, or softly climbing up
By the sweet aid of 'woman's influence';
Successful any way, and caring naught
For any other woman's unsuccess,—
These tell us they have all the rights they want.

Religious women of the feebler sort,—
Not the religion of a righteous world,
A free, enlightened, upward-reaching world,
But the religion that considers life
As something to back out of! – whose ideal
Is to renounce, submit, and sacrifice,
Counting on being patted on the head
And given a high chair when they get to heaven,—
These tell us they have all the rights they want.

Ignorant women – college-bred sometimes,
But ignorant of life's realities
And principles of righteous government,
And how the privileges they enjoy
Were won with blood and tears by those before—
Those they condemn, whose ways they now oppose;
Saying, 'Why not let well enough alone?
Our world is very pleasant as it is,'—
These tell us they have all the rights they want.

And selfish women, – pigs in petticoats,—
Rich, poor, wise, unwise, top or bottom round,
But all sublimely innocent of thought,
And guiltless of ambition, save the one

Deep, voiceless aspiration – to be fed!
These have no use for rights or duties more.
Duties today are more than they can meet,
And law insures their right to clothes and food,—
These tell us they have all the rights they want.

And, more's the pity, some good women, too;
Good conscientious women, with ideas;
Who think – or think they think – that woman's cause
Is best advanced by letting it alone;
That she somehow is not a human thing,
And not to be helped on by human means,
Just added to humanity – an 'L'—
A wing, a branch, an extra, not mankind,—
These tell us they have all the rights they want.

And out of these has come a monstrous thing,
A strange, down-sucking whirlpool of disgrace,
Women uniting against womanhood,
And using that great name to hide their sin!
Vain are their words as that old king's command
Who set his will against the rising tide.
But who shall measure the historic shame
Of these poor traitors – traitors are they all—
To great Democracy and Womanhood!

The Mother's Charge

She raised her head. With hot and glittering eye,
'I know,' she said, 'that I am going to die.
Come here, my daughter, while my mind is clear.
Let me make plain to you your duty here;
My duty once – I never failed to try—
But for some reason I am going to die.'
She raised her head, and, while her eyes rolled wild,
Poured these instructions on the gasping child:

'Begin at once – don't iron sitting down—
Wash your potatoes when the fat is brown—
Monday, unless it rains – it always pays

To get fall sewing done on the right days—
A carpet-sweeper and a little broom—
Save dishes – wash the summer dining-room
With soda – keep the children out of doors—
The starch is out – beeswax on all the floors—
If girls are treated like your friends they stay—
They stay, and treat you like their friends – the way
To make home happy is to keep a jar—
And save the prettiest pieces for the star
In the middle – blue's too dark – all silk is best—
And don't forget the corners – when they're dressed
Put them on ice – and always wash the chest
Three times a day, the windows every week—
We need more flour – the bedroom ceilings leak—
It's better than onion – keep the boys at home—
Gardening is good – a load, three loads of loam—
They bloom in spring – and smile, smile always, dear—
Be brave, keep on – I hope I've made it clear.'

She died, as all her mothers died before.
Her daughter died in turn, and made one more.

Christian Virtues

Oh, dear!
The Christian virtues will disappear!
Nowhere on land or sea
Will be room for charity!
Nowhere, in field or city,
A person to help or pity!
Better for them, no doubt,
Not to need helping out
Of their old miry ditch.
But, alas for us, the rich!
For we shall lose, you see,
Our boasted charity!—
Lose all the pride and joy
Of giving the poor employ,
And money, and food, and love

(And making stock thereof!).
Our Christian virtues are gone,
With nothing to practise on!

It don't hurt them a bit,
For they can't practise it;
But it's our great joy and pride—
What virtue have we beside?
We believe, as sure as we live,
That it is more blessed to give
Than to want, and waste, and grieve,
And occasionally receive!
And here are the people pressing
To rob us of our pet blessing!
No chance to endow or bedizen
A hospital, school, or prison,
And leave our own proud name
To Gratitude and Fame!
No chance to do one good deed,
To give what we do not need,
To leave what we cannot use
To those whom we deign to choose!
When none want broken meat,
How shall our cake be sweet?
When none want flannels and coals,
How shall we save our souls?
Oh, dear! Oh, dear!
The Christian virtues will disappear!

The poor have their virtues rude,—
Meekness and gratitude,
Endurance, and respect
For us, the world's elect;
Economy, self-denial,
Patience in every trial,
Self-sacrifice, self-restraint,—
Virtues enough for a saint!
Virtues enough to bear
All this life's sorrow and care!
Virtues by which to rise
To a front seat in the skies!
How can they turn from this

To common earthly bliss,—
Mere clothes, and food, and drink,
And leisure to read and think,
And art, and beauty, and ease,—
There is no crown for these!
True, if their gratitude
Were not for fire and food,
They might still learn to bless
The Lord for their happiness!
And, instead of respect for wealth,
Might learn from beauty, and health,
And freedom in power and pelf,
Each man to respect himself!
And, instead of scraping and saving,
Might learn from using and having
That man's life should be spent
In a grand development!
But this is petty and small;
These are not virtues at all;
They do not look as they should;
They don't do *us* any good!
Oh, dear! Oh, dear! Oh, dear!
The Christian virtues will disappear!

JOSEPHINE DELPHINE HENDERSON HEARD
1861–19–?

JOSEPHINE DELPHINE HENDERSON HEARD was born in Salisbury, North Carolina. Her parents were slaves but were allowed to work and live on their own. She learned to read and perform music at an early age and was educated at private institutions. Graduating with honours, she began her teaching career in North Carolina, then moved to Tennessee. In 1882 she married W. H. Heard, a postal employee who became a Bishop in the African Methodist Episcopal Church. In the 1890s they lived in Philadelphia. Her poems, most of them religious, were published in the *Christian Recorder* and other evangelical journals, recited in classrooms and collected in *Morning Glories* (1890).

To Clements' Ferry

One lovely summer afternoon when balmy breezes blew,
A charming little buggy, scarce large enough for two,
Dashed down the narrow little street and stopped beside a gate,
Where a charming little woman dwelt whom he had met of late.

Out stepped a little body, looking like a happy bride;
He gently stood and placed her in a safe seat at his side:
'I'm going to show you now,' said he (with eyes that twinkle merry),
'The very prettiest of drives, it leads to Clements' Ferry.'

'If you have never heard of it, my darling little treasure,
I'll tell you all about the place, it will afford me pleasure.'
And on they sped, mile after mile, with chat and laughter merry—
He watched her dimpled, roguish smile and drove toward the ferry.

Through lovely groves, where birds sang sweet their notes of joy so
    merry,
Or partridge, hid in ripened wheat, whistled his 'Bob White' cherry.

Up the shell road and o'er the fields and by the moss-hung oaks,
Where marshy land its rich grain yields or sad-voiced raven croaks.

Then turning off the highway and past the gate of toll,
Then up into a by-way which led straight to the knoll,
''Tis here,' said he, 'the loveliest spot in all the world so wide,
Swept by the breezes from the sea, and kissed by every tide.

Come down beside the river's brink, where the water ripples merry—
A lovely place to rest and think, down here beside the ferry.'
So taking his uplifted hands she gave a little bound,
And very soon they sat them down upon the grassy ground.

'In days that are forever fled, when slavery cursed this nation—
This land was owned by Clements and on his great plantation
Were many slaves who daily tilled this soil, tho' oft in pain—
Their master's coffers must be filled from the fields of golden grain.

'They knew no rest who labored there, but worked from early light—
They ploughed and hoed and reaped and sowed, till the sun went
    down at night;
Then to the river they would come all foot-sore, worn and weary,
Hungry and faint to reach their home they crossed here at the ferry.

'One day they heard a strange sweet voice, not such as wont to lead
    them;
It made their burdened hearts rejoice, for 'twas the voice that freed
    them.
And when the sun went down that night their shouts rose loud and
    merry—
They crossed with footsteps swift and light the last time o'er this
    ferry.

'So here besides this river we have found a rustic seat,'
And still the water rippled on and winds blew soft and sweet—
'I've something else to tell you,' and his laughing eye were merry,
He whispered something in her ear, but not about the ferry.

                            *

The sun was shining in the west and back toward home they drove;
Soft twilight had its shadows cast o'er field and knoll and grove—
The ferry has another name, which lovers oft repeat,
Instead of 'Clements' Ferry', it is now 'Sunset Retreat'.

                                        1890

Tennyson's Poems

On receiving Tennyson's Poems from
Mrs M. H. Dunton, of Brattleboro', Vt.

Dear Friend, since you have chosen to associate
My humble thoughts with England's poet laureate,
I trust that he will bear me pleasant company,
And soon we shall far more than mere acquaintance be.
Since childhood's days his name I have revered,
And more and more it has become to me endeared;
I blush not for the truth, I but confess,
I very wealthy feel since I his 'works' possess.

I've found in the immortal Shakespeare much delight,
Yet, oft his vulgar language shocked me quite;
And I twice grateful am, that I no more shall be
Dependent in spare moments on *his* company.
But I shall roam o'er England's proud domain,
Shall meet her lords and ladies, and her peasants plain,
Attend her royal spreads, and figure at her courts,
On prancing steed with nodding plume, I join their hunting sports.

1890

Thine Own

To live and not to be Thine Own,
Like Springtime is when birds are flown;
Or liberty in prison bars,
Or evening skies without the stars;
Like diamonds that are lustreless,
Or rest when there's no weariness;
Like lovely flower that have no scent,
Or music when the sound is spent.

1890

Love Letters

Dear Letters, Fond Letters,
　　Must I with you part?
You are such a source of joy
　　To my lonely heart.

Sweet Letters, Dear Letters,
　　What a tale you tell;
O, no power on earth can break
　　This strange mystic spell!

Dear Letters, Fond Letters,
　　You my secret know—
Don't you tell it, any one—
　　Let it live and grow.

1890

The Black Sampson

There's a Sampson lying, sleeping in the land,
He shall soon awake, and with avenging hand,
In an all unlooked for hour,
He will rise in mighty power;
　　What dastard can his righteous rage withstand?

E'er since the chains were riven at a stroke,
E'er since the dawn of Freedom's morning broke,
He has groaned, but scarcely uttered,
While his patient tongue ne'er muttered,
　　Though in agony he bore the galling yoke.

O, what cruelty and torture has he felt?
Could his tears, the heart of his oppressor melt?
In his gore they bathed their hands,
Organized and lawless bands—
　　And the innocent was left in blood to welt.

The mighty God of Nations doth not sleep,
His piercing eye its faithful watch doth keep,

And well nigh His mercy's spent,
To the ungodly lent:
   'They have sowed the wind, the whirlwind they shall reap.'

From His nostrils issues now the angry smoke,
And asunder bursts the all-oppressive yoke;
When the prejudicial heel
Shall be lifted, we shall feel,
   That the hellish spell surrounding us is broke.

The mills are grinding slowly, slowly on,
And till the very chaff itself is gone;
Our cries for justice louder,
Till oppression's ground to powder—
   God speed the day of retribution on!

Fair Columbia's filmy garments all are stained;
In her courts is blinded justice rudely chained;
The black Sampson is awaking,
And his fetters fiercely breaking;
   By his mighty arm his rights shall be obtained!

1890

EMILY PAULINE JOHNSON
(TEKAHIONWAKE)
1861–1913

EMILY PAULINE JOHNSON was born and raised on Six Nations Reserve near Brantford, Ontario. She took the name Tekahionwake as an adult. Her mother was a cousin of novelist William Dean Howells, her father a Mohawk leader. Growing up, she learned from relatives the English poetic tradition as well as the Mohawk oral tradition of tales and legends. Her early poems were published in United States periodicals, *Gems of Poetry*, *Mother's Magazine* and *Boys' World*. Selections appeared also in a Canadian anthology, *Songs of the Great Dominion* (1889). She began performing in Toronto literary events around 1890. She quickly became internationally known and toured Canada, the United States and Great Britain from 1892 to 1909, performing her poetry in Native American dress. Her first book, *The White Wampum* (1895), includes poetry and tales; later poems are collected in *Canadian Born* (1903) and *Flint and Feather* (1912). She also published tales and short fiction in *Legends of Vancouver* (1911), *The Shagganappi* and the semi-autobiographical *The Moccasin Maker* (1913). She is regarded today as a forerunner of contemporary Native American literature.

Marshlands

A thin wet sky, that yellows at the rim,
And meets with sun-lost lip the marsh's brim.

The pools low lying, dank with moss and mould,
Glint through their mildews like large cups of gold.

Among the wild rice in the still lagoon,
In monotone the lizard shrills his tune.

The wild goose, homing, seeks a sheltering,
Where rushes grow, and oozing lichens cling.

Late cranes with heavy wing, and lazy flight,
Sail up the silence with the nearing night.

And like a spirit, swathed in some soft veil,
Steals twilight and its shadows o'er the swale.

Hushed lie the sedges, and the vapours creep,
Thick, grey and humid, while the marshes sleep.

1895

Joe

AN ETCHING

A meadow brown; across the yonder edge
A zigzag fence is ambling; here a wedge
Of underbush has cleft its course in twain,
Till where beyond it staggers up again;
The long, grey rails stretch in a broken line
Their ragged length of rough, split forest pine,
And in their zigzag tottering have reeled
In drunken efforts to enclose the field,
Which carries on its breast, September born,
A patch of rustling, yellow, Indian corn.
Beyond its shrivelled tassels, perched upon
The topmost rail, sits Joe, the settler's son,
A little semi-savage boy of nine.
Now dozing in the warmth of Nature's wine,
His face the sun has tampered with, and wrought,
By heated kisses, mischief, and has brought
Some vagrant freckles, while from here and there
A few wild locks of vagabond brown hair
Escape the old straw hat the sun looks through,
And blinks to meet his Irish eyes of blue.
Barefooted, innocent of coat or vest,
His grey checked shirt unbuttoned at his chest,
Both hardy hands within their usual nest—
His breeches pockets – so, he waits to rest
His little fingers, somewhat tired and worn,
That all day long were husking Indian corn.

His drowsy lids snap at some trivial sound,
With lazy yawns he slips towards the ground,
Then with an idle whistle lifts his load
And shambles home along the country road
That stretches on fringed out with stumps and weeds,
And finally unto the backwoods leads,
Where forests wait with giant trunk and bough
The axe of pioneer, the settler's plough.

                                        1895

Wave-Won

Tonight I hunger so,
Belovéd one, to know
If you recall and crave again the dream
That haunted our canoe,
And wove its witchcraft through
Our hearts as 'neath the northern night we sailed the
    northern stream.

Ah! dear, if only we
As yesternight could be
Afloat within that light and lonely shell,
To drift in silence till
Heart-hushed, and lulled and still
The moonlight through the melting air flung forth its fatal
    spell.

The dusky summer night,
The path of gold and white
The moon had cast across the river's breast,
The shores in shadows clad,
The far-away, half-sad
Sweet singing of the whip-poor-will, all soothed our souls
    to rest.

You trusted I could feel,
My arm as strong as steel,
So still your upturned face, so calm your breath,
While circling eddies curled,

While laughing rapids whirled,
From boulder unto boulder, till they dashed themselves to death.

Your splendid eyes aflame
Put heaven's stars to shame,
Your god-like head so near my lap was laid—
My hand is burning where
It touched your wind-blown hair,
As sweeping to the rapids verge, I changed my paddle blade.

The boat obeyed my hand,
Till wearied with its grand
Wild anger, all the river lay aswoon,
And as my paddle dipped,
Thro' pools of pearl it slipped
And swept beneath a shore of shade, beneath a velvet moon.

Tonight, again dream you
Our spirit-winged canoe
Is listening to the rapids purling past?
Where, in delirium reeled
Our maddened hearts that kneeled
To idolize the perfect world, to taste of love at last.

1895

LOUISE IMOGEN GUINEY
1861–1920

LOUISE IMOGEN GUINEY was born in Roxbury, Massachusetts, to Irish Catholic parents. She attended a convent school in Providence, Rhode Island. Her father, a lawyer, politician, and brigadier-general for Union forces in the Civil War, died when she was sixteen. After graduating from high school, she wrote to support herself and her mother. Though her poetry and prose were critically well received and gained her the support of key literary figures, they did not provide a living. She became postmistress of Auburndale, Massachusetts, in 1894 but resigned under sexist and anti-Irish Catholic pressure. From 1899 to 1901 she worked in the Boston Public Library. She moved to Oxford, England, in 1901. Later modernist women poets Louise Bogan and Amy Lowell named Guiney as an influence. She also produced scholarship and criticism, championing the Aesthetes (a British movement advocating art's autonomy) and devoting much work to the seventeenth-century metaphysical poets. Publications include poetry collections, *Songs at the Start* (1884), *The White Sail* (1887), *A Roadside Harp* (1893), *Happy Ending* (1909); essays, *Goose Quill Papers* (1885) and *Patrins: A Collection of Essays* (1897); short fiction, *Lovers' Saint Ruth and Three Other Tales* (1895); biographies, *Robert Emmett* (1904) and *Blessed Edmund Campion* (1908); and an anthology of Roman Catholic poetry, *Recusant Poets* (1938).

Down Stream

Scarred hemlock roots,
Oaks in mail, and willow-shoots
   Spring's first-knighted;
Clinging aspens grouped between,
Slender, misty-green,
   Faintly affrighted:

Far hills behind,
Sombre growth, with sunlight lined,
   On their edges;
Banks hemmed in with maiden-hair,
And the straight and fair
   Phalanx of sedges:

Wee wings and eyes,
Wild blue gemmy dragon-flies,
   Fearless rangers;
Drowsy turtles in a tribe
Diving, with a gibe
   Muttered at strangers;

Wren, bobolink,
Robin, at the grassy brink;
   Great frogs jesting;
And the beetle, for no grief
Half-across his leaf
   Sighing and resting;

In the keel's way,
Unwithdrawing bream at play,
   Till from branches
Chestnut-blossoms, loosed aloft,
Graze them with their soft
   Full avalanches!

This is very odd!
Boldly sings the river-god:
   'Pilgrim rowing!
From the Hyperborean air
Wherefore, and O where
   Should man be going?'

Slave to a dream,
Me no urgings and no theme
   Can embolden;
Now no more the oars swing back,
Drip, dip, till black
   Waters froth golden.

Musketaquid!
I have loved thee, all unbid,

Earliest, longest;
Thou hast taught me thine own thrift:
Here I sit, and drift
  Where the wind's strongest.

If, furthermore,
There be any pact ashore,
  I forget it!
If, upon a busy day
Beauty make delay,
  Once over, let it!

Only, – despite
Thee, who wouldst unnerve me quite
  Like a craven,—
Best the current be not so,
Heart and I must row
  Into our haven!

Garden Chidings

The spring being at her blessed carpentry,
This morning makes a stem, this noon a leaf,
And jewels her sparse greenery with a bud;
Fostress of happy growth is she. But thou,
O too disdainful spirit, or too shy!
Passive dost thou inhabit, like a mole,
The porch elect of darkness; for thy trade
Is underground, a barren industry,
Shivering true ardor on the nether air,
Shaping the thousandth tendril, and all year
Webbing the silver nothings to and fro.
What wonder if the gardener think thee dead,
When every punctual neighbor-root now goes
Adventurously skyward for a flower?
Up, laggard! climb thine inch; thyself fulfil;
Thou only hast no sign, no pageantry,
Save these fine gropings: soon from thy small plot
The seasonable sunshine steals away.

A Reason for Silence

You sang, you sang! you mountain brook
    Scarce by your tangly banks held in,
As running from a rocky nook,
    You leaped the world, the sea to win,
Sun-bright past many a foamy crook,
    And headlong as a javelin.

Now men do check and still your course
    To serve a village enterprise,
And wheelward drive your sullen force,
    What wonder, slave! that in no wise
Breaks from you, pooled 'mid reeds and gorse,
    The voice you had in Paradise?

John Brown: A Paradox

Compassionate eyes had our brave John Brown,
And a craggy stern forehead, a militant frown;
He, the storm-bow of peace. Give him volley on volley,
The fool who redeemed us once of our folly,
And the smiter that healed us, our right John Brown!

Too vehement, verily, was John Brown!
For waiting is statesmanlike; his the renown
Of the holy rash arm, the equipper and starter
Of freedmen; aye, call him fanatic and martyr:
He can carry both halos, our plain John Brown.

A scandalous stumbling-block was John Brown,
And a jeer; but ah! soon from the terrified town,
In his bleeding track made over hilltop and hollow,
Wise armies and councils were eager to follow,
And the children's lips chanted our lost John Brown.

Star-led for us, stumbled and groped John Brown,
Star-led, in the awful morasses to drown;
And the trumpet that rang for a nation's upheaval,

From the thought that was just, thro' the deed that was evil,
Was blown with the breath of this dumb John Brown!

Bared heads and a pledge unto mad John Brown!
Now the curse is allayed, now the dragon is down,
Now we see, clear enough, looking back at the onset,
Christianity's flood-tide and Chivalry's sunset
In the old broken heart of our hanged John Brown!

The Atoning Yesterday

Ye daffodilian days, whose fallen towers
Shielded our paradisal prime from ill,
Fair past, fair motherhood! let come what will,
We, being yours, defy the anarch powers.
For us the happy tidings fell, in showers
Enjewelling the wind from every hill;
We drained the sun against the winter's chill;
Our ways were barricadoed in with flowers:

And if from skyey minsters now unhoused,
Earth's massy workings at the forge we hear,
The black roll of the congregated sea,
And war's live hoof: O yet, last year, last year
We were the lark-lulled shepherdlings, that drowsed
Grave-deep, at noon, in grass of Arcady!

MARY WESTON FORDHAM
b. ?1862

MARY WESTON FORDHAM published a book of poems, *Magnolia Leaves* (1897), through a South Carolina press. Booker T. Washington, then Principal of Tuskegee Institute, wrote an introduction for the volume, expressing the hope that it would inspire other black men and women to earn recognition in the field of poetry. Little else is known about Fordham; her poems include references to ancestors and relatives and suggest that she lost as many as six children in infancy.

Atlanta Exposition Ode

'Cast down your bucket where you are,'
From burning sands or Polar star
From where the iceberg rears its head
Or where the kingly palms outspread;
'Mid blackened fields or golden sheaves,
Or foliage green, or autumn leaves,
Come sounds of warning from afar,
'Cast down your bucket where you are.'

What doth it matter if thy years
Have slowly dragged 'mid sighs and tears?
What doth it matter, since thy day
Is brightened now by hope's bright ray.
The morning star will surely rise,
And Ethiop's sons with longing eyes
And outstretched hands, will bless the day,
When old things shall have passed away.

Come, comrades, from the East, the West!
Come, bridge the chasm. It is best.

Come, warm hearts of the sunny South,
And clasp hands with the mighty North.
Rise Afric's sons and chant with joy,
Good will to all without alloy;
The night of grief has passed away—
On Orient gleams a brighter day.

Say, ye that wore the blue, how sweet
That thus in sympathy we meet,
Our brothers who the gray did love
And martyrs to their cause did prove.
Say, once for all and once again,
That blood no more shall flow in vain;
Say Peace shall brood o'er this fair land
And hearts, for aye, be joined with hand.

Hail! Watchman, from thy lofty height;
Tell us, O tell us of the night?
Will Bethlehem's Star ere long arise
And point this nation to the skies?
Will pæans ring from land and sea
Fraught with untrammelled liberty
Till Time's appointed course be run,
And Earth's millennium be begun?

'Cast down your bucket,' let it be
As water flows both full and free!
Let charity, that twice blest boon
Thy watchword be from night to morn.
Let kindness as the dew distil
To friend and foe, alike, good will;
Till sounds the wondrous battle-call,
For all one flag, one flag for all.

1897

Serenade

Sleep, love sleep,
The night winds sigh,
In soft lullaby.

The Lark is at rest
With the dew on her breast.
So close those dear eyes,
That borrowed their hue
From the heavens so blue,
Sleep, love sleep.

Sleep, love sleep,
The pale moon looks down
On the valleys around,
The Glow Moth is flying,
The South wind is sighing,
And I am low lying,
With lute deftly strung,
To pour out my song,
Sleep, love sleep.

1897

The Coming Woman

Just look, 'tis a quarter past six, love—
    And not even the fires are caught;
Well, you know I must be at the office—
    But, as usual, the breakfast 'll be late.

Now hurry and wake up the children;
    And dress them as fast as you can;
'Poor dearies,' I know they'll be tardy,
    Dear me, 'what a slow, poky man!'

Have the tenderloin broiled nice and juicy—
    Have the toast browned and buttered all right;
And be sure you settle the coffee:
    Be sure that the silver is bright.

When ready, just run up and call me—
    At eight, to the office I go,
Lest poverty, grim, should o'ertake us—
    ' 'Tis bread and butter,' you know.

The bottom from stocks may fall out,
  My bonds may get below par;
Then surely, I seldom could spare you
  A nickel, to buy a cigar.

All ready? Now, while I am eating,
  Just bring up my wheel to the door;
Then wash up the dishes; and, mind now,
  Have dinner promptly at four;

For tonight is our Woman's Convention,
  And I am to speak first, you know—
The men veto us in private,
  But in public they shout, 'That's so.'

So 'by-by' – In case of a rap, love,
  Before opening the door, you must look;
O! how could a civilized woman
  Exist, without a man cook.

                                   1897

ELLA HIGGINSON
1862–1940

ELLA HIGGINSON was born in Council Grove, Kansas, youngest of three children. The family moved to eastern Oregon when she was young. She was educated in local schools and began submitting poems to newspapers while a schoolgirl. Around 1880 she married a pharmacist, Russell Carden Higginson, and moved to Bellingham, Washington. For several years she edited the literary department of the *Seattle Sunday Times*. Her stories were published in national magazines and collected in *The Flower that Grew in the Sand* (1896), *A Forest Orchid* (1897) and *From the Land of the Snow-Pearls* (1897). She published one novel, *Mariella, or Out West* (1904) and six volumes of poetry: *A Bunch of Western Clover* (1894), *Four-Leaf Clover* (1894), *When the Birds Go North Again* (1898), *The Voice of April Land* (1903), *The Vanishing Race and other Poems* (1911). Over fifty composers set her lyrics to music and her songs were performed by Caruso and others. She was named poet laureate of Washington in 1931. She actively participated in the women's club movement and the Washington State Federation of Women's Clubs issued a posthumous collection of her unpublished poems in 1941.

Four-Leaf Clover

I know a place where the sun is like gold,
    And the cherry blooms burst with snow,
And down underneath is the loveliest nook,
    Where the four-leaf clovers grow.

One leaf is for hope, and one is for faith,
    And one is for love, you know,
And God put another in for luck—
    If you search, you will find where they grow.

But you must have hope, and you must have faith,
　　You must love and be strong – and so—
If you work, if you wait, you will find the place
　　Where the four-leaf clovers grow.

Eve

Close to the gates of Paradise I flee;
　　The night is hot and serpents leave their beds,
　　And slide along the dark, crooking their heads,—
My God, my God, open the gates to me!

My eyes are burning so I cannot see;
　　My feet are bleeding and I suffer pain;
　　Let me come in on the cool grass again—
My God, my God, open the gates to me!

I ate the fruit of the forbidden tree,
　　And was cast out into the barren drouth;
　　And since – the awful taste within my mouth!
My God, my God, open the gates to me!

Am I shut out for all eternity?
　　I do repent me of my one black sin,
　　With prayers and tears of blood ... Let me come in!
My God, my God, open the gates to me!

Let me come in where birds and flowers be;
　　Let me once more lie naked in the grass
　　That trembles when the long wind-ripples pass!
Lord God, Lord God, open the gates to me!

Moonrise in the Rockies

The trembling train clings to the leaning wall
　　Of solid stone; a thousand feet below
Sinks a black gulf; the sky hangs like a pall
　　Upon the peaks of everlasting snow.

Then of a sudden springs a rim of light,
   Curved like a silver sickle. High and higher—
Till the full moon burns on the breast of night
   And a million firs stand tipped with lucent fire.

Dawn on the Willamette

Between the pale blue of the morning sky
   And the soft, deeper violet of the hill
   Mount Hood stands like a virgin, white and still.
The purple mists across the valley lie,
Run thro' and thro' with primrose lances – ay,
   With rose and amethyst. Sweet, loud and shrill,
   With little swelling throats, the dawn-birds trill
Their glad hearts out in praise; and proud and high,
The sun vibrates into the blue, and sets
   Willamette burning like a chain of brass,
   And all the steeples into silhouettes
Of flame against the sky. Up from the grass
   A pilgrim skylark soars, and throbbing higher,
   Shakes all the air with passion and desire.

A Dream of Sappho

The little hollows in the pavements shine
   With the soft, hesitating April rain,
   That sifts across the city, gray and fine,
And on the huddling, spent waves of the main,—
Where the wild, silver seabirds wheel and scream.
   It is a day to lie before the fire,
   Turning the key on Thought and Care, and dream
Of dark-eyed Sappho and her passioned lyre;
Her sun-warmed courts columned above the sea;
   Blue skies of Lesbos – ay, and of the kiss
   Of the South wind among her bower's leaves.
Who could regret the day's monotony,

In the full rapture of a dream like this—
Set to the faltering music of the eaves!

'The Opal Sea'

An inland sea – blue as a sapphire – set
   Within a sparkling, emerald mountain chain
   Where day and night fir-needles sift like rain
Thro' the voluptuous air. The soft winds fret
The waves, and beat them wantonly to foam.
   The golden distances across the sea
   Are shot with rose and purple. Languorously
The silver seabirds in wide circles roam.
The sun drops slowly down the flaming West
   And flings its rays across to set aglow
   The islands rocking on the cool waves' crest
And the great glistening domes of snow on snow.
   And thro' the mist the Olympics flash and float
   Like opals linked around a beating throat.

Dawn

The soft-toned clock upon the stair chimed three—
   Too sweet for sleep, too early yet to rise.
   In restful peace I lay with half-closed eyes,
Watching the tender hours go dreamily;
The tide was flowing in; I heard the sea
   Shivering along the sands; while yet the skies
   Were dim, uncertain, as the light that lies
Beneath the fretwork of some wild-rose tree
Within the thicket gray. The chanticleer
   Sent drowsy calls across the slumbrous air;
   In solemn silence sweet it was to hear
My own heart beat ... Then broad and deep and fair—
   Trembling in its new birth from heaven's womb—
   One crimson shaft of dawn sank thro' my room.

The Statue

That I might chisel a statue, line on line,
   Out of a marble's chaste severities!
   Angular, harsh; no softened curves to please;
Set tears within the eyes to make them shine,
And furrows on the brow, deep, stern, yet fine;
   Gaunt, awkward, tall; no courtier of ease;
   The trousers bulging at the bony knees;
Long nose, large mouth ... But ah, the light divine
Of Truth, – the light that set a people free!—
   Burning upon it in a steady flame,
   As sunset fires a white peak on the sky ...
Ah, God! To leave it nameless and yet see
   Men looking weep and bow themselves and cry—
   'Enough, enough! We know thy statue's name!'

CAROLYN WELLS
1862–1942

CAROLYN WELLS was born in Rahway, New Jersey. Scarlet fever at age six led to a progressive hearing loss. A precocious learner, after graduating as valedictorian of her high school she studied literature, languages and science on her own, taking friends as mentors. Early publications appeared in the British humour magazine *Punch*, and *The Lark*, a small San Francisco magazine published by Gelett Burgess, leader of the 1890s craze for nonsense verse, who critiqued her writing. Among her parodies are rewrites of Burgess's 'The Purple Cow' in the styles of famous poets, supposedly penned by a women's club. Her early nonsense verse is collected in *Idle Idyls* (1900). A highly productive woman of letters, Wells is credited with establishing the humour anthology as a commodity. Her best-known collection was *The Nonsense Anthology* (1902). She wrote more than seventy-five mystery and detective stories, and *The Technique of the Mystery Story* (1913, 1929), a pioneer work on the genre, remains well regarded. She also wrote stories for youth. She collected rare books and was known among bibliophiles for her editions of Walt Whitman and Edward Lear. In 1918 she married Hadwin Houghton, who died a year later. Thereafter she lived in New York City. Her auto-biography, *The Rest of My Life* (1937), tells anecdotes of literary life.

Fate

Two shall be born the whole world wide apart,
And speak in different tongues, and pay their debts
In different kinds of coin; and give no heed
Each to the other's being. And know not
That each might suit the other to a T,
If they were but correctly introduced.
And these, unconsciously, shall bend their steps,

Escaping Spaniards and defying war,
Unerringly toward the same trysting-place,
Albeit they know it not. Until at last
They enter the same door, and suddenly
They meet. And ere they've seen each other's face
They fall into each other's arms, upon
The Broadway cable car – and this is Fate!

The Poster Girl's Defence

It was an Artless Poster Girl pinned up against my wall,
She was tremendous ugly, she was exceeding tall;
I was gazing at her idly, and I think I must have slept,
For that poster maiden lifted up her poster voice, and wept.

She said between her poster sobs, 'I think it's rather rough
To be jeered and fleered and flouted, and I've stood it long
    enough;
I'm tired of being quoted as a Fright and Fad and Freak,
And I take this opportunity my poster mind to speak.

'Although my hair is carmine and my nose is edged with blue,
Although my style is splashy and my shade effects are few,
Although I'm out of drawing and my back hair is a show,
Yet I have n't half the whimseys of the maidens that you know.

'I never keep you waiting while I prink before the glass,
I never talk such twaddle as that little Dawson lass,
I never paint on china, nor erotic novels write,
And I never have recited "Curfew must not ring tonight".

'I don't rave over Ibsen, I never, never flirt,
I never wear a shirt waist with a disconnected skirt;
I never speak in public on "The Suffrage", or "The Race",
I never talk while playing whist, or trump my partner's ace.'

I said: 'O artless Poster Girl, you're in the right of it,
You are a joy forever, though a thing of beauty, nit!'
And from her madder eyebrows to her utmost purple swirl,
Against all captious critics I'll defend the Poster Girl.

A Pastoral in Posters

The mid-day moon lights up the rocky sky;
　The great hills flutter in the greenish breeze;
While far above the lowing turtles fly
　And light upon the pinky-purple trees.

The gleaming trill of jagged, feathered rocks
　I hear with glee as swift I fly away,
And over waves of subtle woolly flocks
　Crashes the breaking day!

The Original Summer Girl

After much biologic research,
　From evidence strong, I believe
　　That I have found out
　　Beyond shadow of doubt
　That the first Summer Girl was Eve.

She had unconventional ways,
　She lived out-of-doors, and all that;
　　She was tanned by the sun
　　Until brown as a bun,
　For she roamed 'round without any hat.

To a small garden-party she went,
　Where the men were exceedingly few;
　　But she captured a mate
　　And settled her fate,
　As often these Summer Girls do.

Now, my statement of course I have proved,
　But as evidence that is n't all;
　　A Summer Girl she
　　Is conceded to be
　Because she staid there till the Fall.

A Problem

There's a whimsey in my noddle, there's a maggot in my
    brain,
There's a doubt upon my spirit that I cannot quite explain.

'T is a grave, important question over which I vacillate,—
Does Enlightenment enlighten, and does Culture cultivate?

We are of the Cognoscenti, and intuitively know
Just the shades of thoughtful fancy that an author ought to
    show.

But from our exalted level should we drop a poisoned hint
To the placid ones who wallow in the sordid slums of print?

Should the Unenlightened Readers be sardonically hissed
If they like a Duchess novel better than *The Egoist*?

Should we rare ones who inhabit the exalted realms of
    thought,
Dictate to the Unenlightened what they ought n't or they
    ought?

To the masses should our classes offer Ibsen when we find
Mr Caine and Miss Corelli better please the massy mind?

Should we shudder to discover that they cannot get the pith
Of the tenebrastic subtleties of Mr Meredith?

Should we rudely contradict them when they confidently say,
'Omar wrote *The Iliad* and Holmes' first name was Mary J.'?

Or shall we abandon flatly this whole altruistic fight,
With the philosophic dictum that 'Whatever is, is right'?

Then, instead of wasting time in teaching others how to think,
We can spend those precious moments with Hafiz or
    Maeterlinck.

Let us stop our futile task of pointing to the open door,
Let the Enlightened cease enlightening and the Cultured cult
    no more.

Of Modern Books

(A Pantoum)

Of making many books there is no end,
  Though myriads have to deep oblivion gone;
Each day new manuscripts are being penned,
  And still the ceaseless tide of ink flows on.

Though myriads have to deep oblivion gone,
  New volumes daily issue from the press;
And still the ceaseless tide of ink flows on—
  The prospect is disheartening, I confess.

New volumes daily issue from the press;
  My pile of unread books I view aghast.
The prospect is disheartening, I confess;
  Why will these modern authors write so fast?

My pile of unread books I view aghast—
  Of course I must keep fairly up to date—
Why will these modern authors write so fast?
  They seem to get ahead of me of late.

Of course I must keep fairly up to date;
  The books of special merit I must read;
They seem to get ahead of me of late,
  Although I skim them very fast indeed.

The books of special merit I must read;
  And then the magazines come round again;
Although I skim them very fast indeed,
  I can't get through with more than eight or ten.

And then the magazines come round *again*!
  How can we stem this tide of printer's ink?
I can't get through with more than eight or ten—
  It is appalling when I stop to think.

How can we stem this tide of printer's ink?
  Of making many books there is no end.
It is appalling when I stop to think
  Each day new manuscripts are being penned!

VOLTAIRINE DE CLEYRE
1866–1912

VOLTAIRINE DE CLEYRE was born in Leslie, Michigan. Her father, a freethinker from Flanders, named her after the philosopher Voltaire. She graduated from a convent school in Ontario, then wrote sketches under several pseudonyms, including Fanny Forester, for *The Progressive Age*. Following the 1887 conviction of five labour leaders charged with bombing Haymarket Square in Chicago, she converted to anarchism and began lecturing for the American Secular Union and the Woman's National Liberal Union. She spent much of her life thereafter in Philadelphia, where she tutored immigrants. She helped found the Ladies' Liberal League in 1892, spoke in defence of anarchist-feminist Emma Goldman, and contributed to Goldman's journal *Mother Earth*. Her political poems were widely published and translated into several languages; she also translated works from French and Hebrew and collaborated with fellow activist Dyer Lum on an uncompleted novel. She opposed stereotyped gender roles and rejected marriage, bearing a son with James B. Elliot. Her most enduring relationship was with Lum, who died in 1893. In 1897 she toured France and Britain lecturing for labour organisations. In 1902 she survived an attempted assassination but refused to press charges against her attacker. Though she never fully recovered from her injuries, she remained active in radical causes.

Out of the Darkness

Who am I? Only one of the commonest common people,
Only a worked-out body, a shriveled and withered soul,
What right have I to sing then? None; and I do not, I cannot.
Why ruin the rhythm and rhyme of the great world's songs with
    moaning?

I know not – nor why whistles must shriek, wheels ceaselessly
    mutter;
Nor why all I touch turns to clanging and clashing and discord;
I know not; – I know only this, – I was born to this, live in it
    hourly,
Go round with it, hum with it, curse with it, would laugh with
    it, had it laughter;
It is my breath – and that breath goes outward from me in
    moaning.

O you, up there, I have heard you; I am 'God's image defaced',
'In heaven reward awaits me,' 'hereafter I shall be perfect';
Ages you've sung that song, but what is it to me, think you?
If you heard down here in the smoke and the smut, in the smear
    and the offal,
In the dust, in the mire, in the grime and in the slime, in the
    hideous darkness,
How the wheels turn your song into sounds of horror and
    loathing and cursing,
The offer of lust, the sneer of contempt and acceptance, thieves'
    whispers,
The laugh of the gambler, the suicide's gasp, the yell of the
    drunkard,
If you heard them down here you would cry, 'The reward of
    such is damnation,'
If you heard them, I say, your song of 'rewarded hereafter' would
    fail.

You, too, with your science, your titles, your books, and your
    long explanations
That tell me how I am come up out of the dust of the cycles,
Out of the sands of the sea, out of the unknown primeval
    forests,—
Out of the growth of the world have become the bud and the
    promise,—
Out of the race of the beasts have arisen, proud and
    triumphant,—
You, if you knew how your words rumble round in the wheels
    of labor!
If you knew how my hammering heart beats, 'Liar, liar, you lie!
Out of all buds of the earth we are most blasted and blighted!
What beast of all the beasts is not prouder and freer than we?'

You, too, who sing in high words of the glory of Man universal,
The beauty of sacrifice, debt of the future, the present immortal,
The glory of use, absorption by Death of the being in Being,
You, if you knew what jargon it makes, down here, would be
    quiet.

Oh, is there no one to find or to speak a meaning to *me*,
To me as I am, – the hard, the ignorant, withered-souled worker?
To me upon whom God and Science alike have stamped 'failure',
To me who know nothing but labor, nothing but sweat, dirt, and
    sorrow,
To me whom you scorn and despise, you up there who sing while
    I moan?
To me as I am, – for me as I am – not dying but living;
Not my future, my present! my body, my needs, my desires! Is
    there no one,
In the midst of this rushing of phantoms – of Gods, of Science,
    of Logic,
Of Philosophy, Morals, Religion, Economy, – all this that helps
    not,
All these ghosts at whose altars you worship, these ponderous,
    marrowless Fictions,
Is there no one who thinks, is there nothing to help this dull
    moaning me?

                          1893

Love's Compensation

I went before God, and he said,
    'What fruit of the life I gave?'
'Father,' I said, 'It is dead,
    And nothing grows on the grave.'

Wroth was the Lord and stern:
    'Hadst thou not to answer me?
Shall the fruitless root not burn,
    And be wasted utterly?'

'Father,' I said, 'forgive!
    For thou knowest what I have done;

That another's life might live
   Mine turned to a barren stone.'

But the Father of Life sent fire
   And burned the root in the grave;
And the pain in my heart is dire
   For the thing that I could not save.

For the thing it was laid on me
   By the Lord of Life to bring;
Fruit of the ungrown tree
   That died for no watering.

Another has gone to God,
   And his fruit has pleased Him well;
For he sitteth high, while I – plod
   The dry ways down towards hell.

Though thou knowest, thou knowest, Lord,
   Whose tears made that fruit's root wet;
Yet thou drivest me forth with a sword,
   And thy Guards by the Gate are set.

Thou wilt give me up to the fire,
   And none shall deliver me;
For I followed my heart's desire,
   And I labored not for thee:

I labored for him thou hast set
   On thy right hand, high and fair;
Thou lovest him, Lord; and yet
   'Twas my love won Him there.

But this is the thing that hath been,
   Hath been since the world began,—
That love against self must sin,
   And a woman die for a man.

And this is the thing that shall be,
   Shall be till the whole world die,
Kismet: – My doom is on me!
   Why murmur since I am I?

1898

PRISCILLA JANE THOMPSON
1871–1942

PRISCILLA JANE THOMPSON was born in Rossmoyne, Ohio, daughter of former slaves. Her mother died when she was a child. She and her sister Clara lived with an older brother and were educated in public schools and by tutors. She self-published her first book of poems, *Ethiope Lays* (1900), which she introduced as an endeavour to depict African Americans realistically and positively. Among the poems are a few experiments with dialect, which features in *Gleanings of Quiet Hours* (1907). Clara and a younger brother, Aaron Belford Thompson, also published volumes of poems.

Freedom at McNealy's

All around old Chattanooga,
    War had left his wasteful trace;
And the rebels, quelled and baffled,
    Freed, reluctantly their slaves.

On his spacious, cool, veranda—
    Stood McNealy, gaunt and tall,
With bowed head, and long arms folded,
    Pond'ring on his blacks, enthralled.

Years and years, he'd been their master,
    Harsh and stern his reign had been;
Many an undeserving lashing,
    He had rudely given them.

All his life he'd been a despot;
    Ruling all with iron hand;
Never till this deadly conflict,
    Had he e'er brooked one command.

But his lately rich plantation,
    Sacked by Union men he see:
And the bitter dregs stand waiting:
    He must set his bondmen free.

From their work, they come together,
    At their master's last command,
And at length, well-nigh two hundred
    'Fore the large veranda stand.

Oh! that motley crowd before him,
    Speaks the wrong one man has done;
For his constant, dire oppression,
    Can be seen on every one.

Men of middle age all palsied,
    By hard work and sorrow's pain;
Blighted youths and orphaned infants;
    All had felt his cruel reign.

There were women fair who knew him,
    To be more of brute than man;
There were children clinging to them,
    Through whose veins his own blood ran.

Widowed hearts in swarthy bosoms,
    Ever bled in patient pain,
O'er their loved ones, sold before them,
    To increase McNealy's gain.

All of this preys on McNealy,
    As before his slaves he stands;
And his low'ring, dogged, expression,
    Speaks the power that's left his hands.

And, with quivering voice and husky,
    Tells he that each one is free;
Tells them of his heavy losses,
    Meanly seeking sympathy.

And the soft hearts of his vassals,
    Melts, as only Ethiopes' can;
As with brimming eyes and kind words,
    Each one grasps his tyrant's hands.

One by one, they've all departed;
  Man and woman, boy and girl;
Void of learning, inexperienced,
  Launched upon the crafty world.

But one cabin is not empty,
  Two old souls are kneeling there;
In the throes of desolation,
  They have sought their Lord in prayer.

They have never tasted freedom,
  And their youthful hopes are fled;
Now, the freedom they are seeking,
  Is with Jesus and the dead.

Poor aunt Jude and uncle Simon!
  Freedom brings to them no cheer;
They have served McNealy's fam'ly—
  For three score, or more of years.

Steep and rough, the road they've traveled,
  Many were their heartfelt groans—
Yet they cleave unto their tyrant,
  For his lash, is all they've known.

Like a bird of long confinement,
  Cleaves unto his open cage,
These two wretched slaves, benighted,
  Clave to bondage, in their age.

And they sought McNealy humbly,
  With their hearts filled to the brim;
Told him, all their days remaining,
  They would gladly give to him.

And McNealy, pleased and flattered,
  With no feeling of remorse,
Takes them back into his service,
  As you would a faithful horse.

                                  1900

My Father's Story

There is an ancient story,
That my father used to tell—
When out side all were hoary,
And still the snowdrops fell;
While the rolling hills about us,
Seemed sinking to the dell.
When heavy snows prevented
All outside exercise,
Our fam'ly group, contented,
Sought amusement otherwise;
Then, my father, smiling blandly,
Would tell his tale thiswise:
'When a boy, I well remembah,
How th' ole folks use to tell,
'Bout a rich man, in Virginyah,
Who was mean and close as well;
And his po' slaves late and early,
Tilled his fields, whate'er befell.
All day long with oaths tremendous,
He, his weary slaves would drive,
And his urging lash, malicious,
Did the setting sun survive;
And each sunrise found his bondmen,
Grieving that they were alive.
Oft the piercing cry of woman—
Rent the placid ev'ning air,
And the foul lash, at his summun,
Left her swooning in despair;
While the rude whelks on her person,
Marred the beauty, ling'ring there.
Oft the aged, maimed and feeble,
Fell before his brutal blow,
While he hurried on, unheedful,
Of their groans of utter woe—
Or the look of bitter anguish,
In their tearful eyes of sloe.
One ev'ning, atter set of sun,
When the moon-beams faintly shown,

When two days' work were forced in one,
By the dint of fierceness shown,
This evil man sat on his porch,
Which vines had overgrown.
And the blue smoke, odorif'rous,
Rose up from his pipe of clay,
While his evil mind, assiduous,
Labored o'er a sternah way,
To force from his wornout bondmen,
Greatah tasks the coming day.
Pond'ring thus, with evil foresight,
With his glassy eyes half closed—
Through the smoke and misty moonlight,
An uncanny object rose;
'Though he rubbed his eyes with vigah,
Still it lingered in repose.
'Twas an object, grim and massive,
Lurking near his grand abode;
Crouching ever, calm and passive,
Whilst the misty moonbeams glowed,
And its rude shape, in the dim light,
Loomed up like a giant toad.
Up he sprung, by terrah shakened—
With his hands to temples pressed.
And the spook, as if awakened,
From its deep, still, passiveness
Quivered in a blue blaze, frightful—
Then, dissolved to nothingness.
Long he stood there, terrah strickened,
Staring at the vacance, grim,
And his heart within him sickened—
While a trembling seized his limbs—
And the cold sweat on his forehead,
Glistened in the moonlight, dim.
Thenceforth, when with over fierceness,
He would press his bondmen, sore,
And his cruel, foul, perverseness,
Made them their sad lot deplore,
This grim spook, at fall of ev'ning,
Threat'ningly would haunt his door.
But, by frequent visitation,

Ever harmless, ling'ring near—
'Last, its evil premonition,
Lost its meaning on his ear;
And with recklessness, defiant,
He forgot his cow'ring fear.
Once, when with unusual madness,
He, his viciousness, had shown,
And his bondmen, bowed in sadness—
To their wretched huts, had gone,
In the quietness of even,
He sat on his porch, alone.
Softly, zephyrs from the rushes,
Swept the smooth cut lawn of green.
While the shadows, of the bushes,
Like black dye on grass did seem,
And the dew, on bud and leaflet,
Shown like gems of Orient dream.
As he sat there staring idly,
Out into the lovely night,
Wrapt in blue blaze, quiv'ring wildly.
His old haunt flashed on his sight—
And with sudden impulse, quickly,
Anger took the place of fright.
With an oath, he seized his rifle;
And with coolness, took good aim;
But his gun hung fire a trifle,
Seeming fearful of the game—
And was loath to speed its bullet,
To that ghostly, frightful, flame.
When the rifle rang out clearly,
And the bullet true, had sped,
This old spook, with hiss and groanings,
Leapt into a huge blaze red,
And, with flying sparks, o'er covered,
This vile man, fell backward, dead.
Children, God sent forth that spirit,
As a warning, to that man;
But he passed it by, unheeded;
So God took another plan—
And he called him to his judgment,
As he oft does sinful man.'

Then my father, sadly smiling,
With his patient, worn, hands claspt,
Would, with gentle air, beguiling,
Fall to musing on the past—
Of his earlier life in bondage—
Mindless of the winter's blast.

1900

NOTES

Eliza Lee Follen

p. 3 'Lines on Nonsense': Follen praises nonsense at a time when the word was generally a dismissive pejorative, well before the verse of Edward Lear (1812–88) and Lewis Carroll (1832–98) established nonsense poetry as a modern genre. In the 1832 introduction to *Little Songs* Follen states her wish 'to catch something of that good-humored pleasantry, that musical nonsense, which makes Mother Goose so attractive to children of all ages' – to capture the sensory pleasure of nursery rhymes with folk origins, whose historical references, often political, have been lost, or are lost on children. The heightening of sound and suppression of meaning are common to later nonsense verse, though it often encrypts satire (see Carolyn Wells's poems, pp. 279–83).

p. 5 'For the Fourth of July': Follen uses a common rhetorical strategy of radical abolitionism, inverting patriotic Republican rhetoric with a confrontative denunciation of slavery (e.g., Frederick Douglass condemned celebrations of the Fourth of July in 1852).

Sarah Josepha Hale

p. 8 'Mary's Lamb': Hale's purpose in writing children's poetry contrasts with Follen's (above): 'I know children love to read rhymes, and sing little verses; but they often read silly rhymes, and such manner of spending their time is not good. I intended, when I began to write this book, to furnish you with a few pretty songs and poems which would teach you truths, and, I hope, induce you to love truth and goodness. Children who love their parents and their home, can soon teach their hearts to love their God and their country' ('To all Good Children in the United States', *Poems for Our Children*, 1830).

p. 8 *from* 'Three Hours; or, The Vigil of Love': Hale's long poem, 'Three Hours; or, The Vigil of Love', casts as legend a founding moment in American children's literature, with mothers playing a central role in producing a new kind of subject, free of the pre-modern superstitions that haunt their own minds. The poem follows the thoughts and actions of a seventeenth-century colonial woman as she waits, tending a sick child, from nine to twelve o'clock on a stormy night for her husband to return from a meeting of community leaders. The setting is a cabin at the edge of a wilderness settlement, the precursor to Boston. The stanzas on reading open reveries about her aristocratic origins in England as Lady Grace Talbot and her elopement to the New World with Sydney Morton, a Puritan whom her father had planned to execute. Hale reminds the reader that this was the age of superstition, before minds were freed by the alliance of Christianity with science. Waiting, Grace remembers frightening stories her mother told her, the key one being of a knight imprisoned in a haunted castle who kept demons away by prayer. Her mother taught her to fend off evil by praying every hour as the clock struck. She follows this advice, though she vows not to terrorise her own child with such stories but instead to instil hope in him by teaching him God is love. When her child pleads for water, she discovers that all the water has leaked out of the cracked drinking vessel. Fearful of Indians though mother love has conquered her fear of the supernatural, she takes an Indian trail through the pitch-dark night to fetch water from a spring. She returns too late to pray at midnight and, entering the cabin, sees what she thinks is a fiend bending over her son. It is only her husband Morton.

Hannah F. Gould

p. 10 'Apprehension': compare with Mary Mapes Dodge's 'The Wooden Horse' (p. 155) for a striking sense of the differences between an antebellum and a postbellum view of childhood.

p. 11 'The Butterfly's Dream': mechanics: vulgar manual labourers.

p. 13 'The Child's Address to the Kentucky Mummy': the American Antiquarian Society of Boston had in a display cabinet the naturally mummified body of a woman, found in a cave in Kentucky.

Lydia Huntley Sigourney

p. 15 'Death of an Infant': reaches towards sonnet form but without rhyme and with the last line cut short. Note the many caesuras (grammatical breaks) in the middles of lines.

p. 15 signet-ring: a finger ring engraved with an official seal or stamp, equivalent to a signature.

p. 15 'Indian Names': the condemnatory last two stanzas of this poem were omitted from a luxury edition of Sigourney's revisions, *Illustrated Poems*, in 1856. The softened version of the poem has been frequently anthologised.

p. 20 'Erin's Daughter': years of near-famine conditions in Ireland culminated in the Great Famine of 1845–7 when hundreds of thousands died of starvation. The first major wave of Irish emigration began during this period, with nearly 800,000 Irish entering the United States in the 1840s and nearly a million in the 1850s. More unaccompanied women arrived from Ireland than from other points of origin.

Caroline Gilman

p. 22: Other games included in *Oracles for Youth* lead with the following questions: What is your character? What is your favourite youthful game? What is your favourite study? What are your favourite names? Who is your girlfriend? Who is your boyfriend? What do you like to be, or do? What is your favourite flower? What sport do you prefer? What musical instrument do you love? What will be your profession? What distinguished classical character do you admire? What is your favourite mythological character? What is your favourite constellation? Notably, few of these youth games are differentiated by gender while most of Gilman's adult games (*The Sybil* and *Oracles of the Poets*) are.

p. 23 carriage-and-four: a luxury vehicle drawn by four horses; a status symbol.

p. 23 nabob: a prominent or wealthy person in its general usage. The term originally referred to provincial governors of the Mogul empire in India.

Penina Moise

p. 27 'To Persecuted Foreigners': despite resolutions to uphold Jewish freedoms in the Congress of Vienna (1814), nationalistic anti-Semitic demonstrations swept through Germany in 1819.

p. 28 'The Newspaper': Caliph: a successor to Muhammed as temporal and spiritual head of Islam. In the *Arabian Nights*, the Caliph of Baghdad, Harun al-Rashid, leaves his palace disguised as a merchant 'to see and hear what new thing was stirring'.

p. 28 Vezier: vizier – high executive officer of the Turkish empire.

p. 28 The British prototype of '65: *Oxford Gazette*, later *London Gazette*, first published 1665.

p. 28 Clio: muse of history and heroic poetry.

p. 28 Kent: faithful courtier who serves Lear disguised as a servant and is put in the stocks by Lear's treacherous son-in-law Cornwall. Shakespeare, *King Lear*.

p. 29 One fugitive forsakes the Cotton pod: a slave escapes a cotton plantation.

Jane Johnston Schoolcraft

p. 30 'Otagamiad': combines the name of the Outagamis (Fox tribe) with the Greek suffix '-ad' signifying the title of a poem (as in *Iliad*). Allies in the seventeenth century, the Ojibwa and Outagamis became foe when the latter allied with the Sioux, with whom the Ojibwa were in longstanding conflict over territories.

p. 30 LaPointé: in the Apostle Islands in Lake Superior off the north coast of Wisconsin.

p. 30 Ojeeg: Schoolcraft's grandfather, Waub Ojeeg (d. 1793). His tribe was allied to the French until 1759 when the British took Quebec; they allied with the British in conflicts from the Revolutionary War to the War of 1812. From around 1770–90 Waub Ojeeg was head of his tribe, leading seven campaigns against the Outagamis and Sioux. The 'Otagamiad' probably refers to the last and largest of these campaigns, organised through war-dances and assemblies and drawing fighters from all along the southern coasts of Lake Superior, resulting in Ojibwa victory. The oration that Waub Ojeeg composed for this campaign endured in oral tradition, was rendered in English by Schoolcraft's father John Johnston, and was likely the inspiration for 'Otagamiad'.

p. 32 Camudẃa: a past sound (Henry Rowe Schoolcraft's note).

p. 32 Baimwáwa: the passing thunder (Henry Rowe Schoolcraft's note).

p. 33 Keewaydin: the North Wind (Henry Rowe Schoolcraft's note).

p. 33 Dacota: the Dakota, Native American people of the northern Mississippi valley.

p. 33 Canowakeed: he who takes after the wind (Henry Rowe Schoolcraft's note).

Elizabeth Oakes-Smith

p. 34 'The Sinless Child': a seven-part poem about an ideal self, recalling William Wordsworth's Lucy poems and 'Ode: Intimations of Immortality from Recollections of Early Childhood' (1807) and the preternaturalism of Samuel Taylor Coleridge's 'Christabel' (1816). Albert Linne, a rake and wastrel who only needs a female ideal to reform him, recalls the persona of Byron.

Part I: Eva lives in a humble cottage with her widowed mother. Even as a child, she has a profound communion with nature, perceiving divine agency and hidden truth everywhere. Part II: her hard-working mother does not understand her gift, but Eva tries to explain the presence of spirits in nature and the purpose of human feeling to draw people heavenward. Part III: as Eva matures, her mother worries about her health because of her pallor, strange ways and disinterest in love. Eva explains that, because of her gift, she must be alone. She reveals to her mother that newborn children bear the 'signet-mark' of heaven, which a bad conscience gradually effaces; that human life could be Edenic still if people did not succumb to wickedness. She then describes the effects of various sins, ending with murder. Part IV: Eva and her mother continue discussing Eva's philosophy: a human life is a book on which all one's deeds are recorded. Eva tells the story of old mad Richard, once prosperous and happy, and poor Lucy, an unwed mother whose innocent son Richard apparently murdered. Part V: Eva next tells the story of a woman who abuses her stepchildren while the spirit of their dead mother returns to care for them. Part VI: Eva's meeting with Albert Linne. Part VII: Eva, having fulfilled her destiny, goes to bed and dies. Albert is a changed man and lives a pious, charitable life with his 'spirit bride' always near his heart.

Frances Anne Kemble

p. 43 Sonnet, 'What is my lady like?': the genre is *blason médaillon*, a descriptive inventory, most often in the sonnet tradition a male-authored inventory of the female body.

p. 45 'Faith': Kemble's most popular poem, frequently anthologised.

p. 45 'Sonnet': laurel leaf: emblem of distinction in poetry, from the myth

of Daphne, who was changed into a laurel tree to escape being raped by
Apollo, god of music.

Margaret Fuller

p. 47 'Meditations': thunder: Fuller is musing sceptically about an experience
of theophany such as that experienced by Moses on Mount Sinai when he
received the Ten Commandments.

p. 48 Novalis: pen name of Friedrich Leopold, Freiherr von Hardenberg
(1772–1801), leading poet of early German Romanticism, who believed
man's goal was to regain a lost mystical communion with nature. Fuller read
Novalis while teaching herself German in 1833.

p. 49 'The One in All': Moxen: moksha or moksa. Buddhist term for union
with the divine mind, liberation of the soul from further transmigration;
equated with nirvana in some sources.

p. 51 'Lines Written in Boston on a Beautiful Autumnal Day': Fuller was
involved in the planning of Brook Farm, a communistic experimental community, founded in 1841, aimed at sharing and minimising menial labour
and maximising time for education and spiritual development. Though she
never joined Brook Farm, she visited frequently, making her longest visit in
the autumn of 1842.

p. 51 Adonis' gardens: Adonis was a beautiful youth of Greek mythology,
loved by the goddesses Aphrodite and Persephone, ordered by Zeus to live
half the year in the underworld with Persephone and half on earth with
Aphrodite.

p. 52 Mr Lyell: Sir Charles Lyell (1797–1875), British geologist, made lecture
and study tours of the United States in 1845 and 1849. Lyell's geology was
part of the Victorian scientific challenge to traditional Christian views of the
earth's origin.

Mary S. B. Dana Shindler

p. 53 'Real Comfort': Dana self-mockingly portrays herself as a Bluestocking,
originally a code word that a late-eighteenth-century British literary circle
used to refer to fellow members (male and female), later a stereotype of
eccentricity applied to literary women.

Rebekah Gumpert Hyneman

p. 56 'Judith': a Jewish heroine whose story is told in the book of Judith in the Apocrypha. To save her city Bethulia from the assault of Holofernes, general of Assyrian king Nebuchadnezzar, Judith enters his camp and beheads him as he sleeps off a drunken stupor. See note in 'The Poets and Their Critics' (p. 348). For a different approach to the story, see Adah Isaacs Menken's 'Judith' (p. 197).

p. 57 falchion: broad-bladed curved sword.

p. 58 'Woman's Rights': see 'The Poets and Their Critics' (p. 348). For other statements on women's rights, see Ada, 'The Scroll is Open' (p. 61), and Coolidge, 'My Rights' (p. 174).

Ada (Sarah Louisa Forten)

p. 60 'An Appeal to Women': read at the first Anti-Slavery Convention of American Women (1837).

p. 61 'The Scroll is Open': At the first Anti-Slavery Convention of American Women, women abolitionists initiated the tactic of flooding Congress with anti-slavery petitions, one of their most important contributions to the abolitionist movement. The citizen petition was an established political tradition, but Congress had passed a gag rule against discussions of slavery in 1836. The flood of petitions against slavery precipitated a crisis in Congress over the right to petition. See Hyneman, 'Woman's Rights' (p. 58), and Coolidge, 'My Rights' (p. 174), for other statements concerning women's duties and rights.

Catherine Ana Warfield and Eleanor Percy Lee

p. 64 'The Sun-Struck Eagle': the American bald eagle became an emblem of the United States with approval of the seal design in 1782. Warfield and Lee combine the national emblem with the Romantic idea of genius, drawing on the classical myth of Icarus, a boy who flew too high on artificial wings and fell into the sea. For a contrasting postbellum story of eagles, see Mary Mapes Dodge, 'Taking Time to Grow' (p. 156). See also Dickinson's eagle in 'Victory comes late' (p. 141).

p. 65 'Forests and Caverns': Kentucky landscape was renowned, by early in the nineteenth century, for its vast system of limestone caves, particularly

Mammoth Cave some eighty-five miles south of Louisville where Warfield lived.

Julia Ward Howe

p. 67 'Battle-Hymn of the Republic': see 'The Poets and Their Critics' (p. 346).

p. 68 'Lyrics of the Street': omitted in this selection from the poem cycle are 'The Telegrams', 'The Wedding', 'The Funeral', 'The Charitable Visitor', 'The Fine Lady', 'The Darkened House', 'The Old Man's Walk', 'At a Corner', 'The Black Coach', 'Play'; the cycle ends with 'The Lost Jewel', 'Outside the Party', 'The Soul-Hunter', and 'Street Yarn'. The cycle overall is concerned with gender and class in urban modernity and with traces of the sacred in the secular city.

p. 72 'The House of Rest': see Jackson, 'My House Not Made with Hands' (p. 146); Coolidge, 'A Home' (p. 172); and Charlotte Gilman, 'Homes' (p. 249), for other meditations on houses, homes and domesticity.

Ann Plato

p. 76 'The True Friend': Ruth: Moabite heroine of the Biblical book of Ruth, who vows to remain with her Hebrew mother-in-law Naomi after the death of her husband (Ruth, 1:16). Plato may be speaking of an intimate female friend or of an internal self.

p. 77 That gold most pure: quotes Matthew, 6:19–21 from Christ's Sermon on the Mount.

Alice Cary

p. 78 'The Window Just Over the Street': 'I think of a dear little sun-lighted head': as in Howe's 'Lyrics of the Street', a sexually transgressing woman is a central figure in Cary's urban street scene. In American, British and European nineteenth-century art, literature and non-fiction writing, fallen women (often suicides by drowning) served as icons of male alienation and cautions to women aspiring to public life. Especially interesting in this poem is the voyeurism of the (female) speaker, a stance usually associated with men.

p. 81 'In Bonds': Cary, who supported abolition, uses images from the slave trade and conditions of enslavement to describe a generalised human condition.

p. 82 'The West Country': Gay girls at work in the factories: the mills of New England, which employed young women labourers starting in the 1820s. Compare this view of the prospects for homesteaders' children with that of Mollie Moore Davis, 'Going Out and Coming In' (p. 231); see also Emily Dickinson's 'Her Sweet turn to leave the Homestead' (p. 136) for a variation on this theme.

Margaret Junkin Preston

p. 85 'Erinna's Spinning': besides the suppressed rebellion against gender role expectations evident in this poem, Preston places in a classical setting the contrasting antebellum economic systems of the northern and southern states, and particularly a white woman's role in those systems. Urging her daughter to conform to a heterosexual role, Erinna's mother counsels her to be an industrious producer and skilled consumer of fabrics (northern industrial capitalism), while she longs for the aristocratic leisure to pursue the arts and other personal achievements like Sappho and her group of Lesbian youths, who are accompanied by slaves.

p. 85 Erinna: the name of Preston's heroine associates her with the Erinyes, Furies, snake-haired avenging daughters of Uranus in Greek mythology.

p. 85 Lesbian: pertaining to the Greek island Lesbos, where the poet Sappho lived in the seventh century BC. Sappho led a group of young women musicians and poets devoted to the worship of Aphrodite.

p. 85 Mytilené: the principal city of Lesbos.

p. 86 Acanthus: a prickly herb.

p. 86 Dryad: wood nymph.

p. 86 Isthmian games: sports competition held at the Isthmus of Corinth in ancient Greece.

p. 87 Delphian lyre: stringed instrument of Delphi, ancient city in central Greece.

p. 87 Æolian: Greek people who colonised Lesbos and the nearby coast of Asia Minor. Doubles as a reference to British romantic poetry; Samuel Taylor Coleridge made the 'aeolian harp' a symbol of the oversoul's play on the individual soul.

p. 87 Artemis: virginal goddess of hunting.

p. 87 Pythius: Pythius, surname of Apollo, brother of Artemis.

p. 87 Queen of Heaven: Hera, sister and wife of Zeus.

p. 87 Jove: Jupiter, the Roman equivalent to the Greek Zeus, leader of the gods. 'Olympian Jove' is an odd locution since Olympus is the gods' Greek residence.

p. 87 Hercules, who sat unsex'd: Hercules's punishment for impulsively killing a friend was to be made a slave of Queen Omphale for three years. During this time he dressed as a woman and spun wool with Omphale's handmaidens, while the Queen wore his lion's skin.

p. 87 seer of Chios: Homer. Chios is an island on the west coast of Asia Minor whose poets helped to create the texts attributed to Homer.

p. 87 Milesian: from Miletus, a city on the coast of Asia Minor, a trade centre of the ancient world.

p. 87 Colchian: from Colchis, a district of Asia Minor on the east end of the Black Sea, trade source of the saffron plant in the ancient world.

p. 87 Cyprian: from the Mediterranean island of Cyprus.

p. 88 Sappho's bay: the laurel leaf, symbol of poetic achievement.

Frances Jane Crosby van Alstyne

p. 89 'The Mandan Chief': the Mandan, reduced to two villages by smallpox and cholera in the eighteenth century, were again struck by smallpox in 1837, leaving only 100–150 survivors. The 1837 epidemic began in Fort Clark, North Dakota, where the Mandans then lived, when a fur company's steamboat brought infected passengers. Some Mandans, including Chief Mato Tope (Four Bears), committed suicide to join their dead relatives. However, Mato Tope's suicide was not as Crosby reports it – she has him confused with Ajax (*Iliad*), Saul (1 Samuel, 31) or Brutus (*Julius Caesar*, V.5). Mato Tope determined to starve himself to death, spent several days in meditation in the hills, returned to the village and delivered an oration on the reasons for his suicide, then lay down in his home with the bodies of his family members.

p. 92 'Thoughts in Midnight Hours': Cynthia: a surname of Artemis or Diana, the moon goddess of classical mythology. The unusual stanza form, iambic pentameter rhymed AABB, pairs two heroic couplets. The heroic couplet is associated with the rationalism of eighteenth-century neoclassical poetry; this poem has more in common overall with Romantic meditative odes. The poem is full of intertextual resonances. The title echoes that of Coleridge's associative meditation 'Frost at Midnight' (1798). 'Study what God reveals' revises Alexander Pope's famous couplet from 'An Essay on Man': 'Know then thyself; presume not God to scan. / The proper study of mankind is man.' 'How sweet at such an hour the parting sigh' echoes John Keats's 'Ode to a Nightingale': 'Now more than ever seems it rich to die, / To cease upon the midnight with no pain.' The trope of summoning a departed spirit also invokes the Romantics and, most proximally, Edgar Allan Poe's 'The Raven' (1845).

Elizabeth Drew Barstow Stoddard

p. 99 'Nameless Pain': lotus-eating: in Homer's *Odyssey*, IX, eating the lotus tree makes Odysseus's companions want to live idly in Lotus-land and destroys their desire to return home. In Tennyson's 'The Lotus-Eaters' (1832, revised 1842), lotus-eating figures an aesthetic remove from human toil.

p. 101 'Before the Mirror': the Lady of Shalott: heroine of Tennyson's poem of that title (1832, rev. 1842). The Lady, under a curse, lives in a tower, sees the outside world only in a mirror, and weaves what she sees into a tapestry.

p. 101 Penelope: plagued by suitors during her husband's twenty-year absence, Penelope promised she would choose one when she finished weaving her father-in-law's shroud, but every night she unravelled what she had woven during the day.

p. 101 long-haired Greek: images in this stanza refer to the Homeric legend.

p. 102 Norman knight: Sir Lancelot. A glimpse of him in her mirror causes the Lady of Shalott to look out of the window, thus bringing about her death, the consequence of the curse that held her in the tower. Other images in this stanza refer to Arthurian legend.

p. 102 'Above the Tree': 'I am a part of all that I have met': from Tennyson's 'Ulysses'.

p. 102 The one we thought had made the nation's creed: probably President Abraham Lincoln.

Phoebe Cary

pp. 104, 105 'Homes for All', 'Harvest Gathering': these two poems are adjacent in the Carys' first book (1850) and their having the same stanza form reinforces the impression that Cary composed them as complements, political prayers about the shape of westward expansion. Stanzas about slavery in 'Harvest Gathering' express opposition to its being permitted in the West and belief that Southern slavery will wither away.

p. 106 'Shakespearian Readings': Oh, but to fade ...: parody of Claudio's speech, *Measure for Measure*, III.1.117–31.

p. 107 That very time I saw ...: parody of Oberon's speech, *A Midsummer Night's Dream*, II.1.155–67.

p. 107 My father had a daughter ...: parody of Viola's speech, *Twelfth Night*, II.4.108–16.

Lucy Larcom

p. 111 'What the Train Ran Over': the Boston–Lowell train line, part of the nucleus of the New England rail system, began operating in 1835.

Frances Ellen Watkins Harper

p. 114 'Aunt Chloe': this cycle begins with an untitled poem in which Chloe remembers when her children were sold. 'The Deliverance' follows; then 'Aunt Chloe's Politics', 'Learning to Read', 'Church Building', and finally 'The Reunion' when Chloe's children return to visit her. For other accounts of the emancipation of slaves, see Josephine Heard's 'To Clements' Ferry' (p. 256) and Priscilla Thompson's 'Freedom at McNealy's' (p. 288).

p. 114 Fort Sumpter: Fort Sumter, off the coast of South Carolina. The Civil War began in April 1861 when the Confederate state of South Carolina seized it.

p. 116 Secesh: secession – the Confederacy of southern states.

p. 116 Bull's Run fight: two early battles of the Civil War were fought at Bull Run, a stream in Virginia, both ending in northern troops being routed.

p. 117 slavery was dead: Lincoln issued the Emancipation Proclamation on 1 January 1863. The news was probably delayed in reaching Aunt Chloe's household.

p. 118 another President: Andrew Johnson, who engineered a Reconstruction programme setting terms for the readmission of southern states but vetoed Civil Rights legislation.

p. 118 a circle: in summer 1866 Andrew Johnson toured the east and midwest seeking popular support; this tour was called the 'swing around the circle'. It was a complete failure.

p. 118 But now we have a President: Ulysses S. Grant, the first President elected with the votes of black men, took office in 1868.

p. 118 Ku-Klux Klan: one of several white supremacist secret societies organised just after the Civil War to prevent black men from voting through intimidation and violence. In 1871 Congress passed acts to suppress the Klan.

Rose Terry Cooke

p. 122 Schemhammphorasch: 'ShemhaMeforash': ancient name of the Tetragramaton, the ineffable name of God, which could be uttered only by the high priest on specific holy days. To speak it inappropriately would bring divine retribution.

p. 124 Michael: prince of the angels who returns to do battle with the forces of evil during the Apocalypse; Revelation, 12:7–8.

p. 125 'Che Sara Sara': what will be will be, when an accent is placed on the last a in 'Sara' (Italian). Dr Faustus speaks this phrase to summarise the inevitability of sin and everlasting death as he rejects God in Christopher Marlowe's *Faustus* I.1. The poem uses language from the Song of Solomon, e.g. 1:5, 2:14, 4:16.

p. 125 'A Hospital Soliloquy': 10 April 1865 is the day after Confederate General Lee surrendered to Union General Grant at Appomattox, Virginia.

p. 126 Shenandoah route: the devastating campaign of the Union's Army of the Shenandoah led by General Philip Henry Sheridan, October 1864 to March 1865.

p. 126 Abr'am's hand: England, to defend its economic interests, had contemplated intervening in the Civil War on the South's behalf. Southerners and this northern soldier believed that Lincoln's Emancipation Proclamation of 1863 repelled foreign assistance. It officially changed the North's cause from preserving national unity to abolishing slavery.

p. 126 secesh: secession, the Confederacy.

p. 126 English powder: the industrial North manufactured its own arms, while the Confederacy relied on imports, evading the Northern blockade of southern ports to carry on arms trade through the Caribbean and the Canadian Atlantic coast. Great Britain was the prime supplier.

Achsa W. Sprague

p. 128 'The Poet': a blank-verse drama in four scenes. The Seymours are the ideal family, liberal, literary and progressively moralistic; Mr Seymour's friend Henry Bruce is a yet more progressive and literary bachelor; Kate Walters and Walter Clifton (but especially Kate) are frivolous, idle, weak in principles and conventional in social views. Scene I, a forest near the ocean: a woman poet, seeking to do 'something worthy life', is visited by the spirits of Poesy and Beauty, Genius, various nature spirits, and the Goddess of the Soul, who grant her the gift of improvisation. Scene II, a parlour in the Seymour family's home: Ida, seventeen, enthusiastically discusses with her father a book by the poet of Scene I, both expressing their progressive views on woman, which Kate Walters ridicules. Her fiancé Walter Clifton enters and joins the discussion, seconding Kate's views and relating that Henry Bruce has become entranced with the poet whose book Ida is reading. Bruce enters and convinces those present to attend a performance by the poet. Ida determines to reread *Corinne* (1807), a novel by Mme de Staël about an improvisatrice, and Bruce accompanies her to the library to help her find it. There Ida reveals to Bruce that she has secretly been writing poetry; he agrees to help her improve her writing. Finding Mr Seymour alone in the parlour, Bruce asks and receives his permission to court Ida. Scene III begins with the selection given in this anthology. The poet, now called the Improvisatrice, faces several challenges from doubters in the audience and fully acquits herself. Scene IV, the Seymours' parlour: with Bruce present, Ida reads her parents a poem and reveals that she is the author. Alone with Ida, Bruce reveals his love to her; she reciprocates. The Improvisatrice, now known as Miss Raymond, arrives for a visit, having become a friend of the family, and announces her plan of opening a home for fallen women. Bruce tells Miss Raymond that her poetry helped him win Ida; both anticipate that Ida, too, will become a poet.

p. 129 Don Giovanni: Mozart opera about Don Juan, the legendary libertine; Bruce undoubtedly disapproves of the immorality depicted in the opera.

p. 129 Norma: Bellini opera about a Druid priestess, first produced in New York in 1841.

p. 130 bedight: archaic; equip, array, often referring to a knight's equipment. The young gentleman seems to be saying that unrequited love might turn him into a knight errant.

p. 131 Pharisees: a party of Jewish scribes who devoted themselves to fulfilling the letter of the law. In Luke, 18:11 a Pharisee thanks God he is not sinful like other men.

Emily Dickinson

p. 135 'Fascicle 34': words to the right are alternate phrasings that Dickinson provided in her manuscripts.

p. 136 Curricle: two-wheeled carriage drawn by two horses.

p. 136 'Her Sweet turn to leave the Homestead': compare with Alice Cary's 'The West Country' (p. 82) and Mollie Moore Davis's 'Going Out and Coming In' (p. 231).

p. 137 Guinea Look: the lady looks like a guinea fowl waiting to be fed.

p. 137 Belt: shut

p. 138 Coins: refers to the tradition of placing coins on the eyelids of the dead to keep the eyelids closed.

p. 139 'My Life had stood – a Loaded Gun': see 'The Poets and Their Critics' (p. 333).

p. 139 Vesuvian: volcanic, after the volcano Vesuvius.

p. 139 Eider-Duck: source of eiderdown, the fine feathers used in feather pillows.

p. 140 Anodyne: a drug that allays pain.

p. 141 'Victory comes late': see 'The Poets and Their Critics' (p. 333).

p. 141 Eagle: see note on the eagle as national emblem under Catherine Warfield (p. 302).

Helen Hunt Jackson

p. 146 'My House Not Made with Hands': see Howe, 'The House of Rest' (p. 72); Coolidge, 'A Home' (p. 172); and Charlotte Gilman, 'Homes' (p. 249), for other meditations on houses, homes and domesticity.

p. 147 Bedouins: nomads of the North African, Arabian and Syrian deserts.

p. 149 'Emigravit': Latin; he or she leaves.

Mary Mapes Dodge

p. 151 'The Mayor of Scuttleton': Dodge renders local politics absurd. Compare Follen's and Gould's efforts to explain politics to children.

p. 152 'Fire in the window': Dodge defuses an image that many postbellum parents would have associated with the burning of Southern cities during the Civil War.

p. 152 'The Moon came late': Goggleky Gluck, whose name suggests she is German American – a much-parodied ethnic group – has stumbled onto high society.

p. 152 'Shepherd John': Dodge strangely takes the pastoral figure of a shepherd, associated with Christ, as an uneducated agrarian eager for his child to advance beyond him.

p. 153 'Early to bed': a leisured-class parody of Benjamin Franklin's aphorism, 'Early to bed, early to rise/Makes a man healthy, wealthy, and wise.'

p. 153 'The Way To Do It': the child speaker is demonstrating gestures and stances he has learned in his elocution lessons.

p. 154 'Poor Crow!': probably racial; the crow's narrative parodically recalls that of escaped slaves.

p. 155 'The Wooden Horse': compare Gould's 'Apprehension' (p. 10).

p. 156 Tinker, come bring your solder: Dodge assumes middle- or upper-class readers with an army of trade occupations at their command.

p. 156 'Taking Time to Grow': compare Warfield/Lee on the eagle; Dodge urges middle-class American children to accept a prolonged, protected infancy as a sign of their specialness.

Louisa May Alcott

p. 158 'The Lay of a Golden Goose': an autobiographical parody of Aesop's fable about a goose that lays a golden egg. The couple that owns the goose kill it in search of the gold inside but find none (moral: much wants more and loses all). See 'The Poets and Their Critics' (p. 328) for Alcott's explanation of why she wrote this poem.

p. 159 Socratic: philosophical, specifically relating to Socrates's method of sceptical dialogue.

p. 159 transcendental: Alcott's father Bronson Alcott was a leader of transcendentalism, an American philosophical movement. Opposing scientific rationalism, the transcendentalists believed nature embodied spiritual truth and intuition was the only way to apprehend it. They stressed the unity of all things in a Supreme Mind, with which the individual soul was identical; thus tradition and authority could be disregarded. Margaret Fuller's 'The One in All' (p. 49) meditates on transcendentalist concepts.

Elizabeth Akers Allen

p. 163 jews-harp: a small lyre-shaped instrument held between the lips, producing notes when a metal tongue is struck by the thumb.

p. 164 'Rock Me to Sleep': one of the most popular American poems of the nineteenth century; see biographical note on Allen (p. 163).

p. 166 fiery pillar: Exodus, 13:21: as the Israelites fled bondage in Egypt and wandered in search of a new home, a pillar of fire guided them by night.

p. 166 earthworks: embankments made of earth to fortify a field.

p. 166 picket-fires: the campfires of pickets, detached groups of soldiers assigned to guard an encamped army.

p. 166 guidons: small flags marking units of soldiers.

Mary Abigail Dodge

p. 170 Quaker: John Greenleaf Whittier, who wrote the poem cited in the note, was a Quaker. Hamilton goes on to use Quaker plain speech – 'thee' instead of 'you', intended to signify equality between speaker and addressee – in addressing Whittier.

p. 170 *New York Observer:* weekly evangelical newspaper with a tradition of anti-Catholic and anti-theatre propaganda.

p. 171 **When pulpits preach him:** Whittier's poetry was immensely popular with preachers and women.

Sarah C. Woolsey

p. 172 '**A Home**': see Howe, 'The House of Rest' (p. 72); Jackson, 'My House Not Made with Hands' (p. 146); and Gilman, 'Homes' (p. 249), for other poems about homes.

p. 173 **the old miracle:** Christ's miracles of feeding thousands of people with a few loaves and fishes; e.g. Matthew, 14:15–21, 32–9.

Harriet Prescott Spofford

p. 176 '**Magdalen**': Mary Magdalene, one of Christ's most devoted followers. She is identified with the unnamed sinful woman in Luke, 7:36–50 who washes Christ's feet with her tears. The haemorrhaging woman who touches Jesus's cloak in hope of a cure in Matthew, 9:20–22, Mark, 5:25–33 and Luke, 8:42–8, is probably a part of the conflation resulting in the non-scriptural legend of Mary Magdalene kissing his hem.

Sarah M. B. Piatt

p. 180 '**The Palace-Burner**': Paris, 18 March 1871, following the abolition of Napoleon III's empire and during the establishment of the Third Republic, Parisian revolutionaries declared a Commune (an insurrectionary government) and proclaimed Paris a free town governed only by its citizens. The Communists' siege of Paris ended the last week of May with some 36,000 men and women being massacred by the French army.

p. 182 '**A Child's Party**': ignotus: anonymous.

p. 183 **Were one of these on earth today:** the family heirlooms Piatt describes were probably destroyed or looted by Union raiders in the Civil War.

p. 185 **priestess of the eternal flame:** Piatt compares the cook to Vesta, goddess of the hearth in Roman myth.

Mary Eliza Perine Tucker Lambert

p. 186 Loew's Bridge: Fulton Street Bridge, completed March 1866 and standing only one year. It spanned the intersection of New York City's Broadway and Fulton streets, which was almost impassable by pedestrians because of heavy traffic. Lambert's poem moves among observations, meditations, memories and visions. Among the omissions are observations and judgments on political, religious, theatrical and literary celebrities, including poet William Cullen Bryant and *New York Tribune* publisher Horace Greeley.

p. 186 Greenback: dollar.

p. 186 Wall: 'Wall Street is our temple of Mammon, where men of money "most do congregate" (Lambert's note).

p. 187 Dixie: nickname for the states south of the Mason-Dixon line, which demarcated slave and free states. The popular song of that title was composed by Daniel Decatur Emmett in 1859 and became a favourite of the Confederate army.

p. 187 A one-armed soldier: 'This is no fancy sketch. The writer actually saw this, – saw a Southern soldier give alms to the Northern soldier, who can be seen at any time near the Bridge playing an organ. Indeed everything described was seen, if not precisely in the order mentioned' (Lambert's note).

p. 187 'Yankee Doodle': a popular song dating to colonial days; 'Yankee', a British slur on the American troops during the Revolutionary War, became the North's nickname in the conflict between the states.

p. 188 From e'en a cord: 'Always at the Bridge are venders selling the dancing toys, whose motions depend upon an elastic string, the invention of which has brought a fortune to the inventor' (Lambert's note).

p. 190 Wilcox and Gibbs: 'The "Wilcox and Gibbs sewing machine", celebrated alike for its simplicity, rapidity of movement, as well as its durability, was patented in 1857, first sold in 1859, since which time one hundred thousand have been sold' (Lambert's note).

p. 191 Harper's good 'Bazar', 'Die Modenwelt' or 'Magazine of Madam Demorest': fashion magazines.

p. 191 the rival artists: 'The artists referred to are Madams M. F. Gillespie and Demorest, whose exquisite taste has rendered them renowned in the fashionable circles, not only of New York, but of the whole United States' (Lambert's note). Ellen Louise Curtis Demorest (1824–98) was the leading arbiter of women's fashions in the mid-1860s. *Demorest's Monthly Magazine* was published from 1866–99; each issue included a tissue-paper dress pattern, the mass production of which Demorest originated. She also ran an elite shop on Broadway.

p. 191 Surrogate: judicial officer who has jurisdiction over probate of wills, settlement of estates and appointment of guardians. This final section begins with a parade of images representing the history of the spot where the office of the Surrogate now stands. 'Hon. Gideon J. Tucker, who has held important State offices for more than twenty years, and is one of the first political writers of the age, is the present Surrogate of New York, and has occupied that position for the last five years. It is said of him that he has never been politically wrong in his life' (Lambert's note).

Queen Lili'uokalani

Notes provided by Sue Nance. Lili'uokalani composed her *mele* in Hawaiian and wrote inexact English translations. Hawaiian poetic tradition is rich in *kaona*, disguised references, which Lili'uokalani used to conceal the political significance of her songs from Americans who knew only literal Hawaiian. The *kaona* remain hidden in her translations. Some, but not all, of the *kaona* in the poems here are explained in the following notes.

p. 193 'Aloha'oe': Lili'uokalani's most famous song, traditionally performed throughout Hawaii at the arrivals and departures of ships. Lili'uokalani wrote it as a love song; the most often repeated story of its composition is that she wrote it after observing a young couple (probably her sister Likelike and a lover) parting at the gate of the estate in Maunawili where she was staying. Missionaries began using the song at funerals, to its author's surprise.

p. 193 cliffs: the estate is on the windward side of the cliffs.

p. 193 *liko*: tiny blossoms of the lehua, a flower of dozens of thin threads forming a puff, appearing more fragile than they are. The lehua grows abundantly at higher elevations in Hawaii and is sacred to Pele, goddess of the creative force of the volcanoes. Here *liko* refers to the delicacy and beauty of the young woman. Its poetic meaning is a budding, small and tender being (often a child) in need of nurturing and protection.

p. 194 'Sanoe': composed with Kapeka (Lizzie Chapman Ah Chuck), a close friend of Lili'uokalani's sister Likelike. 'Sanoe' is a disguised word. Hawaiian has no letter 's' and the 's' sound was often used by chanters to disguise words from missionaries who knew Hawaiian. Sanoe refers here to a mist that moves slowly among low-lying vegetation, like a pervasive dew, used poetically in descriptions of skin.

p. 195 'Ku'u Pua I Paoakalani': one of the most beautiful and most frequently performed of Lili'uokalani's *mele*. Composed while she was under house arrest, it speaks of longing for a child, who is likened to a flower. The form, with the last stanza referring back to the topic of the first stanza in an iteration saying 'Now hear my story' or something similar, is common in Hawaiian oral tradition.

p. 195 'Ka Waiapo Lani': this poem indirectly expresses Lili'uokalani's feelings about her imprisonment. Discretion was needed to protect a group of her supporters who had been threatened with execution for their uprising against American rule.

p. 195 heavenly showers: the *kaona* is royal lineage.

p. 196 crownlets: reference to the mouths of volcanoes and thus to the ancient religion. The political suggestion is that by forsaking the old religion for Christianity, Hawaiians opened themselves up to outside political domination.

Adah Isaacs Menken

p. 197 'Judith': a Jewish heroine whose story is told in the book of Judith in the Apocrypha. To save her city Bethulia from the assault of Holofernes, general of Assyrian king Nebuchadnezzar, Judith enters his camp and beheads him as he sleeps off a drunken stupor. Menken probably knew Friedrich Hebbel's tragedy *Judith* (1841) in which Judith becomes Holofernes's lover before killing him.

p. 197 Ashkelon, Gaza: cites in Philistia.

p. 198 Baal-perazim: site of modern Sheikh Bedr south of Jerusalem in the valley of Rephaim, site of David's victory over the Philistines, II Samuel, 5:20.

p. 198 seventh angel: the seventh angel in Judaic tradition is Jeremiel, identified as guardian of souls in the underworld. Revelation, 16:17–21: the seventh angel of the apocalypse causes lightning, thunder and the greatest earthquake humankind has ever known.

p. 199 Magdalene: see note under Spofford (p. 312)

Owl Woman

Each song was sung twice, then twice from the seventh measure, then once from the beginning with slight breaks in tempo between renditions. Densmore, an ethnomusicologist, provided simple rather than literary renditions of the words and did not attempt to capture in English the nuances generated by repetition.

p. 200 'Brown owls': given to Owl Woman by her first guide to the spirit world, the spirit of a man who had been recently killed. She began every treatment with these songs.

p. 200 'The owl feather': given to Owl Woman by the spirit of a man she had treated. The songs express his thoughts when he was waiting for her.

p. 201 'In the dark': given by the spirit of an elderly man who died suddenly.

p. 201 'Poor old sister': given to Owl Woman by the spirit of her brother as she headed towards the home of an old man named Marciano whom she had cared for every night without seeing signs of his recovery. Her brother told her Marciano would die.

p. 201 'Ahead of me' and 'Yonder lies': given to Owl Woman by the spirit of a friend of a man she had treated shortly after the man died. An unusually long song.

p. 201 'Sadly I was treated' and 'A railroad running west': given by the spirit of a man killed in a drunken brawl, then hauled in a buggy to the railroad tracks where he was left so it would appear the train had killed him.

p. 201 'Yonder are spirits' and 'I pity you': given by the spirit of a man returning with his sister on horseback to inspect the condition of his house.

p. 201 'On the west side' (two songs) and 'In the great night': given by a spirit Owl Woman described as follows: 'Jose was not a lively boy, he was slow and sleepy headed.' Both 'On the west side' songs refer to rehearsals for a dance.

p. 202 'I am going', 'Ashes Hill', 'The spirit person': sung just before midnight. The first two concern a journey to the spirit world; in the third, a spirit person is teasing the speaker.

p. 202 'A low range', 'I am not sure', 'I am dead here', 'Black Butte': sung between midnight and early morning. 'I am dead here' and 'Black Butte' were given by the spirit of a man who died at *Vihuhput* by falling in a well as he tried to climb into it for a drink of water after camping in Black Butte (locations later known as Dub's Buttes). The dawn is the light that spirits see, mentioned in other of Owl Woman's songs.

p. 202 'I think I have found out': Owl Woman used this song, after discussing a patient's condition with his relatives, if she saw he was going to die.

Constance Fenimore Woolson

pp. 203, 205 'One' and 'The Other': the first two parts of *Two Women: 1862*. The maiden and the lady meet on the train. Though the lady is taken with the maiden, the maiden thoroughly disapproves of the lady. They discover they are in love with the same man, Meredith Wilmer (whom the maiden calls 'Willie', a name the lady finds childish), a Union soldier. Wilmer has been wounded by Morgan's raiders, a Confederate cavalry that conducted three ruthless campaigns through Kentucky in 1862, destroying rail facilities strategic to the North. Both women are rushing to Wilmer's side in a farmhouse in Kentucky. A long argument follows this discovery, each woman certain Wilmer loved only her and each defending her own way of being (the maiden is a devout Christian, the lady a worldly-wise socialite). Wilmer is dead when they arrive, and the maiden's picture and letters lie on a table, which she takes to mean he loved her to the last. However, the doctor who attended him informs the lady that his last words were for her, and that he left the maiden's letters for her to dispose of. The lady vows not to rob the maiden of her belief in Wilmer's love. The maiden leaves but the lady stays on to grieve by Wilmer's grave, where Morgan's raiders happen on her and, stunned by her beauty, stand silently by, honouring the man they killed. Two years later, the lady, back in Washington, receives a letter from the maiden saying that she is to marry. The lady deprecates the maiden's love for Wilmer, saying that she herself could never marry; however, out of *noblesse oblige*, she continues to entertain wealthy and distinguished admirers. In Lake Erie, Ohio, the maiden prepares for her wedding, asserting that to have prolonged her mourning for Wilmer would have been selfish and that she decided to marry out of a sense of duty to her mother.

p. 204 'The river!': the Ohio River separates the states of Ohio (Union) and Kentucky (Confederacy).

p. 206 Milo Venus: Venus of Milo or Melos, ancient sculpture of the Roman goddess of beauty and sensual love; now in the Louvre, its arms missings.

p. 206 Nubian: refers to tribes that formed an empire in North Africa from the sixth to the fourteenth centuries. The term 'Nubian', whose root refers

to the slave trade on which the empire thrived, was virtually synonymous
with 'negroid' or black in European languages well into the nineteenth
century. Woolson probably means to indicate that the lady is a mulatto.

Ina Coolbrith

p. 208 'Longing': the pardoned pair: Adam and Eve. Coolbrith imagines
God has forgiven them for eating the fruit of knowledge and let them back
into Eden.

p. 209 'My "Cloth of Gold" ': the prosody in this poem shows the influence
of Christina Rossetti, as do many of Coolbrith's most interesting poems (e.g.
her long poem 'Concha' in *Wings of Sunset*). The Field of Cloth of Gold
was a plain in Picardy where Henry VIII of England met Francis I of France
in 1520. Hoping to elicit Henry's support against Emperor Charles V, Francis
had a temporary palace erected in the field, with everything either made of
gold or covered in gold thread. The overall effect was bland rather than
impressive.

p. 212 'Lines On Hearing Kelley's Music to "Macbeth" ': an irregularly
extended sonnet.

p. 212 Kelley: American composer Edgar Kelley (1857–1944) composed
incidental music for *Macbeth*. He worked in San Francisco, where he studied
Chinese music, 1880–6 and 1892–6.

p. 212 Sisters Three: the witches who predict Macbeth's fate at the beginning
of Shakespeare's play.

p. 212 Thane: Scottish feudal lord; refers to Macbeth.

Emma Lazarus

p. 213 'How Long': distant isle: England.

p. 215 'The New Colossus': Colossus: 105-feet-high statue of Helios, the
Greek sun god, erected on the island of Rhodes in 304 BC. The 'new
Colossus' is the 151-feet-high Statue of Liberty Enlightening the World
by Auguste Bartholdi, presented to the American people by France to
commemorate the centenary of the American Declaration of Independence.

p. 216 'Long Island Sound': inlet about a hundred miles long between
Connecticut and Long Island.

p. 217 '1492': the year Columbus first landed on American shores, and Jews were expelled from Spain as a result of the Inquisition, a tribunal for suppressing heresy, established by monarchs Ferdinand and Isabella, who also sponsored Columbus's voyage.

p. 218 Abul Hassan Judah Ben Ha-Levi: Yehuda ben Shemuel ha-Levi (1075–1141), religious philosopher and the most eminent poet of the Jewish Golden Age in Spain.

Henrietta Cordelia Ray

p. 220 'The Quest of the Ideal': this theme is well established in the sonnet tradition from Petrarch (1304–74) on, but the ideal is usually an unattainable woman. Ray's questing subject, 'Fair Hope', is female.

p. 220 Diana: Roman deity identified with Artemis, virginal Greek goddess of hunting.

p. 221 'Toussaint L'Ouverture': Pierre François Dominique Toussaint L'Ouverture (1743–1803), slave who became the ruler of Haiti following an insurrection in 1791 and subsequent factional conflict. He ruled until 1801 when Napoleon sent troops to retake the island. Toussaint L'Ouverture died in prison in France.

Ella Wheeler Wilcox

p. 222 'Communism': Wilcox is referring to the revolutionary government established in 1792 by representatives of the Parisian communes, the smallest administrative districts. The Reign of Terror, a bloody purge of thousands of suspected traitors to the revolution, followed.

p. 223 'Solitude': one of Wilcox's most popular poems.

p. 224 Lamartine: French Romantic poet and liberal republican statesman, 1790–1869.

Rose Hartwick Thorpe

p. 229 'Curfew Must Not Ring Tonight': set during the second phase of the English Civil War (1648–52) which ended with Oliver Cromwell's rule as Lord Protector (1653–8). Basil Underwood is clearly on the wrong side of the conflict, possibly a Royalist. For a reference to this poem's immense popularity, see Carolyn Wells's poem 'The Poster Girl's Defence' (p. 280).

Mollie E. Moore Davis

p. 232 'Going Out and Coming In': see Alice Cary's poem 'The West Country' (p. 82) for an optimistic view of the prospects of western home-steaders' children.

Edith M. Thomas

p. 235 'Cries of the Newsboy': *News, Sun, World, Tribune*: New York newspapers. The New York newspapers began employing newsboys, often orphaned or abandoned immigrant children, to distribute papers on the streets in the 1830s; the practice continued for a century.

p. 235 Mercury: Roman equivalent to Greek god Hermes, associated with both carrying messages and thieving.

p. 235 cuckoo fledgeling: the cuckoo, a brown European bird, lays its eggs in the nests of other birds which hatch and rear the offspring.

Lizette Woodworth Reese

p. 239 'An Old Belle': Cavaliers: knights, Royalists in the English Civil War. Reese is referring to the aristocratic tradition of the Old South and its association with feudal chivalry.

p. 239 Camden street: a block west of the Harbor of Baltimore in a commercial district near the railroad warehouse where goods were transferred from freighters to railway cars. Residences were lower- or lower-middle-class, primarily apartments over stores and businesses.

Zaragoza Clubs

See biographical note (p. 242) and 'The Poets and Their Critics' (p. 363). The genre of these poems is *brindis*, hail or toast. The event commemorated is the Battle of Cinco de Mayo, 5 May 1862, at which Mexican forces under Ignacio Zaragoza (1829–62) checked the advance of French troops at Puebla, south of Mexico City. Ambitious for control of Central America as a trade route, Napoleon III sent forces to Mexico starting in 1861 on the pretence of protecting European economic interests. The invasion arrived just as Benito Juárez (1806–72) assumed national control following a civil war between reactionary forces and the republican government that Juárez had headed since 1857. Persisting after the Cinco de Mayo battle, the French took Mexico City in June 1864. Napoleon III installed Archduke Maximilian of

Austria as Emperor of Mexico. Juárez's government set up a capital in Chihuahua. Maximilian was deposed, tried, and executed in 1867, and Juárez ruled Mexico from then until his death. A full-blooded Zapotec Indian, Juárez promoted political, economic and social reforms and opposed the power of the clergy.

p. 243 Bell Warner: *todo el Norte*/**all the North:** Warner may be referring to the north of Mexico, where Juárez's government was in exile, or to all of the territory that Mexico had ceded to the US in the Treaty of Guadalupe Hidalgo (1848).

p. 244 Refujia Díaz: *a los traidores, A frailes*/**traitors, friars:** Mexican reactionaries and clergy who supported the French occupation.

p. 244 Carlota: Maximilian's wife Charlotte, princess of Belgium, a power behind Maximilian; she urged him to continue ruling when he wanted to abdicate and negotiated with European powers for support of his rule.

p. 244 *un buho*/**an owl:** in pre-Columbian folklore owls appear as omens of good or evil, and Mexican folklore includes many owls with different characters, not all wise as in European tradition. This owl may be something like the lechuza, a being drawn to ill feeling or loss of faith and bringing further evil.

p. 246 Isabel Warner: Rosales: Antonio Rosales (1822–65). Benito Juárez gave him the rank of general for routing French forces at San Pedro, November–December 1864.

p. 247 Teresa Morales: *relicario*/**reliquary:** shrine in which sacred relics are kept.

p. 247 Herrera: Hipólito Herrera (1830–85), a hero of the Battle of Puebla.

p. 247 Refugio Arce de Silva: Rivera: Aureliano Rivera (1832–1904) distinguished himself as a guerrilla fighter against the French.

p. 248 Filomeno Ibarra: Vesta: Roman goddess of the hearth.

Charlotte Perkins Stetson Gilman

p. 249 'Homes': see Howe, 'The House of Rest' (p. 72); Jackson, 'My House Not Made with Hands' (p. 146); and Coolidge, 'A Home' (p. 172); for other perspectives on homes.

p. 249 Sestina: a complicated, strict verse form invented by medieval troubadours: six stanzas of six lines each followed by a three-line envoi, all unrhymed and usually, in English poetry, ten syllables per line. The same six end-words occur in each stanza but in a shifting order which follows a strict pattern. All end-words must appear in the envoi, either in the middle or at the end of the line.

p. 252 an 'L': an annexe or extension.

p. 253 'Christian virtues': bedizen: adorn gaudily.

Josephine Delphine Henderson Heard

p. 256 'To Clements' Ferry': for other accounts of the emancipation of slaves, see Frances Harper's 'The Deliverance' (p. 114), and Priscilla Thompson's 'Freedom at McNealy's' (p. 288).

p. 258 'Tennyson's Poems': Alfred, Lord Tennyson (1809–92) was English poet laureate from 1850 to his death, generally recognised by both British and American critics as the leading poet of the era. His versions of Arthurian legend (e.g. *Idylls of the King*) were important works of Victorian medievalism, seeking alternatives to modern social structures in nostalgia for the feudal age.

p. 259 'The Black Sampson': Sampson was an Israelite hero of prodigious strength, captured by the Philistines through the trickery of Delilah, a Philistine woman with whom he was infatuated. In captivity, Sampson gradually regained his strength and used it while on exhibition in a temple to pull the temple down on himself and all present.

p. 259 Organized and lawless bands: white vigilantes and mobs that perpetrated terrorism against African Americans in the postbellum South, escalating in the 1890s and continuing through the mid-twentieth century. An estimated 10,000 people were lynched from 1878–98, most for social offences and challenges to white authority.

p. 260 They have sowed the wind, the whirlwind they shall reap: paraphrase of Hosea, 8:7.

Emily Pauline Johnson

p. 261 'Marshlands': an unusual sonnet form, seven rhymed couplets, evading the developmental pattern of more complex rhyme schemes.

Louise Imogen Guiney

p. 266 Hyperborean: the modern meaning is arctic, frozen, but the word derives from the name of a primordial virtuous and happy people of Greek legend who lived in a warm paradise on the far side of the North Wind's origin. Later legend described the Hyperborean atmosphere as feathery, a reference to abundant snowfall in the north.

p. 266 Musketaquid: Musquetaquid Pond, West Concord, Massachusetts. Fed by streams and linked downstream to Haywards Pond, then to the Assabet River, on which mills were built in the nineteenth century.

p. 268 'John Brown: A Paradox': in the 1850s, while the anti-slavery movement pursued nonviolent means, John Brown (1800–59) felt called by God to use violence to free slaves. He organised a small band of followers whose first exploits involved killing pro-slavery settlers in Kansas. He became an abolitionist martyr when hanged for leading the seizure of the US arsenal in Harper's Ferry, Virginia (now West Virginia).

p. 269 Chivalry's sunset: the demise of the old South's aristocratic tradition.

p. 269 'The Atoning Yesterday': minsters: a large or important church, similar to a cathedral in status.

p. 269 Arcady: pastoral paradise, after Arcadia, a region of ancient Greece whose people remained primitively rustic as the city-states developed complex civilisations.

Mary Weston Fordham

p. 270 'Atlanta Exposition Ode': Atlanta Exposition: Cotton States and International Exposition held at Atlanta in 1895 with thirty-seven states and thirteen foreign countries participating, one of a series of commercial expositions held in the South (1881–1907) to boost morale during economic depression, attract trade and investment, encourage reconciliation between North and South, and promote pan-Americanism. New additions at the 1895 Exposition were buildings devoted to women and to African Americans, the latter portraying blacks as an economic asset in an effort to allay investors' fears about a Southern 'race problem'.

p. 270 Cast down your bucket where you are: from Booker T. Washington's oration at the Atlanta Exposition. He told a fable of a ship lost at sea, advised by a voice from an approaching vessel to cast a bucket into the sea for drinking water; the bucket brought up fresh water from the mouth of the Amazon. Washington's influential speech set a conciliatory agenda, known as 'The Atlanta Compromise', amid fierce racial tensions: African Americans would yield their political rights if allowed to pursue economic development on their own.

p. 271 On Orient: to the east – dawn is here.

p. 271 ye that wore the blue: Confederate veterans; the Confederate army's uniform was blue.

p. 271 the gray did love: those who supported the Union during the Civil War; the Union army's uniform was grey.

p. 271 Watchman, ... tell us of the night: 1825 hymn by John Bowring, paraphrased from Isaiah, 21:11 and usually sung at Epiphany.

p. 271 Bethlehem's Star: the star that shone over Bethlehem at Jesus's birth, guiding the Magi to the site. Matthew, 2:2, 10.

p. 271 millennium: thousand years; in Christian apocalyptic thought, the period during which Christ will reign with his saints on earth while Satan is in bondage; Revelation, 20:2.

Ella Higginson

p. 274 'Four-Leaf Clover': adopted as a theme song by the 4-H Club, which grew out of agricultural youth clubs in Iowa (1909–10), later becoming national with assistance from the US Department of Agriculture.

p. 275 'Eve': the primordial mother of Judeo-Christian myth, whose tasting first of the fruit of knowledge provided a rationale for women's subordination that was often cited in the nineteenth century, here demands to be let back into the gates of Paradise, closed to humankind since Adam and Eve's fall from grace. Genesis, 3:24.

p. 275 'Moonrise in the Rockies': the Rocky Mountain Range, extending from Alaska to New Mexico and to heights above 14,000 feet. The single greatest impediment to transcontinental travel before the completion of railroads.

p. 276 'Dawn on the Willamette': the Willamette River in north-west Oregon.

p. 276 Mount Hood: 11,245-foot peak in the Cascade Mountains, northwest Oregon, the highest point in the state.

p. 276 'A Dream of Sappho': Sappho: poet of the Greek island of Lesbos, seventh century BC, associated with superior lyric craft, passion, and bonds among women. Fragments of her poems were preserved by other authors; papyri ascribed to her were discovered in the late nineteenth century and a new edition published in 1887.

p. 277 'The Opal Sea': refers to Puget Sound, an eighty-mile arm of the Pacific extending into Washington State.

p. 277 Olympics: mountain range in north-west Washington.

p. 278 'The Statue': the figure Higginson describes would be readily recognised as Abraham Lincoln.

Carolyn Wells

p. 279 'Fate': an unrhymed sonnet.

p. 280 Escaping Spaniards: Spaniards had been stock villains in English melodrama since the Renaissance, but Wells's proximal reference is to sensational descriptions of Spanish colonial officials in the American press. Reports of Spanish atrocities in Cuba roused American public opinion to war hysteria, contributing to declaration of war against Spain in April 1898.

p. 280 Broadway: a thoroughfare in New York City.

p. 280 'The Poster Girl's Defence': Poster Girls were a turn-of-the-century fad, allegorical representations of gigantic young women symbolising American virtue and glory. Strangely hued and unlifelike, Poster Girls conflated the media-promoted 'New Woman' image (defining women as independent, physically adept, mentally acute, men's social equals at work and study) with a new attitude in American foreign relations as westward movement ended at the Pacific coast and expansionist drives turned towards the Caribbean: will is supreme, the desire for love absent. Wells has her Poster Girl benefit by contrast to the American Girl type, a junior version of the New Woman, at once sensuous and innocent, strong-minded and eager for experience, busy filling the leisure afforded by her family's prosperity.

p. 280 'Curfew Must Not Ring Tonight': popular recitation piece by Rose Hartwick Thorpe, included in this anthology (p. 228).

p. 280 a joy forever, though a thing of beauty, nit: paraphrase of John Keats, 'A thing of beauty is a joy for ever,' *Endymion*, Book 1, 1.1.

p. 281 'A Pastoral in Posters': compare to Higginson's 'Moonrise in the Rockies' (p. 275).

p. 281 'The Original Summer Girl': a 'summer girl' was an 'American Girl' spending the summer at a resort, which provided escape from city heat and a marital hunting ground.

p. 282 'A Problem': cognoscenti: connoisseurs, arbiters of good taste.

p. 282 Duchess: pseudonym of once-fashionable Irish novelist Margaret Wolfe Hamilton Hungerford, 1855?–97.

p. 282 *The Egoist*: 1879 novel by British author George Meredith.

p. 282 Ibsen: Henrik Johan Ibsen (1828–1906), Norwegian playwright, a founder of modern drama, known for supplanting traditional dramatic formulas with psychological and social realism.

p. 282 Mr Caine: Thomas Henry Hall Caine (1853–1931), best-selling British adventure novelist.

p. 282 Miss Corelli: Marie Corelli (1855–1924), author of extravagant, mystical romantic novels full of superlative heroines.

p. 282 Omar: the speaker has confused Homer with Omar Khayyam, author of the *Rubaiyat*, popular in Edward FitzGerald's translation in the late nineteenth century.

p. 282 Holmes: Oliver Wendall Holmes, Sr (1809–94), American poet and essayist.

p. 282 Mary J.: Mary Jane Holmes (1825–1907), prolific writer of popular sentimental novels.

p. 282 Whatever is, is right: Alexander Pope, 'An Essay on Man', 1.289; satirically quoted in Voltaire's *Candide*.

p. 282 Hafiz or Maeterlinck: rarefied reading, ancient and modern. Hafiz (meaning a scholar who has memorised the Koran) was the pen name of Persian poet Shams-ud-din Muhammad (*c.* 1300–88). Maurice Maeterlinck (1862–1949) was a Belgian writer whose first two books of mysterious and dreamy poetry appeared in the late nineteenth century.

p. 283 'Of Modern Books': Pantoum: verse form adapted by nineteenth-century French poets from the Malay *pantun*, established in English in the late nineteenth century. Of indeterminate length, a pantoum is composed of quatrains; the second and fourth lines of each stanza form the first and third lines of the following stanza, and the first line of the poem repeats as its last line.

p. 283 Of making many books there is no end: adapted from the first line of Elizabeth Barrett Browning's *Aurora Leigh*, 'Of writing many books there is no end'.

Voltairine de Cleyre

p. 286 'Love's Compensation': de Cleyre conflates the parable of the Talents (Matthew, 25:14–30), in which a master punishes a servant for storing rather than investing the one coin he is allotted, with the story of Jesus's blasting a fig tree that bore no fruit (Matthew, 21:18–22).

p. 287 *Kismet*: fate, lot, portion.

Priscilla Jane Thompson

p. 288 'Freedom at McNealy's': see Harper, 'The Deliverance' (p. 114), and Heard, 'To Clements' Ferry' (p. 256), for other accounts of emancipation.

p. 288 Chattanooga: city in south-east Tennessee.

THE POETS AND THEIR CRITICS

In this section, the poets appear alphabetically for ease of reference.

Louisa May Alcott

Louisa May Alcott: Her Life, Letters, and Journals, *ed. Ednah D. Cheney (Boston: Roberts Brothers, 1889), p. 243*
The following letter of 7 August 1870 accompanied 'The Lay of a Golden Goose' when Alcott sent it to her editor, Thomas Niles, from Switzerland.

Dear Mr Niles, – I keep receiving requests from editors to write for their papers and magazines. I am truly grateful, but having come abroad for rest I am not inclined to try the treadmill till my year's vacation is over. So to appease these worthy gentlemen and excuse my seeming idleness I send you a trifle in rhyme, which you can (if you think it worth the trouble) set going as a general answer to everybody; for I can't pay postage in replies to each separately, – 'it's very costly.' Mr F. said he would pay me $10, $15, $20 for any little things I would send him; so perhaps you will let him have it first.

The war makes the bankers take double toll on our money, so we feel very poor and as if we ought to be earning, not spending; only we are *so* lazy we can't bear to think of it in earnest...

Elizabeth Akers Allen

The Nation, *vol. 3 (1866), p. 306*
... readers of late minor poetry will recognise in Mrs Akers a favorite verse writer when we say that she is the author of the touching lines, 'Rock me to sleep' ... It is no wonder that they have been sung everywhere, for they give sweet and unaffected expression to the sentiment of the purest tie between human hearts; they present it as it exists ... in the tender light of memory, and with all its sweetness increased by contrast with the harsh experiences of the world...

... We do not pronounce her work equal to [Shakespeare or Poe] ... [but she] not only may permit herself to write and publish verses for her own amusement or as a means of self-culture, but also earns the thanks of readers of poetry, to whom much that she writes will certainly give genuine pleasure.

Alice and Phoebe Cary

Rufus W. Griswold, The Female Poets of America *(Philadelphia: Moss, Brother & Co., 1849), p. 372*

In the west, song gushes and flows, like the springs and rivers, more imperially than elsewhere, as they will believe who study ... young poets, whose minds seem to be elevated, by the glorious nature there, into the atmosphere where all thought takes a shape of beauty and harmony. A delicious play of fancy distinguishes much of the finest poetry of the sex; but Alice Carey evinces in many poems a genuine imagination and a creative energy that challenges peculiar praise. We have perhaps no other author, so young, in whom the poetical faculty is so largely developed. Her sister writes with vigor, and a hopeful and genial spirit, and there are many felicities of expression ... She refers more than Alice to the common experience, and has perhaps a deeper sympathy with that philosophy and those movements of the day, which look for a nearer approach to equality, in culture, fortune, and social relations.

Sarah Josepha Hale, Woman's Record *(New York: Harper & Brothers, 1854), p. 615*

Two striking peculiarities enhance the interest of the poems of Alice; the absence of learning, properly so called; and the capacity of the heart to endow the true poet for the high office of interpreter of nature without the aid of learning ... the magic of genius is felt most powerfully, when it triumphs over obstacles seemingly insuperable; the poems we are now considering are fairly entitled to higher praise than though written by a scholar, with all appliances and means for study and composition at command ... In the sentiment of these songs we find the secret of their inspiration; the Bible is the fount from which these young poetesses have quaffed. With the Bible in her hand, and its spirit in her heart, woman can nourish her genius, and prove a guiding angel to all who look heavenward for the Temple of Fame.

Emily Dickinson

*William Dean Howells, 'Emily Dickinson Announced', W. D.
Howells as Critic, ed. Edwin H. Cady (Routledge & Kegan Paul,
1973), pp. 189–95*
Originally published in *Harper's*, January 1891. Howells, a writer of
realist fiction and an influential critic, enhanced reception of the first
published volumes of Dickinson's poetry with his high praise.

> The strange *Poems of Emily Dickinson* we think will form something like
> an intrinsic experience with the understanding reader of them ... She
> could not have made such poetry without knowing its rarity, its singular
> worth; and no doubt it was a radiant happiness in the twilight of her
> hidden, silent life ...
>
> Occasionally, the outside of the poem ... is left so rough, so rude, that
> the art seems to have faltered. But there is apparent to reflection the fact
> that the artist meant just this harsh exterior to remain, and that no grace
> of smoothness could have imparted her intention as it does. It is the soul
> of an abrupt, exalted New England woman that speaks in such brokenness.
> The range of all the poems is of the loftiest; and sometimes there is a kind
> of swelling lift, an almost boastful rise of feeling, which is really the spring
> of faith in them ...
>
> If nothing else had come out of our life but this strange poetry we
> should feel that in the work of Emily Dickinson America, or New England
> rather, had made a distinctive addition to the literature of the world, and
> could not be left out of any record of it; and the interesting and important
> thing is that this poetry is as characteristic of our life as our business
> enterprise, our political turmoil, our demagogism, our millionairism.

*James Fullarton Muirhead, 'Some Literary Straws', The Land of
Contrasts: A Briton's View of His American Kin (Lamson, Wolffe &
Co., 1898), pp. 179, 181, 186*
> [Emily Dickinson's] poems are all in lyrical form – if the word form may be
> applied to her utter disregard of all metrical conventions. Her lines are
> rugged and her expressions wayward to an extraordinary degree ...
>
> ... While tenderly feminine in her sympathy for suffering, her love of
> nature, her loyalty to her friends, she is in expression the most unfeminine
> of poets. The usual feminine impulsiveness and full expression of emotion
> is replaced in her by an extraordinary condensation of phrase and feeling
> ... In her poems ... one is rather impressed with the deep well of poetic
> insight and feeling from which she draws ... In spite of frequent strange
> exaggeration of phrase one is always conscious of a fund of reserve force.

The subjects of her poems are few, but the piercing delicacy and depth of vision with which she turned from death and eternity to nature and to love make us feel the presence of that rare thing, genius. Hers is a wonderful instance of the way in which genius can dispense with experience...

... The reader ... will surely own, whether in scoff or praise, the essentially American nature of her muse. Her defects are easily paralleled in the annals of English literature; but only in the liberal atmosphere of the New World, comparatively unshadowed by trammels of authority and standards of taste, could they have co-existed with so much of the highest quality.

Allen Tate, 'Emily Dickinson', On the Limits of Poetry: Selected Essays, 1928–48 *(The Swallow Press and William Morrow & Co., Publishers, 1948), pp. 197–213*
From comments originally published in 1928 and 1932. Tate was an influential critic of the New Criticism movement, the dominant force in American criticism from the 1930s through the 1960s.

Great poetry needs no special features of difficulty to make it mysterious. When it has them, the reputation of the poet is likely to remain uncertain. This is ... true of Emily Dickinson, whose verse appeared in an age unfavorable to the use of intelligence in poetry. Her poetry is not like any other poetry of her time; it is not like any of the innumerable kinds of verse written today ... It is a poetry of ideas, and it demands of the reader a point of view – not an opinion of [current events], but an ingrained philosophy that is fundamental, a settled attitude that is almost extinct in this eclectic age ... It requires also, for the deepest understanding ... a highly developed sense of the specific quality of poetry – a quality that most persons accept as the accidental feature of something else that the poet thinks he has to say...

A culture cannot be consciously created. It is an available source of ideas that are imbedded in a complete and homogeneous society. The poet finds himself balanced upon the moment when such a world is about to fall, when it threatens to run out into looser and less self-sufficient impulses. This world order is assimilated, in Miss Dickinson, as medievalism was in Shakespeare, to the poetic vision; it is brought down from abstraction to personal sensibility.

... Miss Dickinson ... was born into the equilibrium of an old and a new order. Puritanism could not be to her what it had been to the generation of Cotton Mather – a body of absolute truths; it was an unconscious discipline timed to the pulse of her life.

The perfect literary situation: it produces, because it is rare, a special and perhaps the most distinguished kind of poet ... The two poles of the mind are not separately visible; we infer them from the lucid tension that may be most readily illustrated by polar activity. There is no thought as such at all; nor is there feeling; there is that unique focus of experience which is at once neither and both.

... in Emily Dickinson the Puritan world is no longer self-contained ... her sensibility exceeds its dimensions. She has trimmed down its supernatural proportions ... instead of the tragedy of the spirit there is a commentary upon it. Her poetry is a magnificent personal confession, blasphemous and, in its self-revelation, its honesty, almost obscene. It comes out of an intellectual life towards which it feels no moral responsibility. Cotton Mather would have burnt her for a witch.

Louise Bogan, 'A Mystical Poet', Emily Dickinson: Three Views by Archibald MacLeish, Louise Bogan and Richard Wilbur (Amherst: Amherst College Press, 1960), pp. 27–34

We have ... in Johnson's edition of the poems published in 1955, as complete a record of the development of a lyric talent as exists in Literature ... We ourselves can discover, in the index to the three volumes, that her favorite subject was not death, as was long supposed; for life, love and the soul are also recurring subjects. But the greatest interest lies in her progress as a writer, and as a person. We see the young poet moving away, by gradual degrees, from her early slight addiction to graveyardism, to an Emersonian belief in the largeness and harmony of nature. Step by step, she advances into the terror and anguish of her destiny; she is frightened, but she holds fast and describes her fright ... Nature is no longer a friend, but often an inimical presence. Nature is a haunted house. And – a truth even more terrible – the inmost self can be haunted.

Adrienne Rich, Parnassus: Poetry in Review, 'Vesuvius at Home: The Power of Emily Dickinson', 5:1 (Fall–Winter, 1976), pp. 49–74
Rich is a leading feminist poet and critic, and this essay is one of her most influential.

I know that for me, reading [Dickinson's] poems as a child and then as a young girl already seriously writing poetry, she was a problematic figure. I first read her in the selection heavily edited by her niece which appeared in 1937; a later and fuller edition appeared in 1945 when I was sixteen, and the complete, unbowdlerised edition by Johnson did not appear until fifteen years later ... More than any other poet, Emily Dickinson seemed to tell me that the intense inner event, the personal and psychological, was inseparable from the universal; that there was a range for psychological poetry beyond mere self-expression. Yet the legend of the life was troubling, because it seemed to whisper that a woman who undertook such explorations must pay with renunciation, isolation, and incorporeality. With the publication of the *Complete Poems*, the legend seemed to recede into unimportance beside the unquestionable power and importance of the mind revealed there...

There is one poem ['My life had stood – a Loaded Gun –'] which is the real 'onlie begetter' of my thoughts here about Dickinson ... I think it is a poem about possession by the daemon, about the dangers and risks of such possession if you are a woman, about the knowledge that power in a woman can seem destructive, and that you cannot live without the daemon once it has possessed you ... But this woman poet also perceives herself as a lethal weapon ... the poet sees herself as split, not between anything so simple as 'masculine' and 'feminine' identity but between the hunter, admittedly masculine, but also a human person, an active, willing being, and the gun – an object, condemned to remain inactive until the hunter – the *owner* – takes possession of it ... It is the gun, furthermore, who *speaks for him*. If there is a female consciousness in this poem it is buried deeper than the images: it exists in the ambivalence toward power, which is extreme. Active willing and creation in women are forms of aggression, and aggression is both 'the power to kill' and punishable by death. The union of gun with hunter embodies the danger of identifying and taking hold of her forces, not least that in so doing she risks defining herself – and being defined – as aggressive, as unwomanly ... and as potentially lethal...

The poet experiences herself as loaded gun, imperious energy; yet without the Owner, the possessor, she is merely lethal. Should that possessor abandon her – but the thought is unthinkable: 'He longer *must* – than I.' The pronoun is masculine; the antecedent is what Keats called 'The Genius of Poetry'.

I do not pretend to have ... explained this poem ... But I think that for us, at this time, it is a central poem in understanding Emily Dickinson, and ourselves, and the condition of the woman artist, particularly in the nineteenth century.

Shira Wolosky, Emily Dickinson: A Voice of War *(New Haven and London: Yale University Press, 1984), pp. 61–2, 93–5*

Written in 1862, and presumably commemorating the death of Frazer Stearns [son of the president of Amherst College who was killed in the Civil War], this poem ['Victory comes late –'] nevertheless evades specificities. Its opening image of victory delayed and especially of freezing corpses makes its war context clear. But Dickinson then immediately pursues her own primary interest. The political and historical spheres give way to the pressing metaphysical enigmas raised by them...

Written in 1863, it is perhaps not merely gratuitous that the poem ['My Life had stood – a Loaded Gun –'] posits firearms as its controlling figure. In this light, the poem's religious resonances may also be taken literally. Preachers were repeatedly insisting that war is a manifestation of divine power, and man, God's instrument in waging it...

A radical inversion is here implied. The poem's speaker would not be the poet or any human agent, but God; and the poem would examine divine power in conjunction with human agency...

This power, at least as dreadful as it is majestic, becomes, with the poem's inversion, a human implement. Here, man is not God's instrument, but God man's ... Murder committed in God's name – as was certainly the case with both northern and southern crusaders – may imply a terrible misuse of heavenly power.

... The strange counterpoint between innocence and murder for which this poem is famous becomes functional and systematic in the framework of a martial God – who, during the time of this poem's composition, was a concrete and historical, not just a figurative, Being.

... Whether the poem is read finally in terms of psychic or divine forces, the problem of destructive power in the order of the world and, therefore, of the contradictions involved in a benevolent and omnipotent God remains preeminent for Dickinson. It extends beyond the fact of war, which finally becomes an instance – and at times a model – for Dickinson's confrontation with evil and suffering. And the theodicy invoked for war, as for suffering in general, becomes less and less satisfactory. War emerges as one aspect of a problem that has for Dickinson broader implications.

Sharon Cameron, Choosing Not Choosing: Dickinson's Fascicles *(Chicago: University of Chicago Press, 1992), pp. 4, 34*

... to understand Dickinson's piecemeal lyrics as governed by a fascicle structure would seem to imply a unity produced by a reading of connections between and among poems. But ... to the contrary ... unity is not produced by reading Dickinson's lyrics in the fascicle context ... what is revealed in the fascicles is not only connections *among* poems about the same thing, not only intertextuality in the sense that different poems might be *about* the same thing, or present problems about the same or similar topic/s, or even reiterate aspects of each other. What is more radically revealed is a question about what constitutes the identity of the poem...

Susan Howe, My Emily Dickinson *(Berkeley: North Atlantic Books, 1985), p. 76*
Howe, a poet and critic, discusses resonances of 'My Life had stood – a Loaded Gun –'

POSSIBILITIES
My Life: a Soul finding God.
My Life: a Soul finding herself.
My Life: a poet's admiring heart born into voice by idealising a precursor poet's song.
My Life: Dickinson herself, waiting in corners of neglect for Higginson to recognise her ability and help her to join the ranks of other published American poets.
My Life: the American continent and its westward moving frontier. Two centuries of pioneer literature and myth had insistently compared the land to a virgin woman (bride and queen). Exploration and settlement were pictured in terms of masculine erotic discovery and domination of alluring/threatening feminine territory.
My Life: the savage source of American myth.
My Life: the United States in the grip of violence that threatened to break apart its original Union.

Betsy Erkkila, 'Emily Dickinson and Class', The American Literary History Reader, *ed. Gordon Hutner (New York: Oxford University Press, 1995), pp. 310–11*
In her own writing Dickinson appears to have been more interested in being immortal than in being merely useful, helpful, dutiful, or moral. Adhering to an essentially aristocratic ... notion of literature as the production of mind and genius for eternity, she set herself against not only the new commercialisation and democratisation but against the sentimental women writers of her time who had gained money and fame in the American marketplace...

Folding, sewing, and binding four to five sheets of paper together in groupings of eighteen to twenty poems, Dickinson ... converted traditional female thread and needle work into a different kind of housework and her own form of productive industry. She appears to have been engaged in a kind of home or cottage industry, a precapitalist mode of manuscript production and circulation that avoided the commodity and use values of the commercial marketplace. Along with the manuscripts that she produced, threaded, and bound herself, Dickinson also engaged in a private, essentially aristocratic form of 'publication' by enclosing and circulating her poems in letters to her friends. The irony ... is that while

Dickinson contested the values of the capitalist marketplace in her life and work, by retreating from historical time and social representation toward writing as a subjective, private, and aestheticised act, she, like other Romantic poets, ended by enforcing the separation of art and society and the corresponding feminisation, trivialisation, and marginalisation of art in the new bourgeois aesthetics.

Timothy Morris, Becoming Canonical in American Poetry *(Urbana and Chicago: University of Illinois Press, 1995), p. xiii*

Of all American women poets, Emily Dickinson is the most indisputably canonical. But it remains an anomaly that she achieved this status at all, let alone as early and as firmly as she did. Unlike any other woman writer of the United States, her canonicity has been unassailable from the beginnings of the discipline of American literature ... Clearly, there was no attempt to include Dickinson in the developing American canon *because* she was a woman or spoke to women's concerns. In fact, male critics overcame their considerable prejudice against her gender to promote her to a status as unchallenged as Mark Twain's.

Dickinson's early critics rearranged the terms of their prejudice rather than radically revising it. Critics of the early twentieth century undoubtedly heard Dickinson's voice as feminine. But they heard it as a voyeur (an *auditeur?*) might hear it: not as the distinctive idiom of a particular Victorian woman, but as the secret, unrepressed voice of Everywoman – a voice that was largely the creation of their own fantasies ... Dickinson became the woman poet as virginal site, pried loose from Victorian prudery by publication after her death and made to submit to the critical urges of liberal males. Dickinson was female but nonthreatening; she was dead before she entered critical discourse, and she had been cloistered even during her lifetime. She was the ideal fantasy plaything for male critics.

Mary Mapes Dodge

The Nation, *vol. 19 (1874), p. 369*

Parents will have only to read a short way into 'Rymes and Jingles' to want it, and to read it all through to determine to keep it as a volume of unequalled entertainment for small fry if scarcely less for themselves. It is full of comical wise nonsense and the most felicitous absurdities of language.

Margaret Fuller

Margaret Vanderhaar Allen, The Achievement of Margaret Fuller *(University Park, Pennsylvania: The Pennsylvania State University Press, 1979), pp. 70–71*

[Fuller's] gift for poetic communication seldom found an effective voice in her poems. Many other Transcendentalists, like Fuller, aspired to poetry but succeeded in prose. Her lyric poems are often moralistic or pious, filled with undigested sadness and dejection. Unable to break out of eighteenth-century diction and conventions, she disparaged her verses as 'all rhetorical and impassioned' ... Fuller knew that much of her poetry was occasional poetry and said that 'for us lesser people [she meant less than geniuses like Goethe or Byron], who write verses merely as vents for the overflowings of a personal experience', it is inexcusable to take the public for a confidant by means of autobiographical poetry not sufficiently universalised and objectified to be of lasting merit ... As always, Fuller's self-criticism was too harsh ...

Fuller's infatuation with the German Romantics probably contributed to her inability to find a wholly satisfying form for her utterance. Many German Romantics spoke as she did of dissatisfaction with 'mere' words, a wish to go beyond existing forms and wield 'an enchanter's mirror' ... Fuller, in describing the kind of poetry she wanted to write, was describing something like the poetry that the French Symbolists developed later in the century ... Once again her ideas were far ahead of her time. But she could not write the poetry she envisioned. 'In early years I aspired to wield the sceptre or the lyre; for I loved with wise design and irresistible command to mould many to one purpose, and it seemed all that man could desire to breathe in music and speak in words, the harmonies of the universe. But the golden lyre was not given to my hand, and I am but the prophecy of a poet.'

Charlotte Perkins Stetson Gilman

Henry Austin, review of In This Our World, The Bookman, *vol. 1, no. 5 (June 1895), pp. 335–7*

The contents of this little volume fully justify the first opinions formed by various critics of Mrs Stetson's capacity. Here is a woman with a sense of humour and at the same time, in spots, peculiarly without that saving sense; for some things in the book, if read by themselves, would tempt a critic to class it simply as another curiosity of literature ...

... *malgré* her infelicitous eccentricities of thought and technique, much of her work is lofty in tone ... There is a fine, throbbing, human quality about it. There are passages of grave and potent eloquence ...

Mrs Stetson has very little Nature-worship in her verse, very little word-painting of the scenic sort. Her concern, chiefly, is Human Nature – Man and Woman – and especially the New Woman of whose arrival we have heard so much lately that some of us are weary in advance. But occasionally Mrs Stetson can throw words together, as Turner threw colours, and produce an intense sense of picture ...

... In most of that class of her verses ... where she assails with the cold logic of science and the charming warmth of ridicule the present industrial system ... Mrs Stetson's humorous and vigorous muse is at her best, because at her largest. The *Weltschmerz* blots out the Ego ...

'*Charlotte Perkins Stetson, A Daring Humorist of Reform*', The American Fabian, *vol. 3, no. 1 (January 1897), pp. 1–3*
[*In This Our World*] is a collection of singularly fresh and vigorous pieces – not poetry in the lofty meaning of the word, and, indeed, the author lays no claim to the title of poet, but in the trenchant parables she deftly cuts into her page is teaching of the highest order. If it is not poetry it certainly is not prose ...

Harry Thurston Peck, 'The Cook-Stove in Poetry', The Bookman, *vol. 8, no. 1 (September 1898), pp. 50–51*
[Mrs Stetson's] verse shows an improvement in technique during the past three years until now both in the aptness of her thought, the terseness of her phrase, and the general compactness of her style as a whole, she stands head and shoulders above any of the other minor poets of her sex. In fact, did we not know the author's name, we should have selected many of the poems collected in [*In This Our World*] as having been written by a man.

Mrs Stetson is most interested in life and its various problems. She does not deal very much in sentiment, but she goes out among men and women and looks at them from a semi-sociological point of view and hammers away at what she thinks she sees. Almost everything that she writes is strong and effective, from the way in which she has dealt with it. In her milder moods (which are not frequent) she sometimes shows a touch that is truly poetical. She is at her best, however, and also most at her ease, when she is dealing with questions that are partly ethical.

Hannah F. Gould

Sarah Josepha Hale, Woman's Record, *p. 680*
Hale's assessment of Gould's poetry reveals much about Hale's influential poetics and her opposition to the concepts of poetic value that male Romantic poets brought to dominance.

> The great popularity of Miss Gould we consider a most encouraging omen for the lovers of genuine poetry, of that which is true in thought and natural in description. She charms by the rare merit of imparting interest to small things and common occurrences. These make up far the greater part of life's reality, and, if truth be the essence of poetry, they must be poetical ... Passion has too often usurped the place of reason, and a selfish sensitiveness been fostered, instead of that healthful sentiment of complacency in the happiness of others, which all high exercise of the mental faculties should exalt and encourage. It is this enlarging and elevating the affections, which improves the heart and purifies the taste. And this is one important office of true poetry – such poetry as Miss Gould has written.
>
> She also possesses great delicacy and scope of imagination; she gathers around her simple themes imagery of peculiar beauty and uncommon association – and yet this imagery is always appropriate. Then she has a very felicitous command of language, and the skill of making the most uncouth words 'lie smooth in rhyme', which the greatest poet of the age might envy...
>
> Wit is a much rarer quality than wisdom in female writers ... Miss Gould's sprightly wit has the advantage of appearing quite original. She, however, uses it with great delicacy, and always to teach or enforce some lesson ... the great power of her poetry is its *moral* application...
>
> The mania for melancholy and despairing poetry, which the Byronian era introduced, never found any favour in the clear, calm, sensible mind of our poetess. Her philosophy is as practical and contented as her piety is ardent...
>
> Her poems will be popular while truth has friends and nature admirers, and while children are readers. And what praise is sweeter to a pure, good mind than the praise of childhood, in which the *heart* is always given with the *lips*?

Rufus W. Griswold, The Female Poets of America *(1860), p. 45*
Griswold notes Gould's humour, an attribute rarely credited to women writers.

> Miss Gould's poems are short, but they are frequently nearly perfect in

their kind ... Her most distinguishing characteristic is sprightliness. Her
poetical vein seldom rises above the fanciful, but in her vivacity there is
both wit and cheerfulness ... Often by a dainty touch, or lively prelude,
the gentle raillery of her sex most charmingly reveals itself, and in this
respect Miss Gould manifests a decided individuality of genius.

Louise Imogen Guiney

Bliss Carman, 'Louise Imogen Guiney', The Chap-Book, vol. 2, no.
1 (15 November 1894), pp. 27–36

[Guiney's] second venture in the sea of letters, *The White Sail* ... shows a
marked advance upon the first and contains a number of distinctly original
and notable poems. It is full of that delightful freshness of health which
lends her words their inspiring quality ... Even natural sorrow is so
infused with the perennial gladness of this beautiful world as to become
scarcely more poignant than an ancient tale of pathos ... Not to be
overborne by the turbulence of our days, nor too much moved by any
sadness, is the first lesson of art, – art, that helper and continual solace of
the world's life. So that the great artist must be first of all joyous, then
assured, then fervent, then unrestrained and out of all bounds save those
of his own conscience and contriving. His only patent is originality ...

The true artist ... in these qualities of courage and hope must be
distinctly the most manly of his fellows, and there is no more manly note
in American letters today than that which rings through the lyrics of the
little lady of Auburndale ... She can put more valor in a single line than
one can squeeze from our periodical poets in a twelve month. For it is a
sorry but certain fact that our magazines are fast becoming the nin-
compoopiana of literature. And this is not because they are ill-conducted,
but because their practical success depends upon it. We must always make
allowance in any art for the influence of popular demand. When we
consider the circulation necessary to make a book or a magazine a practical
success, the wonder is, not that contemporary letters are so poor, but that
they are so good.

Alice Brown, Louise Imogen Guiney (New York: The Macmillan
Co., 1921), pp. 41–50

The White Sail, part legend and part lyric, with an academic ballast of
sonnets, sang out in fuller tone [than Guiney's first volume of poetry],
though with no less individual a measure. The legends ring curiously
scholastic in these days when the industrious versifier celebrates the small
beer of his own 'home town' in untrained eccentricities all too faithful to

his villageous mood. Her legends were the tall pines of the fairy grove she wandered in. There were pillared aisles and porticos, not New England dooryards, tapestries shaken by winds of the past, not leaves, red and gold, blown her from the swamps and hills she knew . . .

Louise Bogan, Achievement in America Poetry *(Los Angeles: Henry Regnery Co., 1951), p. 22*
Miss Guiney's interest in the English Carolinian and Recusant poets of the seventeenth century gave her work a learned base; she wrote in a gallant spirit which foreshadowed the more masculine attitudes of certain women poets of the twenties.

Emily Stipes Watts, The Poetry of American Women from 1632 to 1945 *(Austin and London, University of Texas Press, 1977), p. 139*
The verse of Guiney is generally associated with the *fin de siècle* movement in England, with a further basis in the Pre-Raphaelite verse of the Rossettis . . . She urged Americans to find other cultural values in other lands, and her early verse, especially, represents a conscious . . . attempt to reflect 'international' or more general humanistic qualities . . .

Sarah Josepha Hale

Rufus W. Griswold, The Female Poets of America *(1860), p. 57*
. . . in 1848 appeared her Three Hours; or, The Vigil of Love, and Other Poems . . . upon which altogether must rest her best literary reputation . . . Mrs Hale has a ready command of pure and idiomatic English, and her style has frequently a masculine strength and energy. She has not much creative power, but she excels in the aggregation and artistical disposition of common and appropriate imagery . . . [Her works] are all indicative of sound principles, and of kindness, knowledge, and judgment.

Ruth E. Finley, The Lady of Godey's: Sarah Josepha Hale *(Philadelphia and London: J. B. Lippincott Co., 1931), pp. 20–21*
Finley's biographical study contextualises Hale's career and the style of genteel activism that it exemplifies.
[Hale's] real contribution lies in the fact that, having the soul of a modern, she understood – and deliberately employed – Victorianism as a link, a transition, between the lethargic indifference of the eighteenth century, that regarded woman as a highly prized chattel, and the nineteenth century's dream of a woman's destiny – economic and moral freedom. With the subtlety of the true leader she never antagonised her Victorian public; she saw clearly that the affectations and absurdities of her times

were mere reactions against the preceding age of great rudeness and she dealt with them accordingly – her deeper self meanwhile focused on the morrow.

... she knew the uncouth frankness, brutality and immorality of the seventeen-hundreds as harsh realities. For, though many a modern historian still retains enough of late Victorian inhibitions to ignore or gloss over the culmination of the crude and licentious in the social fabric of post-Revolutionary America, there remain the facts, clearly attested, of highways infested with 'gentlemen of the road', rape, preferment, slavery, dueling, hanging for petty theft, public whipping, wife-beating, child-selling ... general as well as individual beastliness. These grim things the editor of *Godey's* knew to have existed in Victorianism's immediate past. And these she knew as but a few of the outrages Victorianism struggled to correct.

... Mrs Hale never lost patience with the prudishness and evasions that were the inevitable results of the nineteenth-century revolt. That she deplored the self-satisfaction of the age, its stubborn adherence to out-moded methods and customs and above all its willful blindness to changing educational and labor conditions, is evidenced in every issue of her magazine. But she was too far-seeing to put herself outside the pale of conformity. Having visioned her goal, she set herself down in genteel effacement, feathered quill in hand, and for the full measure of fifty years proceeded to cajole her public into one reform after another.

Patricia Okker, Our Sister Editors: Sarah J. Hale and the Tradition of Nineteenth-Century American Women Editors *(Athens and London: University of Georgia Press, 1995), pp. 142–4, 166*
Okker discusses Hale's views of poetry as innovative and enabling to women.

In her essay 'Woman the Poet of Nature', published in the *Lady's Book* in 1837, Hale directly refuted the notion that women's poetic achievements were naturally inferior to men's. Rather than describing the highest poetic achievement in masculine terms, Hale created a feminised critical discourse for poetry ... Hale did not equate feminine poetry with limited achievement. On the contrary, she asserted that all poets, especially the great ones, should strive for feminine goals.

... Hale inverted the hierarchy used by many of her contemporaries, who assumed men's poetry to be innately superior to women's. Indeed, Hale argued that women, not men, were 'morally gifted to excel' in poetry. Although she recognised exceptions, she believed that generally 'the poetry of man' focused on the individual 'intellect', 'passions', and 'pride', but the 'poetry of woman' expressed the greatest human truths, including 'impressions of the Beautiful and the Good', 'the love of truth and nature', and 'faith in God' (*Godey's Lady's Book*, May 1837, 194–5). Such a distinction between men's and women's poetry reinforced the genteel association of women with emotions and men with intellect, but Hale believed that men's poetry was capable of greater human truths only when it accepted a female perspective. Like a mother or wife who exerted a positive moral influence on her family through love, poets, according to Hale, achieved their highest calling when they appealed not to readers' rational faculties but to ... their 'impressions', 'faith', and 'love'. Significantly, this understanding of poetry's aims did not imply that it had a didactic purpose. Indeed, elsewhere Hale distinguished between 'didactic' poetry and that which achieved its moral purpose through 'indirect influence' (*Ladies' Magazine*, Feb. 1829, p. 73)...

According to Hale's literary history, women's voices transformed and ultimately improved poetry, especially in its subject matter: 'War, the chace, the wine-cup and physical love are the themes of song in which men first delight and excel; nor is it till feminine genius exerts its power to judge and condemn these, always earthly, and often coarse and licentious, strains that the tone of the lyre becomes softer, chaster, more pure and polished and finally, as her influence increases, and she joins the choir, the song assumes that divine character which angels might regard with complacency.' Although she associated men here with a greater topical range, Hale directly refuted the charge that she restricted women poets. She objected to those 'critics who always speak of the "true feminine style" – as though there was only one manner in which ladies could properly write poetry', and she noted the variety of such poets as ... Lydia Sigourney and Hannah Gould. Furthermore, Hale explained that although women poets have a more limited 'range of subjects' than men, 'in the manner of treating those within her province, she has a freedom as perfect as his' ... Hale insisted that 'the delicate shades of genius are as varied and as distinctly marked in one sex as its bold outlines are in the other. There are more varieties of the rose than of the oak' (*Godey's Lady's Book*, May 1837, p. 194)...

The power of a public female space is ... the greatest legacy of Hale's career ... At a time when many middle-class women struggled to find adequate employment and few people of either sex found financial success through literary pursuits, Hale worked successfully as an editor and writer for over fifty years ... her editorial columns consistently reveal both the power of the sisterly editorial voice and the flexibility of Victorian ideologies of separate spheres. With this editorial voice and Victorian ideologies of gender, Hale used her magazine to create and to comment on literary and women's cultures. That Hale envisioned these cultures as including the professionalisation of authorship and improved wage-earning opportunities for women suggests the extent to which she rejected conservative interpretations of separate spheres.

Frances Ellen Watkins Harper

W. E. B. Du Bois, 'Writers', The Crisis, vol. 1, no. 6 (April 1911), pp. 20–21

It is ... for her attempts to forward literature among colored people that Frances Harper deserves most to be remembered ... She took her writing soberly and earnestly; she gave her life to it, and it gave her fair support.

J. Saunders Redding, 'Let Freedom Ring', To Make a Poet Black (McGrath Publishing Co., 1968), pp. 39, 42

In 1861 Mrs Harper ... wrote to Thomas Hamilton, the editor of the *Anglo African*, a monthly journal that had been established the year before: 'If our talents are to be recognised we must write less of issues that are particular and more of feelings that are general. We are blessed with hearts and brains that compass more than ourselves in our present plight ... We must look to the future which, God willing, will be better than the present or the past, and delve into the heart of the world.'

... In some of Miss Watkins's verse one thing ... is to be noted especially. In the volume called *Sketches of Southern Life* the language she puts in the mouths of Negro characters has a fine racy, colloquial tang. In these poems she managed to hurdle a barrier by which Dunbar was later to feel himself tripped. The language is not dialect. She retained the speech patterns of Negro dialect, thereby giving herself greater emotional scope ... than the humorous and the pathetic to which it is generally acknowledged dialect limits one ...

Joan R. Sherman, Invisible Poets: Afro-Americans of the Nineteenth Century (Urbana: University of Illinois Press, 2nd ed., 1989), pp. 73–4

[Harper] shows a ... talent for matching technique and subject in the charming series of poems which makes up most of *Sketches of Southern Life* (1872). Aunt Chloe, the narrator, is a wise, practical ex-slave who discusses the war and Reconstruction with earthy good humor, as Uncle Jacob, a saintly optimist, counsels prayer, 'faith and courage'. These poems are unique in Mrs Harper's canon for their wit and irony; the colloquial expressions of Aunt Chloe's discourse form a new idiom in black poetry which ripens into the dialect verse of Campbell, Davis, and Dunbar in the last decades of the century ... The Aunt Chloe series is successful because a consistent, personalised language and references to everyday objects give authenticity to the subjects while directly communicating the freedmen's varying attitudes of self-mockery, growing self-respect, and optimism without sentimentality.

Melba Joyce Boyd, Discarded Legacy: Politics and Poetics in the Life of Frances E. W. Harper, 1825–1911 *(Detroit: Wayne State University Press, 1994), p. 151*
Boyd compares the personae of *Aunt Chloe* to those in Harper's novel *Iola Leroy.*

By avoiding existing examples of dialect, as exemplified by Stowe and other popular writers, Harper evaded the pitfalls of an over-apostrophied dialect with stilted articulations. Harper's personae speak fluidly and intelligently about enslavement, the Civil War, literacy, religion, and electoral politics. Speaking their own consciousness, their tongues are rounded from injustice and embellished with insightful imagery...

Ironically, Harper ... whose diction was trained for elocutionary delivery from public lecterns – revolutionised the presentation and adaptation of black American English. Unlike many of her contemporaries, she ignored the prejudices of the bourgeois imagination and thereby transcended the cultural and class contradictions of traditional writing. Her aesthetic motivations determined an oral approach for the written language for the benefit of culture rather than exploiting the experience of the culture for the benefit of the literature. Hence, her dialect poetry, written for the historicisation of a people and to promote a positive vision for their future, advanced the democratic tradition of American literature and envisioned the dialect achievements of twentieth-century writers.

Ella Higginson

Review of When the Birds Go North Again, The Dial, *vol. 26 (1899), p. 52*
At first sight Mrs Higginson's collection of poems, 'When the Birds Go North Again', seems to be the usual sort of thing. There are sonnets, and lyrics, and bits of religious or didactic verse – all upon such themes as every versifier attempts. A closer examination, however, reveals the fact that this writer, while often amateurish in manner and crude in technique, has an unusual gift of passionate imagination, and at her best rises high

above the plane whereon most minor poets disport themselves...

Julia Ward Howe

Julia Ward Howe, Reminiscences: 1819–1899 *(New York: Houghton Mifflin Co., 1899), pp. 273–5*

Howe tells of composing the 'Battle-Hymn of the Republic' the morning after attending a review of Union troops in Washington, DC. Anxious to help the war effort but busy with her children, she decided to write a song.

> I went to bed that night as usual, and slept, according to my wont, quite soundly. I awoke in the gray of the morning twilight; and as I lay waiting for the dawn, the long lines of the desired poem began to twine themselves in my mind. Having thought out all the stanzas, I said to myself, 'I must get up and write these verses down, lest I fall asleep again and forget them.' So, with a sudden effort, I sprang out of bed, and found in the dimness an old stump of a pen which I remembered to have used the day before. I scrawled the verses almost without looking at the paper. I had learned to do this when, on previous occasions, attacks of versification had visited me in the night, and I feared to have recourse to a light lest I should wake the baby, who slept near me. I was always obliged to decipher my scrawl before another night should intervene, as it was only legible while the matter was fresh in my mind. At this time, having completed my writing, I returned to bed and fell asleep, saying to myself, 'I like this better than most things that I have written.'

Edmund Wilson, Patriotic Gore: Studies in the Literature of the American Civil War *(New York: Oxford University Press, 1962), pp. 59–98*

A leading critic, Wilson ridiculed Howe's lyrics while analysing them in detail.

> It is significant that in 'John Brown's Body', the Federals' favorite song, John Brown should be 'a soldier in the army of the Lord'; and that Julia Ward Howe, when asked to provide for the popular tune a more dignified set of words, should have produced, in the 'Battle-Hymn of the Republic', a more exalted version of the same idea. It will be worthwhile to scrutinise this poem, which, carried along by the old rousing rhythm, has persisted so long and become so familiar that we have ceased to pay attention to its sense...
>
> ... The advent of the Union armies represents ... the coming of the

Lord, and their cause is the cause of God's truth ... The Confederacy is a serpent, which God's Hero must slay, and in proportion to the punishment inflicted by this Hero on God's enemies, who are also his own, the Deity will reward the Hero ... As is often the case with Calvinists, Mrs Howe, though she feels she must bring [Jesus] in, gives Him a place which is merely peripheral. He is really irrelevant to her picture, for Christ died to make men holy; but this is not what God is having *us* do: He is a militant, a military God, and far from wanting us to love our enemies, He gives 'the Hero' orders to 'crush the serpent with his heel'. The righteous object of this is to 'make men [the Negroes] free', and we must die to accomplish this. Note that Christ is situated 'across the sea': he is not present on the battlefield with His Father, yet, intent on our grisly work, we somehow still share in His 'glory'. I have not been able to guess where Julia Ward Howe got these lilies in the beauty of which Jesus is supposed to have been born ... In any case, they serve to place Him in a setting that is effeminate as well as remote. The gentle and no doubt very estimable Jesus is trampling no grapes of wrath. And now come on, New England boys, get in step with the marching God! If you succeed in crushing the serpent, God will reward you with 'grace'. (This cheats on Predestination, but Mrs Howe, 'brought up', as she says, 'after the strictest rule of New England Puritanism', had afterwards become more liberal.)

Rebekah Gumpert Hyneman

Diane Lichtenstein, Writing Their Nation: The Tradition of Nineteenth-Century American Jewish Women Writers *(Bloomington: Indiana University Press, 1992), pp. 64–8*

Although they resembled Christian women in their familial obligations, Jewish women did not need to fight the image of the helpless, fainting 'child-woman'. Because so many of them felt they played a vital role in preserving the Jewish nation through the Jewish home, Jewish women had a strong sense of purpose and identity. They believed in their duties as women particularly because they perceived them as special and necessary for the survival of the Jews. They accepted the responsibility for being teachers of morality, for example, not to guide children and husband past 'maelstroms of atheism and uncontrolled sexuality' as was the Christian woman's duty ... but, rather, to save them from spiritual annihilation (through a loss of Judaism) and literal annihilation (through overt anti-Semitism). Despite these significant differences ... [Jewish American women writers] conformed on some levels to the myths of American womanhood...

... [In her poem 'Judith'] Hyneman extols Judith's courage but assures us that her actions grow out of love of country and God. She is not hardened to battle or murder but, rather, masters her feelings of repugnance in order to serve. Hyneman uses the contrast between the woman's 'gentle hand' and the blood of the battle to heighten the incongruity of the scene. Neither the True Woman, nor even the Mother in Israel, has a regular place on the battlefield; the proper woman's war is against immorality, nonobservance of religious laws, and family members' illnesses.

The poem 'Woman's Rights' ... makes this last point explicit. Despite the provocative title, the poem tells us not that a woman has the right to vote or work, but rather she has the 'right' 'to soothe the couch of pain' as well as to make man's home an earthly paradise and 'to teach the infant mind'.

Helen Hunt Jackson

Emily Stipes Watts, The Poetry of American Women, *pp. 141–2*

... Her primary contribution to women's verse is ... in her desire to give a specific prosodic 'form', an artistic discipline, to her themes and 'feelings'. While the Romantic and Transcendental poets sought an 'organic' poetic structure, Jackson (and Dickinson) reaffirmed the value of traditional verse forms. It is possible to understand such a tendency in terms of a 'reactionary' movement at this time in the verse of both men and women in the ebb and flow of 'the meter-making argument', which Edwin Fussell has identified as 'the soul of American poetry' ...

... Jackson and Dickinson and Guiney and Lazarus seem to represent the growing awareness among American women of the relationship of prosodic structure and meaning ... As women's poetry developed throughout the nineteenth century, the poets had emphasised meaning, thoughts, and themes and ignored prosody. Again and again, we find that the bold and often original content is buried in poorly contrived metrics ... and common rhyme patterns. On the other hand, from 1880 to 1900, there existed in the verse of American women four distinct kinds of prosodic methods, none of which is related to the prosody of Emerson or Whitman or other American male poets at this time. Women's verse was certainly more rich in this sense at this time than that of the American men.

[Among these prosodic methods are] Jackson's emphasis on a tight stanzaic structure, through which vigorous emotions or thoughts are allowed to play ... Jackson herself believed the universe was a 'Form' ... and applied such a standard to her own poetry. Her discursive sonnets ... exhibit her attempts to structure thoughts through form, but other poems clearly indicate her emphasis upon the stanza as a means of controlling feeling and thought.

Emily Pauline Johnson

Review of The White Wampum, The Dial, *vol. 20 (1896), p. 116*
The poems of Miss Johnson derive an adventitious interest from the fact that they are written by an Indian girl, the daughter of a well-known Mohawk chief. As might be expected, these poems are distinctly outdoor songs and ballads, and the barbaric strain of passion is not lacking. But they have also claims to consideration on their own account, for they display delicacy of sentiment and felicity of expression in a remarkable degree.

Frances Anne Kemble

Henry James, 'Frances Anne Kemble', Essays in London and Elsewhere *(Harper & Brothers, 1893), pp. 81–120*
Her prose and poetical writings are alike unequal; easily the best of the former, I think, are the strong, insistent, one-sided *Journal of a Residence on a Georgia Plantation* (the most valuable account – and as a report of strong emotion scarcely less valuable from its element of *parti-poris* – of impressions begotten by that old Southern life which we are too apt to see today as through a haze of Indian summer), and the copious and ever-delightful *Record of a Girlhood* and *Records of Later Life*, which form together one of the most animated autobiographies in the language. Her poetry, all passionate and melancholy and less prized, I think, than it deserves, is perfectly individual and really lyrical. Much of it is so off-hand as to be rough, but much of it has beauty as well as reality, such beauty as to make one ask one's self ... whether her aptitude for literary expression had not been well worth her treating it with more regard. That she might have cared for it more is very certain – only as certain, however, as it is doubtful if any circumstances could have made her care. You can neither take vanity from those who have it nor give it to those who have it not. She really cared only for things higher and finer and fuller and happier than the shabby compromises of life, and the polishing of a few verses the more or the less would never have given her the illusion of the grand style. The matter comes back, moreover, to the terrible question of 'art'; it is difficult after all to see where art can be squeezed in when you have such a quantity of nature ... What she had in verse was not only the lyric impulse but the genuine lyric need ... She made a very honest use of

it, inasmuch as it expressed for her what nothing else could express – the inexpugnable, the fundamental, the boundless and generous sadness which lay beneath her vitality, beneath her humor, her imagination, her talents, her violence of will and integrity of health. This note of suffering, audible to the last and pathetic, as the prostrations of strength are always pathetic, had an intensity all its own, though doubtless, being so direct and unrelieved, the interest and even the surprise of it were greatest for those to whom she was personally known. There was something even strangely simple in that perpetuity of pain which the finest of her sonnets commemorate and which was like the distress of a nature conscious of its irremediable exposure and consciously paying for it. The great tempest of her life, her wholly unprosperous marriage, had created waves of feeling which, even after long years, refused to be stilled, continued to gather and break.

Lucy Larcom

Rufus W. Griswold, The Female Poets of America *(1860), p. 360*
Cites John Greenleaf Whittier on Larcom's poems.

That they were written by a young woman whose life has been no long holyday of leisure, but one of toil and privation, does not indeed enhance their intrinsic merit, but it lends them an interest in the eyes of those who, like ourselves, long to see the cords of cast broken, and the poor niceties of aristocratic exclusiveness, irrational and unchristian everywhere, but in addition ridiculous in a country like ours, vanish before the true nobility of mind – the natural graces of a good heart and a useful life – the self-sustained dignity of a spirit superior to the folly of accounting labor degradation, and usefulness a calamity, and which can not count as common and unclean the duties which God has sanctified.

The Dial, vol. 5 (1885), p. 265

The three hundred closely printed pages which are needed to contain the verse of Lucy Larcom bear unmistakable witness to the industry of one of our most estimable women of letters. Her verses are simply written, and are such as may have a strong hold upon simple minds. Of the heights and depths of poetry, there can be no question in their consideration. Most regions of the imagination and most phases of passion are entirely unknown to her; but she has attained to a considerable facility in the expression of a mild form of religious sentiment, and of the gentler aspect of nature as seen in her New England home ... A refined and delicate fancy is her substitute for imagination, and kindly feeling what she has to give in the place of passion. While these offer nothing to the true lover of poetry, there are many who, lacking the artistic perceptions needed for its enjoyment, may find in such verse as this a pleasure analogous at least – although far lower – to that which persons of acuter sensibilities find in the works of the genuine poets.

Emma Lazarus

James Russell Lowell, letter to Emma Lazarus dated 17 December 1883, Letters to Emma Lazarus in the Columbia University Library, ed. Ralph L. Rusk (New York: Columbia University Press, 1939), p. 74

I must write ... to say how much I liked your sonnet about the Statue ['The New Colossus'] – much better than I like the Statue itself. But your sonnet gives its subject a *raison d'être* which it wanted before quite as much as it wants a pedestal. You have set it on a noble one, saying admirably just the right word to be said ...

Rachel Cohen, 'Emma Lazarus', The Reform Advocate, vol. 74, no. 8 (24 September 1927), p. 189

Emma Lazarus, with the power of her pen, helped to regenerate her people. Her endeavors helped to make easier the way for those who, following in her footsteps, came years after her. She foresaw and foretold what no other Jewess had seen. She wrote in English for the world to read. She was at one with the meanest Jewish refugee, the greatness of kin that knows of no barriers ... It is, indeed, small wonder that one who had felt with all intensity the sufferings of the terror, pogrom-hounded Jews, was able to pen the spirit of that Colossus, the immense woman who stands, with uplifted lamp in hand, waiting to welcome, with mother-love, the sufferers and weary of the Old World to the glorious promise of the New ...

Max I. Baym, 'Emma Lazarus and Emerson', Publications of the American Jewish Historical Society, vol. 38, no. 4 (June 1949), pp. 261–87

... the ... estimate of [Lazarus] as a poet has been obfuscated by three pervasive interested parties: those who would present her as an orthodox Jewess interested in the dates of holidays and memorials; those who would link in her character and work Jewish ardour with social revolution; and those who ... would suppress her Jewishness and true origin. As a result, she has fared ill indeed at the bar of accredited literary history ...

Dan Vogel, Emma Lazarus *(Twayne Publishers, 1980), pp. 161–2*
[Lazarus] left to her literary progeny an American public prepared and willing to accept the writings of American Jews and other Americans from minority groups ... The conditioning of the American public to interest itself in – indeed, to see itself in – the troubles and victories of the Jew began with Emma Lazarus's essays and poems...

Diane Lichtenstein, Writing Their Nation, *pp. 55–7*
Throughout her career, Lazarus sought justification in order to claim a patch of 'native ground' upon which she could establish her literary identity. We see this private search veiled by a public exhortation in an early poem, 'How Long?' ... We hear Lazarus expressing frustration with America's insecurity about its literature. It is time, she writes, to protect ourselves against that British song which cannot accurately or honestly express America's uniqueness. But it is not only America's uniqueness she is defending; it is also her own. In calling for an authentic American 'strain', she sought to stake out a national as well as a personal 'native ground'...

Ironically, Lazarus became [a] literary insider by valorising the outsider. 'The New Colossus', her best-known contribution to mainstream American literature and culture, is the culminating symbol of this process. In the poem, Lazarus valorises the alien who finds in America a home – a native ground composed of many alien grounds. Through the celebration of otherness, Lazarus conveyed her deepest loyalty to the best of both America and Judaism and, ironically, strengthened her 'outsider' status so that it would become valuable.

Another poem, written in 1883, also projects the Jewish pride and gratitude to America Lazarus felt during this fruitful period of American and Jewish literary production. As the title suggests, '1492' focuses on the 'two-faced year' when Spain expelled its Jews and Columbus landed in America. As Lazarus imagines the historical irony of 1492, the Jews, the 'children of the prophets of the Lord', will find haven in a 'virgin world where doors of sunset part' ... Echoing 'The New Colossus' in sonnet form and exuberant rhetoric, '1492' more explicitly focuses on Jews – rather than the generalised 'huddled masses' – and their unique historical experiences.

Adah Isaacs Menken

Diane Lichtenstein, Writing Their Nation, *pp. 105–6*

'Judith', a poem included in *Infelicia*, reveals Menken's histrionic and emotional understanding of Judaism ... Unlike the Old Testament's figure, Menken's Judith violently revels in blood and gore. And unlike Hyneman's timidly courageous 'Female Scriptural Character', Menken's character derives power from sexual passion as well as from national pride. This hero plays to an audience, reciting a climactic soliloquy at the end of a moving scene. Concerned less with Judith's faith and more with her dramatic triumph, Menken, the poet and actor, saw in the hero the potential for a moving part she herself wanted to play.

Penina Moise

Diane Lichtenstein, Writing Their Nation, *p. 99*

At first glance, the poem ['To Persecuted Foreigners'] offers an unambivalent portrait of what America represents and offers. It can be felt as a sincere celebration of American democracy and tolerance. A poem that so passionately and publicly expresses its sentiment, however, might be carrying another encoded message, about insecurity and displacement. By reading through the code, we can see how Moise used her loud proclamation to reassure both herself and her audience that America truly insures liberty and justice for all, and that the poem provided a means for the author to inscribe herself as an American even on the grammatical level of repeating the inclusive pronoun 'our'.

Elizabeth Oakes-Smith

Rufus W. Griswold, The Female Poets of America *(1849), pp. 177–83*

... through all her manifold writings ... there runs the same beautiful vein of philosophy, viz.: that truth and goodness of themselves impart a holy light to the mind, which gives it a power far above mere intellectuality; that the highest order of human intelligence springs from the moral and not the reasoning faculties ...

The simplicity of diction, and pervading beauty and elevation of thought, which are the chief characteristics of The Sinless Child, bring it undoubtedly within the [category of works of genius] ... in every heart, unless thoroughly corrupted by the world – in every mind, unless completely encrusted by cant, there lurks an inward sense of the simple, the beautiful, and the true; an instinctive perception of excellence which is both more unerring and more universal than that of mere intellect. Such is the cheering view of humanity enforced in The Sinless Child, and the reception of it is evidence of the truth of the doctrine it so finely shadows forth ... the writer, in unconsciously picturing the actual graces of her own mind, has made an irresistible appeal to the ideal of soul-loveliness in the minds of her readers.

Edgar Allan Poe, 'Elizabeth Oakes-Smith' (review of The Poetical Writings of Elizabeth Oakes-Smith, *1st ed.),* The Works of Edgar Allan Poe, *vol. 7 (Philadelphia: J. B. Lippincott Co., 1906), pp. 122, 123, 126, 128*

'The Sinless Child' was originally published in the *Southern Literary Messenger,* where it at once attracted much attention from the novelty of its conception and the general grace and purity of its style. Undoubtedly it is one of the most original of American poems ...

... The general thesis of the poetess may, perhaps, be stated as the demonstration that the superior wisdom is moral rather than intellectual; but it may be doubted whether her subject was ever precisely apparent to herself ... At one time we fancy her, for example, attempting to show that the condition of absolute sanctity is one through which mortality may know all things and hold converse with the angels; at another we suppose it her purpose to 'create' ... an entirely novel being, a something that is neither angel nor mortal, nor yet fairy in the ordinary sense ...

In looking back at its general plan, we cannot fail to see traces of high poetic capacity ... She is evidently discontented with the bald routine of commonplace themes, and originality has been with her a principal object. In *all* cases of fictitious composition it should be the *first* object ...

... She enables us to see that she has very *narrowly missed* one of those happy 'creations' which now and then immortalise the poet. With a good deal more of deliberate thought before putting pen to paper, with a good deal more of the constructive ability, and with more rigorous discipline in the minor merits of style, and of what is termed in the school-prospectuses, composition, Mrs Smith would have made of 'The Sinless Child' one of the best, if not the very best of American poems ... The originality of 'The Sinless Child' would cover a multitude of greater defects than Mrs Smith ever committed, and must forever entitle it to the admiration and respect of every competent critic.

Owl Woman

Frances Densmore, Papago Music *(Washington, DC: US*
Government Printing Office, 1929), p. 116

The phonographic recording of Owl Woman's songs occupied an entire
day. She did not wish to sing into the phonograph and insisted that
[Silvariano] Garcia [to whom she had taught her songs] record the songs.
She sang each song softly in order to recall it to his mind, and toward the
latter part of the day she sang with him, but not loud enough for her voice
to be recorded ... In the first two hours Garcia's interest did not falter
and he sang one song after another at her dictation. But there came a time
when he left out two or three words. There was much talking in Papago.
The old woman was suddenly full of animation and fire. The interpreter
said, 'She is telling him that he must not be discouraged because he forgot
those few words. She says he must go on as if nothing had happened.'
Garcia rallied to his task and the work continued, but the old woman
gave closer attention to her singer. Even to one who did not understand
the language it was evident that she was encouraging him and holding his
interest. She was bright, active, with an occasional witticism at which
they laughed heartily. At the close of the afternoon Garcia was singing
steadily with little sign of weariness but her face was drawn and tired, as
of one who had been under a long strain. How many long nights she had
held her singers at their task by the force of her personality, while she
watched the flickering life of a sick man!

Sarah M. B. Piatt

Review in The Dial, *vol. 6 (1886), p. 251*

The publication of Mrs Piatt's select poems was the result of a fortunate
inspiration. The six or seven volumes of her work have been drawn upon
for their choicest treasures; and these, taken together, form a collection
which exhibits very marked excellence. The graceful and suggestive verse
of Mrs Piatt at her best is equal to anything that has yet been done by her
sex in America. Its quality is clearly feminine, and its range is narrow; but
we need not make of either of these limitations matter for unfavorable
criticism, when a collection of verse exhibits, as this does, so marked a
degree of imagination, so great a refinement of feeling, and so large a
sense of the solemn significance of life and death. Her work has been
deemed to be suggestive both of Mrs Browning and Miss Rossetti. Her
spiritual kinship with the latter is asserted not without some show of
reason, although this may not be based upon any resemblance of their

work in detail. It appears rather in their common realisation of the essential nature of human life, of its transitory joys, of its ever-attendant pathos, and of the unreality of all its shadowy phantasmagoria.

Henrietta Cordelia Ray

Joan R. Sherman, Invisible Poets, *p. 134*
> Like so many nineteenth-century poets, H. Cordelia Ray versified only socially acceptable sentiments and a picture-book world. She suppressed natural feelings and thoughtful scrutiny of human relationships, actions, and ideas to serve a Muse for whom poetry was more a skill than an art … Miss Ray's technical virtuosity makes her fidelity to artificiality and respectability the more regrettable, for when she shed the inhibiting Muse, her potential talent could be glimpsed.

Lizette Woodworth Reese

Louise Bogan, Achievement in American Poetry, *pp. 21–2*
> The obscure publication in 1887 of Lizette Woodworth Reese's *A Branch of May* announced the new feminine sincerity of emotion and approach. Miss Reese … wrote her lyrics well outside the conventional literary scene, in what were then rural and provincial surroundings. She conveyed her emotions by means of an almost weightless diction and by a syntax so natural that its art was very nearly imperceptible. The romantic locutions and faded ornaments of the nineteenth-century lyric here drop away; expression is molded by feeling … Miss Reese might be a young woman talking to herself in a garden, but this colloquy with the self is accomplished in form.

Mary S. B. Dana Shindler

In the preface to *The Parted Family, and Other Poems* (1842), Shindler explained the hastiness of her composition in terms of the fast pace of the times:

> 'Tis said that ancient authors on the shelf
> Laid by their works till years had roll'd away;
> But ah! they did not, like my humble self,
> Live in an age of steam! Each passing day
> Now flies, and with it, many a sparkling ray
> Of native genius flies – for want of time,

Lost to our darken'd world. 'Tis true they say
Men never wrote so much, both prose and rhyme;
But then their writings range from silly to sublime.

Lydia Huntley Sigourney

Edgar Allan Poe, review of Zinzendorff and Other Poems, The
Southern Literary Messenger, *vol. 2, no. 12 (January 1836), pp.
112–17*
Poe accused Sigourney of imitating English poet Felicia Hemans:

... in an invincible inclination to apostrophise every object, in both
moral and physical existence – and more particularly in those mottoes or
quotations, sometimes of considerable extent, prefixed to nearly every
poem, not as a text for discussion, nor even as an intimation of what is
to follow, but as the actual subject matter itself, and of which the verses
ensuing are, in most instances, merely a paraphrase...

Having expressed ourselves thus far in terms of nearly unmitigated
censure, it may appear in us somewhat equivocal to say that, as Americans,
we are proud – very proud of the talents of Mrs Sigourney. Yet such is the
fact. The faults which we have already pointed out ... are but dust in the
balance, when weighted against her ... distinguishing excellences. Among
those high qualities which give her, beyond doubt, a title to the sacred
name of the poet are an acute sensibility to natural loveliness – a quick
and perfectly just conception of the moral and physical sublime – a calm
and unostentatious vigor of thought – a mingled delicacy and strength of
expression – and above all, a mind nobly and exquisitely attuned to all
the gentle charities and lofty pieties of life.

Sarah Josepha Hale, Woman's Record, *p. 783*
The predominance of hope with devotional feeling has inclined Mrs
Sigourney to elegiac poetry, in which she excels. Her muse has been a
comforter to the mourner. No poet has written such a number of these
songs, nor are these of necessity melancholy. Many of hers sound the
notes of holy triumph and awaken the brightest anticipations of felicity
... She 'leaves not the trophy of death at the tomb', but shows us the
'Resurrection and the Life'. Thus she elevates the hope of the Christian
and chastens the thoughts of the worldly-minded. This is her mission, the
true purpose of her heaven-endowed mind; for the inspirations of genius
are from heaven, and, when not perverted by a corrupt will, rise upward...

Rufus W. Griswold, The Female Poets of America *(1849), pp. 91–3*
Mrs Sigourney has acquired a wider and more pervading reputation than many women will receive in this country. The times have been favorable for her, and the tone of her works such as is most likely to be acceptable in a primitive and pious community. Though possessing but little constructive power, she has a ready expression, and an ear naturally so sensitive to harmony that it has scarcely been necessary for her to study the principles of versification in order to produce some of its finest effects. She sings impulsively from an atmosphere of affectionate, pious, and elevated sentiment, rather than from the consciousness of subjective ability. In this respect she is not to be compared with some of our female poets, who exhibit an affluence of diction, a soundness of understanding, and a strength of imagination, that justify the belief of their capability for the highest attainments in those fields of poetical art in which women have yet been distinguished. Whether there is in her nature the latent energy and exquisite susceptibility that, under favorable circumstances, might have warmed her sentiment into passion, and her fancy into imagination; or whether the absence of any deep emotion and creative power is to be attributed to a quietness of life and satisfaction of desires that forbade the development of the full force of her being; or whether benevolence and adoration have had the mastery of her life, as might seem, and led her other faculties in captivity, we know too little of her secret experiences to form an opinion...

Review of Routledge's Edition of the American Poets *(1852),* The London Review, *vol. 17 (October 1861), pp. 67–73*
This lady has been called the American [Felicia] Hemans... But, although we often find, on topics which suggest a similar train of thought, this close resemblance between the two, Mrs Sigourney has a wider range of subjects; and in her treatment of them has a freshness and variety... The American songstress can also be sprightly, and – at least, as far as her intention goes – facetious and humorous... Of Mrs Sigourney's poetry a far greater proportion [than of Hemans's] will probably remain... Many of her pieces have great merit; many more, though pleasant enough, and not apparently lacking any of the requisites of good poetry, induce no desire for a second perusal; and this we regard as fatal to all high pretensions ... Longfellow excepted, no American poet is better known on this side of the Atlantic...

Louise Bogan, A Poet's Alphabet: Reflections on the Literary Art
and Vocation, *ed. Robert Phelps and Ruth Limmer (New York:*
McGraw-Hill, 1970), p. 426

> Mrs Sigourney was provincial and naive enough to glory in two titles: the
> 'American Hemans' and the 'Sweet Singer of Hartford'. She reigned,
> however, over a long period as the head of American female letters – from
> shortly after Washington's second term as president until just after the
> death of Lincoln ... She was fluent, industrious, and rather pushing; but
> she managed to put feminine verse-writing on a paying basis, and give it
> prestige ... She gave simple men and women along the eastern seaboard
> and in the backwoods of the West something to be proud of; it is pleasant
> for a young nation to have a vocal tutelary goddess.

Emily Stipes Watts, The Poetry of American Women, *pp. 96–7*

> Sigourney's prosody is as confined to eighteenth-century verse forms as
> was that of most of her contemporaries; in her 'adult' poems, she was
> careless and euphemistic in diction. Her resolution of problems and many
> of her sentiments are traditional ones, but she opened new areas for poetic
> exploration and she showed a sensitivity to the roles of women in the
> quickly industrialising society of her time ... [She] realised that something
> had happened to the role of women, to their identity in nineteenth-century
> society. As a professional herself and as a housewife/mother, she sensed
> that something was wrong and expressed her knowledge through the
> images of dead mothers and children. We find her dull because she never
> developed and, later in her career, simply repeated her earlier poems. We
> find her poetically unsatisfying because she was sloppy and too often
> unaware of her craft. And yet she was a unique voice in American poetry
> at her time.

Nina Baym, American Women Writers and History, 1790–1860
(New Brunswick, NJ: Rutgers University Press, 1995), p. 81

> ... Lydia Sigourney ... urged the study of history on women of all ages
> and conditions, and wrote it herself in every genre and on many topics.
> Although Sigourney has come to symbolise the overwrought emotionality
> of female poetasters, her work as a whole contains a strong admixture of
> republican severity. Her wide-ranging historical subjects fall into four
> main categories: ancient and sacred history; local history of the region
> around Hartford, Norwich, and New London, Connecticut, from white
> settlement through Revolution; the American Revolution; and the history
> of the American Indians after European settlement. The core story of
> Native American history after the European arrival presented in Sig-
> ourney's writings is of Indian generosity answered by European brutality.

Elizabeth Drew Barstow Stoddard

The Dial, *vol. 20 (1896), p. 111*

[With] Mrs Stoddard's volume, we are in the presence of poetry in a more serious sense. It would be difficult to do justice to the intensity of noble feeling that throbs beneath the stern grave simplicity of these poems ... her song rarely fails to reach into the very heart of nature and of life ... The impression of Mrs Stoddard's work, as a whole, is a sombre one, but she has the power to compel to her mood by sheer force of sincerity; the poetic vision is hers in a remarkable degree, and the power to impart it ... In all our choir of American singers, there is no woman's voice more distinctly individual than this, or more compulsive in its appeal.

Edith M. Thomas

The Dial, *vol. 18 (1895), p. 83*

'In Sunshine Land' is a collection of verses ostensibly for children, but they have a serious poetic value, and must be classed with such books as Miss Rossetti's 'Sing-Song' ... Miss Thomas has exhibited in this volume a surprising daintiness of touch and delicacy of feeling; a surprising insight, also, into the workings of the child mind.

Rose Hartwick Thorpe

The Dial, *vol. 3 (1882), p. 175*

The thrilling poem, 'Curfew Must Not Ring Tonight', by Rose Hartwick Thorpe, has fared better in the hands of the illustrator than it is the fate of most works of the kind to do. The devoted and high-spirited girl who dared for the rescue of her lover what few of the stoutest-hearted men would undertake for any cause, is admirably represented in the frontispiece. It is the face of a heroine that we see, young, fair, distressed, desperate, resolute. Its owner will confront the stake if need be, and not hesitate or draw back. The succeeding designs reflect with equal accuracy the spirit of the poem, with one notable exception. The tragic element is evaded in the illustration of the culminating incident, 'Out she swung, far out', etc. It is a confession of weakness by the artist, and a disappointment to the reader.

Catherine Ana Warfield and Eleanor Percy Lee

Rufus W. Griswold, The Female Poets of America *(1849), p. 333*
The reception of [*The Wife of Leon, and Other Poems*] vindicated their publication. They were reviewed with many expressions of approval in the most critical journals, and with especial praise in the *New York Evening Post* and the *New Mirror* ...

... Among [the poems] are many specimens of ingenious and happy fancy, of bold and distinct painting, and of tasteful, harmonious, and sometimes sparkling versification; but not a few of them would have been much better if the authors had recollected that the word 'thing' can never be properly applied to a human intelligence except in expression of contempt, and that 'redolent', 'fraught', 'glee', and some half dozen other pet phrases of poetasters, convenient enough for rhyming and filling out lines, have ... become offensive, unless used sparingly and with the most exact propriety.

Carolyn Wells

Thomas L. Masson, 'Carolyn Wells', American Humorists, *revised ed. (1931; reprinted by Books for Libraries Press, Inc., 1966), pp. 306–7, 309*
Quotes from an interview with Wells.

I don't believe in unappreciated genius, and besides, appreciated or otherwise, I am not a genius. I'm an honest, respectable working girl, and I couldn't be a genius if I tried ... I work pretty hard, but I get a lot of fun out of my work ... I believe in having all the fun one possibly can. Writing nonsense came naturally to me, but, like most other things in their natural state, my faculty was quite worthless until I began training it. I kept sending things to the papers, and the stuff came back. It came back because it was trash. I knew it was trash, but at the same time I had faith in myself ... I had made up my mind I was going to write nonsense verse. I was inspired by the genius and example of Lewis Carroll ... All I needed was a trainer, a teacher, and I knew it. At last I found him in Mr Gelett Burgess ...

... One of the first lessons I was taught by Mr Burgess was the ability to distinguish between silliness and nonsense. Silliness is chaotic, while nonsense – that is, nonsense manufactured for commercial purposes – has got to be organic, well ordered, and, you might say, almost mathematical in its precision, and in its certainty to hit the reader or listener straight between the eyes, as it were.

In real genuine nonsense, there is always a most ludicrous, and, at the same time, a most logical surprise awaiting. Without the element of surprise nonsense fails to be nonsense. Not only must it be logical, but it must not be too obvious, and it must always be truthful, that is it must be truthful and convincing within the range of probabilities set forth in the argument and proposition. That is what I mean by a mathematical precision of a genuine nonsense verse. You see, we nonsense poets like to think that the mechanism of our art rests on principles as unalterable and as fundamental as Greek tragedy.

Ella Wheeler Wilcox

Louise Bogan, Achievement in American Poetry, *pp. 20–21*
It was Ella Wheeler [Wilcox] ... who brought into popular love poetry the element of 'sin' ... By 1900 a whole feminine school of rather daring verse on the subject of feminine and masculine emotions had followed Mrs Wilcox's lead. In this thoroughly middle-class 'poetic' *genre*, the combination of an air of the utmost respectability with the wildest sort of implications was strange indeed.

Emily Stipes Watts, The Poetry of American Women, *p. 144*
Wilcox wrote two distinct kinds of 'adult' poems: those which might appeal today to the television soap-opera set and those which are poetically and intellectually interesting in themselves. She mixed the two together in her volumes of poetry, along with poems apparently meant for children. Thus she tuned her verse directly to the housewife and mixed poems asserting a tough and aggressive individualism (and feminism) with poems of sentimentalism and traditional values. Nevertheless, her firm belief in woman and in her talents springs from the tendencies of earlier American women poets and marks a step to women's poetry today. In her own way, she foreshadows the verse of Edna St Vincent Millay and, later, Sylvia Plath.

Sarah C. Woolsey (Susan Coolidge)

The Nation, *vol. 31 (1880), p. 430*
Susan Coolidge's 'Verses' are as unpretending as their title. The author's muse is of a grave, tender, pensive cast of inspiration, and most of the lyrics that the book contains are penetrated with a mild seriousness that is perhaps their main attraction. Of other than their moral qualities it is difficult to speak positively, since in workmanship they are chiefly remark-

able for the absence of blemish. A contained and quiet diction, and a kind of well-bred air denoting a decent rhetorical reserve and literary equipoise, may be said to characterise them; here and there, for example, this plainly holds in check any disposition towards what a less careful writer would consider the legitimate pathetic or otherwise emotional tendency of the theme. There is considerable metrical variety, but in general little effort or ambitiousness of any kind...

Zaragoza Clubs

Luis A. Torres, The World of Early Chicano Poetry, *1846–1910*
(Encino, California: Floricanto Press, 1994), pp. 473–6
The Zaragoza clubs represent the only poetry by nineteenth-century Chicana women that Torres located in his extensive research.

Two extra-literary items of interest regarding this poetry must be noted. First is that the Battle of Puebla was already regarded as cause for a special day of commemoration ... only three years after the actual Battle ... Second, these poems were all written by Chicana women ... As even a cursory view of these poems in their original Spanish shows, these women poets were committed to advanced principles of poetic techniques and to a variety of poetic forms. Such commitment is evident, for example, in the complexity of rhythm and rhyme scheme in ... '¿Qué hombre será ...' by Belarde and in ... '¡Méjico! tu que ...' by García...

[Francisca García's] 'Mexico! You in whose' [is] lyrical in its description of the Mexican countryside and in her expression of love for Mexico ... As do the additional poets in this group, she views Mexico as essentially her country though she was living in the United States. She uses the occasion of the writing of the poem as cause for her to express her love for Mexico, and she ignores the French as if they were no more than a fleeting inconvenience, refusing to sully her devotion for Mexico by directly recognising the French, the Mexican traitors, or Maximilian and his wife Carlota, yet this poem is one of the most powerful in this group in its desire to see her beloved country free of foreign influences...

These poems serve well as representatives of the additional poems in this division ['Diversified' or indigenous poetry, responding to events in the United States] ... these ... poems followed many of the conventions of traditional poetry; but it is in the subject of social and even political involvement that the distinctions from the Romantic poems [imitative of European Romanticism] are drawn so sharply ... the poets speak out to a wide audience, once again to two countries as some of the earlier 'indigenous' poets likewise did, distinct from the 'Romantic' poets who spoke to the self, or to the individualised lover (often absent), or to no one in particular. In fact, these ... poems are intended to be spoken to an audience ... in public ceremony. These women, then, add to this new and different poetics, and they do so with a social involvement and a sense of immediacy and seriousness of purpose unsurpassed by the other poets in this division.

General Sources

Bogan, Louise, *Achievement in American Poetry* (Los Angeles: Henry Regnery Co., 1951).

Griswold, Rufus W., *The Female Poets of America* (Philadelphia: Moss, Brother & Co., 1849, 1860).

Hale, Sarah Josepha, *Woman's Record* (New York: Harper & Brothers, 1854).

Lichtenstein, Diane, *Writing Their Nation: The Tradition of Nineteenth-Century American Jewish Women Writers* (Bloomington: Indiana University Press, 1992).

Read, Thomas Buchanan, *The Female Poets of America* (Philadelphia: E. H. Butler & Co., 1849).

Sherman, Joan R., *Invisible Poets: Afro-Americans of the Nineteenth Century*, 2nd ed. (Urbana: University of Illinois Press, 1989).

Watts, Emily Stipes, *The Poetry of American Women from 1632 to 1945* (Austin and London: University of Texas Press, 1977).

SUGGESTIONS FOR FURTHER READING

See also works listed as *General Sources*
in The Poets and Their Critics, p. 364.

On Nineteenth-Century American Literary History

Baym, Nina, *American Women Writers and the Work of History, 1790–1860* (New Brunswick: Rutgers University Press, 1995).

Brodhead, Richard H., *Cultures of Letters: Scenes of Reading and Writing in Nineteenth-Century America* (Chicago: University of Chicago Press, 1993).

Coultrap-McQuin, Susan, *Doing Literary Business: American Women Writers in the Nineteenth Century* (University of North Carolina Press, 1990).

Foster, Frances Smith, *Written by Herself: Literary Production by African American Women, 1746–1892* (Bloomington: Indiana University Press, 1993).

Howe, Susan, *The Birth-Mark: Unsettling the Wilderness in American Literary History* (Hanover and London: Wesleyan University Press, 1993).

Morrison, Toni, *Playing in the Dark: Whiteness and the Literary Imagination* (New York: Random House, 1992).

Ruoff, A. LaVonne Brown, *American Indian Literatures: An Introduction, Bibliographic Review and Selected Bibliography* (New York: Modern Language Association of America, 1990).

Showalter, Elaine, *Sister's Choice: Tradition and Change in American Women's Writing* (Oxford: Clarendon Press, 1991).

Tompkins, Jane, *Sensational Designs: The Cultural Work of American Fiction, 1790–1860* (New York: Oxford University Press, 1985).

Walker, Cheryl, *The Nightingale's Burden: Women Poets and American Culture Before 1900* (Bloomington: Indiana University Press, 1982).

Walker, Nancy A., *A Very Serious Thing: Women's Humor and American Culture* (University of Minnesota Press, 1988).

Warren, Joyce W., ed., *The (Other) American Traditions: Nineteenth-*

Century Women Writers (New Brunswick: Rutgers University Press, 1993).

Wiget, Andrew, ed., *Critical Essays on Native American Literature* (Boston: G. K. Hall & Co., 1985).

On Gender in Nineteenth-Century American Cultural History

Banta, Martha, *Imaging American Women: Idea and Ideals in Cultural History* (New York: Columbia University Press, 1987).

Clark, Gregory and Halloran, Michael S., *Oratorical Culture in Nineteenth-Century America: Transformations in the Theory and Practice of Rhetoric* (Carbondale: Southern Illinois University Press, 1993).

Clinton, Catherine and Silber, Nina, eds., *Divided Houses: Gender and the Civil War* (New York: Oxford University Press, 1992).

Hansen, Karen, *A Very Social Time: Crafting Community in Antebellum New England* (Berkeley: University of California Press, 1993).

Hewitt, Nancy A. and Lebsock, Suzanne, eds., *Visible Women: New Essays on American Activism* (University of Illinois Press, 1993).

Martin, Theodora Penny, *The Sound of Our Own Voices: Women's Study Clubs 1860–1910* (Boston: Beacon Press, 1987).

Matthews, Glenns, *The Rise of Public Woman: Woman's Power and Woman's Place in the United States, 1630–1750* (New York and Oxford: Oxford University Press, 1992).

McCarthy, Kathleen D., *Women's Culture: American Philanthropy and Art, 1830–1930* (University of Chicago Press, 1991).

Sacks, Maurie, ed., *Active Voices: Women in Jewish Culture* (Urbana: University of Illinois Press, 1995).

Yellin, Jean Fagan, *Women & Sisters: The Antislavery Feminists in American Culture* (Yale University Press, 1989).

Issues and Methods in Women's Literary History

Ezell, Margaret, J. M., *Writing Women's Literary History* (Johns Hopkins University Press, 1993).

Ezell, Margaret and O'Keeffe, Katharine, eds., *Cultural Artifacts and the Production of Meaning: The Page, the Image and the Body* (Ann Arbor: University of Michigan Press, 1994).

Finke, Laurie, *Feminist Theory, Women's Writing* (Cornell, 1992).

Ruoff, A. LaVonne Brown and Ward Jr., Jerry W., eds., *Redefining American Literary History* (New York: Modern Language Association, 1990).

Criticism on Dickinson

Bennett, Paula, *My Life a Loaded Gun: Dickinson, Plath, Rich & Female Creativity* (Urbana and Chicago: University of Illinois Press, 1990).

Dobson, Joanne, *Dickinson and the Strategies of Reticence: the woman writer in nineteenth-century America* (Bloomington: Indiana University Press, 1989).

Juhasz, Suzanne, Miller, Christianne and Smith, Martha Nell, *Comic Power in Emily Dickinson* (Austin: University of Texas Press, 1993).

Oberhaus, Dorothy Huff, *Emily Dickinson's Fascicles: Method and Meaning* (University Park: Pennsylvania State University Press, 1995).

Smith, Martha Nell, *Rowing in Eden: Rereading Emily Dickinson* (Austin: University of Texas Press, 1992).

Wolff, Cynthia Griffin, *Emily Dickinson* (New York: Addison-Wesley Publishing Co., 1988).

Recent Editions of Prose Works by the Authors

Alcott, Louisa May, *Louisa May Alcott unmasked: collected thrillers*; edited with an introduction by Madeleine B. Stern (Boston: Northeastern University Press, 1995).

Alcott, Louisa May, *Freaks of genius: unknown thrillers of Louisa May Alcott*; edited by Daniel Shealy; Madeleine B. Stern and Joel Myerson, associate editors (New York: Greenwood Press, 1991).

Alcott, Louisa May, *Louisa May Alcott: selected fiction*; introduction by Madeleine B. Stern; edited by Daniel Shealy, Madeleine B. Stern and Joel Myerson (Boston: Little, Brown & Co., 1990).

Alcott, Louisa May, *Little Women*; edited with an introduction by Valerie Alderson (Oxford and New York: Oxford University Press, 1994).

Alcott, Louisa May, *Moods*; edited with an introduction by Sarah Elbert (New Brunswick: Rutgers University Press, 1991).

Alcott, Louisa May, *Louisa May Alcott's fairy tales and fantasy stories*; edited by Daniel Shealy (Knoxville: University of Tennessee Press, *c.* 1992).

Cary, Alice, *Clovernook sketches and other stories*; edited with an introduction by Judith Fetterley (New Brunswick: Rutgers University Press, 1987).

Cooke, Rose Terry, *'How Celia changed her mind' and selected stories*; edited with an introduction by Elizabeth Ammons (New Brunswick: Rutgers University Press, 1986).

Dodge, Mary Abigail, *Gail Hamilton, selected writings*; edited with an introduction by Susan Coultrap-McQuin (New Brunswick: Rutgers University Press, 1992).

Fuller, Margaret, *The portable Margaret Fuller*; edited with an introduction by Mary Kelley (New York: Penguin Books, 1994).

Fuller, Margaret, *Woman in the nineteenth century and other writings*; edited with an introduction by Donna Dickinson (Oxford and New York: Oxford University Press, 1994).

Fuller, Margaret, *The essential Margaret Fuller*; edited with an introduction by Jeffrey Steele (New Brunswick: Rutgers University Press, 1992).

Fuller, Margaret, *These sad but glorious days: dispatches from Europe, 1846–1850*; edited by Larry J. Reynolds and Susan Belasco Smith (New Haven: Yale University Press, 1991).

Fuller, Margaret, *Summer on the lakes in 1843*; introduction by Susan Belasco Smith (Urbana: University of Illinois Press, 1991).

Gilman, Charlotte Perkins, *Benigna Machiavelli* (Santa Barbara, California: Bandanna, 1994).

Gilman, Charlotte Perkins, *The diaries of Charlotte Perkins Gilman*; edited by Denise D. Knight (Charlottesville: University Press of Virginia, 1994).

Gilman, Charlotte Perkins, *The Yellow Wallpaper*; edited with an introduction by Thomas L. Erskine and Connie L. Richards (New Brunswick: Rutgers University Press, 1993).

Gilman, Charlotte Perkins, *Charlotte Perkins Gilman: a nonfiction reader*; edited by Larry Ceplair (New York: Columbia University Press, 1991).

Gilman, Charlotte Perkins, *The living of Charlotte Perkins Gilman: an autobiography*; introduction by Ann J. Lane (Madison, Wisconsin: University of Wisconsin Press, 1991).

Harper, Frances E. W., *A brighter coming day: a Frances Ellen Watkins Harper reader*; edited with an introduction by Frances Smith Foster (Boston: Beacon Press, c. 1994).

Harper, Frances E. W., *Iola Leroy, or Shadows uplifted*; introduction by Frances Smith Foster (New York: Oxford University Press, 1988).

Johnson, E. Pauline, *The moccasin maker*; introduction, annotation and bibliography by A. LaVonne Brown Ruoff (Tucson: University of Arizona Press, 1987).

Kemble, Frances A. and Leigh, Frances A. Butler, *Principles and privilege: two women's lives on a Georgia plantation*; introduction by Dana D. Nelson (Ann Arbor: University of Michigan Press, 1995).

Spofford, Harriet Elizabeth Prescott, *The amber gods, and other stories*; edited with an introduction by Alfred Bendixen (New Brunswick: Rutgers University Press, 1989).

Stoddard, Elizabeth, *The Morgesons and other writings, published and unpublished by Elizabeth Stoddard*; edited with an introduction by Lawrence Buell and Sandra A. Zagarell (Philadelphia: University of Pennsylvania Press, 1984).

Woolson, Constance Fenimore, *Women artists, women exiles: 'Miss Grief' and other stories*; edited with an introduction by Joan Myers Weimer (New Brunswick: Rutgers University Press, 1988).

Related Anthologies

Ashton, Dianne and Umansky, Ellen M., eds., *Four Centuries of Jewish Women's Spirituality: a sourcebook* (Boston: Beacon Press, 1992).

Hollander, John, ed., *American Poetry: The Nineteenth Century* (2 volumes) (New York: Library of America, 1993).

Kane, Paul, *Poetry of the American Renaissance: A Diverse Anthology from the Romantic Period* (Braziller, 1995).

Lauter, Paul, ed., *The Heath Anthology of American Literature* (Lexington, Mass.: D. C. Heath, 1990).

Sherman, Joan R., ed., *African-American Poetry of the Nineteenth Century: An Anthology* (Urbana and Chicago: University of Illinois Press, 1992).

Walker, Cheryl, ed., *American Women Poets of the Nineteenth Century: An Anthology* (New Brunswick: Rutgers University Press, 1992).

ACKNOWLEDGEMENTS

Members of the internet lists AMLIT, AMSTDY, CHICLE, E-GRAD, SLAVERY, STUMPERS, T-AMLIT, VICTORIA and WMST contributed advice, suggestions and information to this project. The Princeton University Library's Reference, Inter-library Loan and Special Collections staff provided needed assistance. Attenders at the conference Spiritual Renewal for Educators, Pendle Hill, were a supportive audience for my first oral transmission of materials in this book; residents of Medford Leas Retirement Community and members of Moorestown Friends Meeting were enthusiastic subsequent audiences; and Molly Weigel, Bill Piper and George Mahlberg took part in the thinking through of selections. Thanks to Gabrielle Welford for suggesting inclusion of one of Emily Dickinson's fascicles; to Sue Nance for providing *mele* by Queen Lili'uokalani; to Luis J. Torres for providing the *brindis* of the Zaragoza clubs; to Natalie Houston for highlighting the sonnet; and to Bill Gleason, U. C. Knoepflmacher, Deborah Epstein Nord and Elaine Showalter for their encouragement and support.

The editor and publishers would like to thank the following for their kind permission to use copyright material:

The Trustees of Amherst College for material from *The Poems of Emily Dickinson*, Thomas H. Johnson, ed., Cambridge, Mass.: The Belknap Press of Harvard University Press, Copyright © 1951, 1955, 1979, 1983 by the President and Fellows of Harvard College. Reprinted by permission;

Little, Brown and Company for material from *The Complete Poems of Emily Dickinson*, T. H. Johnson, ed. Copyright © 1929, 1935 by Martha Dickinson Bianchi; copyright © renewed 1957, 1963 by Mary L. Hampson. By permission of Little, Brown and Company;

Michigan State University Press for material from *The Literary Voyager or Muzzenyegun*, ed., Philip P. Mason, 1962;

W. W. Norton & Company, Inc. and the author for material from Adrienne Rich, 'Vesuvius at Home: The Power of Emily Dickinson' in *On Lies, Secrets, and Silence: Selected Prose 1966–78*. Copyright © 1797 by W. W. Norton & Company, Inc.;

Oxford University Press for material from *Essay; Including Biographies and Miscellaneous Pieces, in Prose and Poetry*, by Ann Plato, ed., Kenny J. Williams. Copyright © 1988 by Oxford University Press, Inc. Reprinted by permission; *Complete Poems of Frances E. W. Harper*, ed., Maryemma Graham. Copyright © 1988 by Oxford University Press, Inc. Reprinted by permission; *Collected Black Women's Poetry*, vols. 1–4, ed., Joan R. Sherman. Copyright © 1988 by Oxford University Press, Inc. Reprinted by permission;

University of Georgia Press for material from Patricia Okker, *Our Sister Editors: Sarah J. Hale and the Tradition of Nineteenth-Century American Women Editors*, 1995, pp. 142–4, 166;

University of Texas Press for material from Emily Stipes Watts, '1800–1850, Sigourney, Smith, and Osgood', Chapter 4, pp. 96–7, and '1850–1900, Refinement and Achievement', Chapter 5, pp. 139, 141–2, 144 in *The Poetry of American Women from 1632 to 1945*. Copyright © 1977.

Every effort has been made to trace all the copyright holders, but if any have been inadvertently overlooked the publishers will be pleased to make the necessary arrangement at the first opportunity.

INDEX OF FIRST LINES